Unsettled Boundaries

Fraser Gold and the British-American Northwest

by

Robert E. Ficken

Washington State University Press
Pullman, Washington

WASHINGTON STATE
UNIVERSITY

Washington State University Press
PO Box 645910
Pullman, Washington 99164-5910
Phone: 800-354-7360
Fax: 509-335-8568
E-mail: wsupress@wsu.edu
Web site: wsupress.wsu.edu

Library of Congress Cataloging-in-Publication Data

Ficken, Robert E.
     Unsettled boundaries : Fraser gold and the British-American Northwest /
     Robert E. Ficken.
        p. cm.
     Includes bibliographical references (p.) and index.
     ISBN 0-87422-268-0 (pbk. : alk. paper)
     1. Fraser River Valley (B.C.)—Gold discoveries. 2. Gold mines and mining—
British Columbia—Fraser River Valley—History—19th century. 3. Gold miners—British Columbia—Fraser River Valley—History—19th century. 4. Americans—British Columbia—Fraser River Valley—History—19th century. 5.
Frontier and pioneer life—British Columbia—Fraser River Valley. 6. Northwest
boundary of the United States—History—19th century. 7. United States—Relations—Canada. 8. Canada—Relations—United States. 9. Hudson's Bay Company—History. I. Title.

F1089.F7F53 2003
971.1'302—dc22   2003022359

WSU PRESS
YEARS   *Fine Quality Books from the Pacific Northwest*

Table of Contents

Illustrations

Acknowledgments

A number of individuals and institutions contributed in significant ways to the research and the preparation of this book. The staff at the Provincial Archives of Manitoba facilitated access to the extensive records of the Hudson's Bay Company. Likewise, assistants at the University of Washington and the University of British Columbia libraries provided essential help in the use of key manuscripts and other printed materials. At the Washington State University Press, Editor-in-Chief Glen Lindeman did a fine job working on the final text, with assistance from Nancy Grunewald, Jean Taylor, Caryn Lawton, Jenni Lynn, and WSU Press Director Mary Read.

A portion of *Unsettled Boundaries* previously appeared in different form as "The Fraser River Humbug: Americans and Gold in the British Pacific Northwest," in the *Western Historical Quarterly* (Autumn 2002). The assistance provided by the editors and staff of that publication also has been greatly appreciated.

This account relies heavily on several major sources. The voluminous gold-era files of the Hudson's Bay Company, located in Manitoba, proved especially key to the writing of this work. Of further importance, the official British government version of events are contained in *Papers Relative to the Affairs of British Columbia*, published in four volumes, 1859–62. Additional significant documents can be found in Frederic W. Howay's *The Early History of the Fraser River Mines*, published by the Provincial Archives of British Columbia in 1926.

American experiences and views of the gold rush, on the other hand, are extensively covered in contemporary West Coast newspapers of the times—from Puget Sound and Bellingham Bay, Portland and the Willamette Valley, and San Francisco. In particular, the San Francisco *Alta California* provided close to daily coverage of events during the gold rush's height in 1858. Invaluable journalistic commentary also was found in Victoria newspapers, the London *Times*, and the *New York Times*.

My son Matthew aided with technical computer matters, and went along for an enjoyable visit to one of *Unsettled Boundaries*' truly bizarre places—border-isolated Point Roberts.

—Robert E. Ficken
November 2003

"British and United States Boundary Line—Yahk River." This river drainage is situated primarily in what today is extreme northwest Montana. R. C. Mayne, *Four Years in British Columbia and Vancouver Island* (1862).

Introduction

Where mighty waters foam and boil,
And rushing torrents roar,
In Frazer River's northern soil,
Lies hid the golden ore.

With luck at last, our hardships past,
We'll start for home once more,
And greet the sight, wild with delight,
Of California's shore.

"Miner's Song of Frazer River"
Hutching's California Magazine (September 1859)

O N JUNE 24, 1858, the annual Hudson's Bay Company brigade rode into Fort Hope on the lower part of the Fraser River, two months after departing from its assembly point in faraway central New Caledonia. "There was much excitement among the men," reported Governor James Douglas of the offshore Vancouver's Island colony, who greeted the firm's trail-worn servants in his private business capacity as Hudson's Bay Company chief factor. The 180 packhorses coming into the post, after all, carried furs—beaver, mink, otter, fox, and bear—valued at $300,000. More to the point, however, the down river party had unexpectedly come face to face with thousands of prospectors who, in a matter of weeks, had come by sea and were rushing up the Fraser to dig for gold on the river bars.

The mainland British Pacific Northwest—a region so obviously insignificant to the distant home government in London that the latter had not formed an official local administration to govern the area—was quickly being transformed into a wet-weather El Dorado, the apparent successor to California's gold-rich Sierra Nevada. The arriving H.B.C. employees readily had fallen under the influence of the new prevailing emotion, noted Douglas, for "a man can make as much in one week at the gold mines as their wages for the year amount to." Here at Fort Hope, the traditional fur trade—the mainstay of European and American economic activity in northwest North America since the time of captains James Cook, John Meares, and Robert Gray seven decades before—was symbolically giving way to mining and rudimentary industrial and commercial endeavors.[1]

Writing of the Fraser River gold rush in 1938, Canadian scholar T. A. Rickard asserted that "no episode in the history of the…Northwest has been recounted so often." The claim was at one time valid. The *British Columbia Historical Quarterly*, for example, published many articles and relevant primary documents about this seminal event. In recent decades, however, Rickard's observation has long since lost force, and only a few notable additions to the gold rush literature have appeared, such as Netta Sterne's *Fraser Gold 1858! The Founding of British Columbia* (WSU Press, 1998).[2]

In the United States, a misleading assumption promulgated long ago by the Fraser rush's disenchanted California miners and merchants—that the events of 1858 represented a terminal humbug—has since permeated the commonplace historical view of this event, both in the popular and the professional historian's mind. The habitual American lack of knowledge about Canadian history and political affairs also has figured into this dismissive conventional wisdom. *Unsettled Boundaries* attempts to correct this erroneous "Californian" view. Actually, post-1858 events would prove that the Fraser gold rush was an essential event in regional development.

Also, *Unsettled Boundaries* focuses on the confusing and often negative consequences of the 49th parallel—an international line created by poorly informed diplomats in London and Washington, D.C. The boundary arbitrarily splits what otherwise is an environmentally and geographically compatible region into two political zones. A number of things compelled my interest in the implications of a borderline that is both meaningful and meaningless. Some years ago at an annual Pacific Northwest History Conference, the most instructive argument to emerge from an engaging panel discussion held that modern political boundaries ought to be ignored in attempting to interpret the greater West Coast's fundamental historical essence.

Then, when visiting an Eastsound gallery on Orcas Island in the San Juan Islands, I purchased an intriguing front-page illustration from the November

9, 1872, *Illustrated London News*, depicting a section of the British-U.S. boundary line at that time. Running straight as a proverbial arrow up and down forested hillsides, the cleared-down-to-tree-stump line bisected exactly the same scenery to the right and left.

A true absurdity of the 49th parallel came best to light, however, during my visit to Point Roberts, Washington, the six-mile square peninsular stub in the Gulf of Georgia that turned out to be on the wrong side, so far as common sense was concerned, of the border. The brief trip from the mainland's Blaine, Washington, to Point Roberts requires two crossings of the international boundary. Upon arrival, the American excursionist finds restaurant prices in Canadian dollars, while grocery and liquor stores cater almost entirely to bargain hunters and Sabbath breakers from nearby greater Vancouver, British Columbia.

A century and a half after local Indians brought the first gold dust into Hudson's Bay Company outposts, the 49th parallel still complicates everyday life along the border. Residents of Vancouver's easternmost suburbs protest against the construction of a power plant in Washington because, while the energy goes south, the noxious emissions will drift into their communities. Although the North American Free Trade Agreement has long since been approved, hapless motorists traveling between Vancouver and Seattle still can expect, depending on the season and time of day, to spend about as much time negotiating the backup at the customs and immigration checkpoints as on the remainder of the drive. Misunderstandings and a lack of knowledge still prevail, particularly south of the parallel, and especially in regard to Canadian politics. A recent survey, for instance, revealed that hardly anyone in Seattle, the sophisticated home of a major public university, Microsoft, and Boeing, not to mention Starbucks Coffee, knew the name of British Columbia's premier.[3]

Unsettled Boundaries was written with the view in mind that British Columbia ought to be fully incorporated into American perceptions of Pacific Northwest history. With a few noteworthy exceptions, scholars have failed to move beyond nationalistic conceptualizations in the direction of an integrated view of the overall region's past. The Columbia River, along with such major interior tributaries as the Kootenai and Okanogan, all flow, after all, through both British Columbia and the United States. The Cascade Range, the Northwest's great mountainous backbone, extends from the British Columbia interior to northern California. The Strait of Juan de Fuca leads from the Pacific into all of the key Canadian and American waterways. The people of Washington, Oregon, Idaho, Montana, and British Columbia cannot fully comprehend their populations' experiences, past and present, without understanding the lives of natives, whites, Asians, and blacks on each side of the parallel.[4]

This historical narrative also particularly deals with the cross-the-line collision between the citizens of one nation and the customs, laws, and business practices they encountered in another country's territory. The focus primarily is on group behavior, with one notable exception—James Douglas emerges as the key figure in this internationalized Pacific Northwest history.

A fur trader transformed—and eventually ennobled—into an imperial factotum, Sir James Douglas held multiple positions and effectively handled befuddling contradictory responsibilities. Often maligned in his own time as an agent of foreign despotism and corporate greed, he nevertheless capably accommodated the needs and requests of the fortune hunters, while adhering to British law and regulations and Hudson's Bay Company rights. Douglas was a worthy successor—in developing frontier commerce and in the management of sometimes unruly Americans—to his Pacific Northwest wilderness mentor, the great John McLoughlin of earlier fur trade fame.

Chapter One

An Unsettled Boundary

A part of the boundary between the United States and Great Britain, on the north-west, remains unsettled.—Olympia *Columbian*[1]

L IKE THE GREAT COLUMBIA, its neighbor in the deep-shadowed trenches on the west side of the Rocky Mountains, the Fraser River at first follows a southeast to northwest course toward the northern interior. Finally changing direction in the first of several big bends, the stream turns west, and then south through open, grassy New Caledonia, so-named by early 19th century Scottish-Canadian adventurers in the employ of the old North West Company. Motivated by dim kilt and bagpipe recollections of their high, green homeland of yore, the Nor'Westers and their successors in the honorable trade for furs, the Hudson's Bay Company, eventually applied the name to the entire Fraser drainage—the defining geographical feature of the Crown's continental possessions in western North America. The H.B.C.'s James Douglas reported to London superiors that the river, though badly obstructed in places, was the region's "only great artery," affording "access to the remotest valleys." Sweeping to tidewater within a daytime stroll of the international boundary, the Fraser was for New Caledonia what the Columbia eventually running far south of the 49th parallel was to Washington and Oregon territories.[2]

However, in contrast to the Columbia, which was served at least on its lower waters by steamboats in the early 1850s, the rugged Fraser, on balance, was poorly suited for extensive commercial navigation. On the positive side, the long dark flank of Vancouver Island protected the Fraser's mouth from violent Pacific storms. (Simon Fraser admitted to "great disappointment in not seeing the *main ocean*" upon completing his epic 1808 downstream voyage.) This was a major advantage over the frightful and dangerous sandbars at the Columbia's mouth.

Large vessels of the type sailing between San Francisco and Puget Sound, however, could not enter the Fraser. The Royal Navy warned of "extensive sand banks, sweeping five miles from the land" into the Gulf of Georgia. Given the prevailing tidal and weather conditions and the lack of markers, mariners experienced considerable difficulty in locating the main channel, particularly when fog and rain, by no means irregular factors, hampered visibility. The closest holding ground where passengers might safely transfer to shallow draft river craft was at Point Roberts, just below the 49th parallel, a place imperfectly sheltered from westerly winds. English men-of-war regularly anchored off the beach, their officers recreating ashore while domiciled in tents and dining on clams served on fine chinaware.[3]

When safely negotiating the "somewhat tortuous and narrow passage" through the sand, careful masters of small steamers experienced few serious problems on the lowermost Fraser. "All that would be required," a naval surveyor noted, is "knowledge of the channel, which never alters." The steamer *Otter* and other Hudson's Bay Company vessels ran upstream as far as fifty miles from the Gulf of Georgia. Navigation and commerce ceased altogether, though, at that point. The Fraser was a deadly maelstrom where it broke the back of the mountains, dashing canoes to bits on brutal outcroppings and drowning travelers amidst watery froth and piles of drift. The Cascade Range, too, rendered movement by land as unappealing and nearly as dangerous as transit by water. The country above Fort Yale was "for all practical purposes, nearly inaccessible," wrote James Douglas, "…in consequence of a range of mountains running north and south which…interpose an almost insurmountable barrier to the progress of trade."[4]

Truly horrific, the Fraser's great upriver chasm included two distinct canyons. Commencing on a downstream run, the first began 18 miles below the mouth of the Thompson River, and the second, a half dozen miles before Fort Yale. From lesser-of-two-evils necessity, persons traveling for subsistence or business reasons sometimes resorted, with knees trembling and brows sweating, to goat-appropriate mountain pathways. "The ground over which the trail passes," reported Richard Mayne, an intrepid lieutenant in Her Majesty's Navy, "is the roughest over which I have ever traveled, the greater part of it being over sharp pointed rocks or granite boulders." After days spent clinging desperately to inches-wide ledges while working up the Fraser to the Forks, an early British Columbia official apologized for failing to submit a detailed account of his journey, because "with perpendicular ascents

Hell's Gate Canyon, Fraser River. *UW Libraries, Frank La Roche 2143½, ca. 1887*

and dangerous descents my eyes and thoughts were wholly engrossed with the safety of my life."

The canyons represented a distinct point of division. Below, life was oriented toward tidewater. Upstream, the focus was on interior New Caledonia, with the sea safely accessible only by extreme roundabout routes. "It is impossible to conceive," said fur trade veterans aware of the commercial implications, of anything "more formidable or imposing than is to be found in that dangerous defile which cannot for one moment be thought of as a practicable water Communication for the transport of valuable property."[5]

Far traveling agents of the North West Company became aware of this basic fact at an early date. Exploring en route to the sea in 1793, Alexander Mackenzie heeded Indian advice that he "might be able to penetrate with more safety and in a shorter period, to the ocean by the inland, western communication." Abandoning the Fraser at the West Road River, Mackenzie and his companions eventually crossed to the Bella Coola River to reach saltwater. In 1808, Simon Fraser actually explored down to the Fraser's mouth and his vivid journal account depicts swamped canoes, "narrow escape from perdition," and ultimate frustration with the death-defying nature of the achievement. "Our lives hung as it were upon a thread," he wrote when

Map from John Domer, *New British Gold Fields...* (London, 1858).

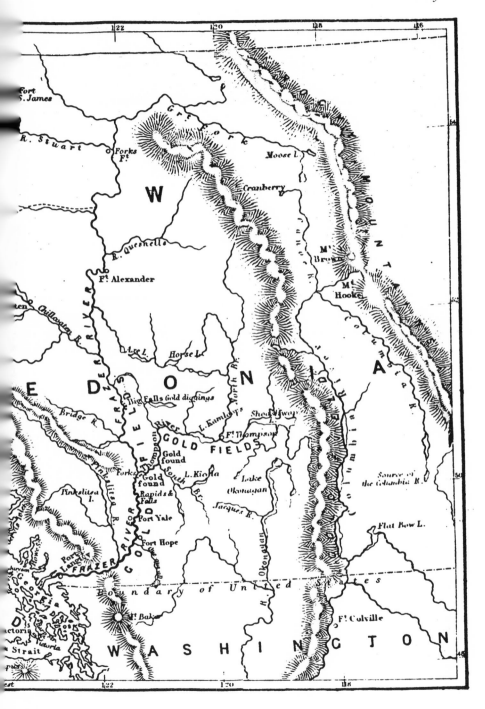

negotiating the rapids. Outfitted with poles, native guides "drew us up, one after another" above the torrent. "We had to pass," Fraser observed in the closest thing to an overall summation of the voyage, "where no human being should venture."[6]

Under a reorganization managed by the British government in the early 1820s, the H.B.C. eventually had taken over the Nor'Westers' Pacific slope operations, including management of the distant interior New Caledonia fur posts—Fort George and Fort Alexandria along the upper Fraser, and Fort Kamloops on the Thompson River. Meanwhile, an agreement between Britain and America had guaranteed to citizens of both countries unrestricted access to the entire Oregon Country, which at the time was claimed by both nations. The vast Oregon Country included all of the area north of Mexican-held California and south of Russian Alaska, and west of the Rocky Mountain continental divide to the Pacific Ocean. This essentially included today's central and southern British Columbia, all of Washington, Oregon, and Idaho, and most of western Montana and parts of western Wyoming. In 1824, the H.B.C.'s governor for North America, George Simpson, visited the Oregon Country with two primary goals—to improve the H.B.C.'s operational efficiency, and to anticipate the probable location of the international boundary when joint occupancy ended (which eventually occurred 22 years later, in 1846).

While wintering in the Oregon Country, Simpson founded Fort Vancouver on the north bank of the lower Columbia (in today's Washington) as the H.B.C.'s new regional headquarters. The locating of the establishment, as well as naming it after the famous coastal explorer, Captain George Vancouver of the Royal Navy, was part of a deliberate attempt to fortify British claims to the north side of the Columbia River. Other new Simpson-inspired experiments in agriculture and administration enhanced the H.B.C.'s regional self-sufficiency and provided, through the sale of grain to Alaska and milled lumber in California and Hawaii, a profitable complement to the traditional fur commerce. Acting in accordance with Simpson's advice, the H.B.C. management ordered John McLoughlin, Fort Vancouver's imposing chief factor, to "work the southern portion of the [Oregon] Country as hard as possible [for furs], while it continues to be free to the subjects of both

Nations," in anticipation of the Columbia eventually becoming the Anglo-American border. (Soon, the H.B.C also established a presence in the southern Puget Sound lowland by constructing Fort Nisqually in 1833, and forming an agricultural colony on the Cowlitz River in 1839.)[7]

Simpson's strategic thinking also had figured into the founding of Fort Langley on the lower Fraser in 1827—a "Tout ensemble" measuring 40 by 45 yards with two "artillery" bastions. In part, the post was supposed to thwart Americans or "Bostons" (as the Indians called Yankee sea-borne traders), who might think of venturing into the Fraser or of exploiting maritime trade opportunities in the vicinity. Anticipating a worst case contingency, the governor also conceived of Langley as a replacement "depot" for Fort Vancouver "in the event of the Columbia being given up to the Americans." Should that unhappy and not entirely unrealistic development take place, the Fraser River would, by process of imperial elimination, become the sole means of H.B.C. "communication between the coast and the interior." Another shift in company plans, however, made Fort Langley an apparently superfluous installation.[8]

Ignoring the conclusions of earlier North West Company expeditions, George Simpson believed that the Fraser had not been "thoroughly examined," a task he personally undertook in the course of an 1828 tour west of the Rockies. Traveling in considerably more comfort than either Alexander Mackenzie or Simon Fraser, nevertheless the H.B.C. governor experienced enough danger to radically alter his thinking about the river. Propelled among the canyons into rapids festooned with "grotesque and fantastic" rocks, his party's small vessel "shot like the flight of an Arrow, into deep whirlpools which seemed to sport in twirling us from one to another...leaving our water logged craft in a sinking state." His conclusion was immediate and entirely dismissive: "I shall...no longer talk of it as a navigable stream." Simpson now considered the Fraser "of little or no use to England as a channel of communication with the interior." He was convinced that the H.B.C. must retain at least the north bank of the lower Columbia in any boundary resolution with the United States. "Lose the right of navigating" the famed River of the West, Simpson warned, and Great Britain would "virtually cut off the interior and the coast of her own shore from each other."[9]

Previously, the New Caledonia fur trade had been administered and supplied by land and river routes coming from the east over the Great Plains and Rocky Mountains. Definitively implemented in 1825, however, a new managerial scheme directly linked New Caledonia with Fort Vancouver, which was served by ocean-going vessels. Early each summer, personnel from the various interior posts assembled at Fort Alexandria, then they traveled south with furs packed on horseback to Kamloops and on to the Okanogan River, and then down the Columbia by boat to Fort Vancouver. Later in the season, the "brigade" returned by the same route, carrying trade goods and supplies for the annual "outfit." With the New Caledonia posts served at what the London directors considered "a moderate cost"—a complete roundtrip normally took four months—Fort Langley on the Fraser largely languished in isolation. The place, however, became a modest emporium of its own. Fraser River salmon, cured and packed in stout barrels, went to Hawaii. Company agents also disposed of produce from a farm, described by one visitor as "many acres…covered with a healthy looking green sward," at opportune markets along the coast.[10]

Possible rivalry with the United States, always a guiding concern of H.B.C. management, also had diverted the company's attention from the Fraser to huge, indifferently explored Vancouver Island, located west across the Gulf of Georgia from Fort Langley. By the early 1840s, American missionaries and settlement advocates in the Willamette Valley, apparently the stealthy advance agents of U.S. expansionism, had aroused increasing H.B.C. concern over security in the Oregon Country in the event of a substantial overland American migration. In addition, the "danger on every side" of crossing the Columbia River bar, a graveyard for sailors, also influenced the H.B.C. to search for a better-situated site for a regional headquarters.

The southern end of Vancouver Island conformed to the principal requirements, being doubly secure by distance from the Americans in the Willamette Valley and by a relative lack of navigational hazards for British trade and naval vessels. Surveying "the most promising points on that coast" from the deck of the schooner *Cadboro* in the summer of 1842, James Douglas settled upon "Camosack" as the most eligible point. The place was hardly superior, or even equal, to alternative locations in the neighborhood as a harbor. However, "at Camosack," Douglas stressed, "there is a range of plains nearly six miles square, containing a great extent of valuable tillage and pasture land equally well adapted for the plough or for feeding stock."[11]

Completed in 1843, Fort Victoria was, George Simpson claimed, "very Elysian in point of climate & scenery." Standing atop a harbor-side bluff, the wooden palisade enclosed company storehouses and traders' residences within four or five acres. Gallery-mounted cannon and a careful attention to security—the gates never were opened between dusk and dawn—also acknowledged the potentially troublesome fact that 18,000 Indians, by careful estimate, resided on Vancouver Island. The place, moreover, often was visited by aggressive tribal delegations from distant archipelagos and fjords even farther north. These were powerful peoples who invariably became embroiled in violent disputes among themselves or with the local H.B.C.-influenced Indian villagers. Fort Victoria had no civilized streets. Governor Simpson's Elysian views to the contrary, pretenders to gentlemanly status donned high sea boots before negotiating deep mud churned up during seemingly endless downpours. As originally constituted, Victoria was a typical Simpson establishment—equal parts trade mart, farm, and rudimentary industrial center. Among the early attempts to generate profit, Victoria copied Langley in exporting salmon, as well as timber and shingles, to Hispanic California and the ever-bustling native kingdom in Hawaii.[12]

Fort Victoria commenced its uncertain business in a period of intense diplomatic activity. Upon concluding the Webster-Ashburton treaty of 1842—a U.S.-British agreement settling the long-vexatious Maine boundary dispute—the English suggested that "the line west of the Rocky Mountains" also be addressed, thereby removing "all cause, however remote, of even contingent risk to the good understanding now so happily restored between two countries which ought never to be at variance with each other." Although the United States responded favorably, various difficulties prevented a pursuit of the proposal at that time.

When negotiations finally did earnestly begin later, the United States basically recommended an earlier proposal—that the existing 49th parallel boundary east of the Rockies be extended west to the Pacific, with the notable exception of leaving Vancouver Island entirely in British hands. The latter, intent upon protecting H.B.C. interests, largely insisted on a long-held view that the demarcation line should follow the Columbia River to the ocean. Meanwhile, the "Oregon Question" had emerged as an emotional issue in the 1844 U.S. presidential campaign, which diverted attention from the orderly conduct of diplomacy. Some fervent American expansionists now were demanding immediate abrogation of joint occupation, the prompt dispatch of "thirty thousand rifles" to the Pacific Northwest, and occupation of "the valley of the Columbia, north as well as south of the river."

Despite considerable public bluster, it was fortuitous that neither government truly desired to resort to arms—Britain from a genuine principle not to do so (preferring to maintain an ever more profitable international commercial order, and concerned with Irish famine, revolt in India, and domestic issues), and the U.S. due to wiser council and an approaching and more potentially advantageous war with Mexico for control of California and the Southwest. Consequently, a final diplomatic settlement came with the Oregon Treaty of June 15, 1846. America gained sovereignty to all the mainland below the 49th parallel, while Britain received sole hegemony over New Caledonia and all of Vancouver Island.[13]

Initially, the treaty had little impact. The habitual informalities of the region's small white populations continued to prevail. With an official boundary survey indefinitely delayed, the occasional tree trunk hatchet slash—marks "liable at any moment," a federal patronage appointee warned, "to be swept away by summer fires...or overthrown by winter winds"—delineated a porous border. The Royal Navy and the Hudson's Bay Company continued to freely utilize Point Roberts, on the wrong side of the 49th parallel. In the San Juan Islands, distant diplomatic contentions soon arose over an ambiguous international boundary line through the islets, but the citizens of both countries continued to cultivate acreage and graze stock there, with some difficulties arising when American officials attempted to levy taxes on all parties. The treaty, meanwhile, guaranteed H.B.C. property rights and occupation of its posts south of the 49th parallel in the American sector, including the farming subsidiaries at Nisqually and Cowlitz (the Puget's Sound Agricultural Company) and provided for open British navigation of the Columbia River. Continuing business in a minimally disturbed fashion, the English firm dominated the economy of the early American settlements.[14]

The accelerating pace of American migration over the Oregon Trail in the late 1840s and 1850s, however, endangered the H.B.C.'s properties on the lower Columbia, and at Cowlitz Farm and on the southern Sound. By early 1858, the H.B.C.'s James Douglas (also by then, governor of the Crown Colony of Vancouver's Island) reported of the incoming settlers: "They have been preying upon us here since their arrival in the country." American immigrants, many of whom bore long-held anti-British feelings, filed claims on H.B.C. fields and orchards, harvested British wheat, and founded the town of Steilacoom among H.B.C. holdings on the southern Sound. "In the history of squatting," George Simpson fumed upon receiving reports that Americans had physically expropriated the Fort Vancouver sawmill, "I never heard of such a case." The other forms of trespass were "bad enough," said the governor, "but it is beyond all bounds to squat in our very buildings." The H.B.C.'s London-based management had expected the 1849 inauguration of a formal American territorial government to end "the unsettled state of things." Appeals to territorial authorities, however, generated only insincere advice that the courts must be relied upon for redress (under the prevailing political conditions, however, it was unlikely that judges would rule in favor of the British).[15]

Recognizing that H.B.C. holdings in the U.S. were eventually for all practical purposes lost anyway, the company actively pursued, under the 1846 treaty, the sale of its holdings south of the 49th parallel to the American government. Beginning in the winter of 1849, George Simpson undertook periodic missions to Washington City in pursuit of this goal. Anticipating an eventual compromise, he submitted on the advice of "several lawyers in the States," a deliberately inflated assertion of H.B.C. property and legal rights in Oregon Territory. Simpson admitted, "Such wide indefinite claims might not be recognized & would no doubt be much curtailed, but by making large demands we are more likely to be confirmed in the possession of the comparatively small but valuable portions."

The talks dragged on for years, with no productive end in sight. Regular changes in presidential administrations, from Polk, to Taylor, to Fillmore, to Pierce, to Buchanan, forced Simpson to frequently "begin the work de novo." Presidents, cabinets, and congress would scatter to the winds for months at a time, escaping the climatic challenges of life in the capital. And, when these officials actually were on the scene, Simpson noted that "angry discussions about Kansas, Slavery, [and] Mormons" dominated political discourse, both public and private, diverting attention from matters of secondary importance.[16]

At least in theory thanks to the treaty, the H.B.C. ironically held a more substantive legal position south rather than north of the 49th parallel. For its possessory rights within British territory, the company depended upon an 1838 grant of exclusive right for 21 years to trade with the Indians. Hudson's Bay officials held "a more extended application" to the document, however, contending that the language would have specifically embraced non-Indians as well, had significant numbers of such persons been in residence at the time.

The H.B.C. realized, however, that an explicit legislative enactment was imperative, and therefore petitioned the British government for recognition of its possessory entitlement, at minimum, to Vancouver Island. After a series of exchanges, the colonial office agreed to a favorable charter drafted by the H.B.C.'s London directors. Reflecting belated opposition from free traders, however, the charter issued on January 13, 1849, creating the Crown Colony of Vancouver's Island also required that the company "dispose of all lands hereby granted…at a reasonable price" to bona fide settlers. The H.B.C.'s parliamentary critics gained a further point against the firm by securing the appointment of Richard Blanshard, a determined adversary, as governor of the new Vancouver's Island colony. Resigning in 1851, however, after much controversy in Victoria, Blanshard opened the way for a congenial successor.[17]

Born on August 15, 1803, in British Guiana, James Douglas had joined the H.B.C. in 1821 and spent his adult life in fur trade employment, emerging at a relatively young age as the principal assistant and appropriate successor to the well-known John McLoughlin at Fort Vancouver. He was, George Simpson concluded in an enduring 1833 assessment, "well qualified for any Service requiring bodily exertion[,] firmness of mind and the exercise of Sound judgement." Even his adversaries in Victoria's commercial community expressed personal admiration for the new governor. In most respects—including his tendency toward stoutness and a preference for doddering

Sir James Douglas—Hudson's Bay Company chief factor, and colonial governor of Vancouver's Island (1851–64) and British Columbia (1858–64).

about in his private rose garden—Douglas was considered "a true English gentleman," albeit one of a necessarily uncouth and socially undisciplined background in a frontier fur-trade setting. Official contemporary portraits, featuring grim expression, dark circles beneath the eyes, and pasted-down thinning hair, reflected a temper sometimes barely contained and something akin to untreated dyspepsia.[18]

Douglas, however, now filled what the London *Times* called "apparently incompatible offices," a charge sure to provoke his sour disposition. That is, by continuing to serve as an H.B.C. chief factor at Fort Victoria he represented a private monopoly, but at the same time he was the chief British colonial official on the Pacific coast. Many superiors in the home government were unsympathetic to such political-business creations, particularly because of the H.B.C.'s outmoded and arbitrary hierarchical governing philosophy. Although Douglas claimed he took every precaution to "avoid even the suspicion…of undue influence being used on my part in favouring the objects of the Hudson's Bay Company," his actions were bound to provoke second guessing and bitter whisperings. Compounding the problem, the London colonial office failed to provide him with a staff or financial assistance, forcing Douglas to rely on H.B.C. personnel and facilities in the everyday administration of duties. Public and private business was indeed entangled, with a later audit finding "separate accounts were not kept…as might easily & should have been done, had the Governor & Company's Agent been independent of each other."[19]

H.B.C. chief factors, the *Times* also claimed, were "better fur-traders than colonists." The shortcomings in Victoria, however, were to a considerable extent institutional in nature, rather than the result of any dereliction on Douglas's part. The necessity of conducting public business through the medium of a private enterprise was bound to compromise efficiency to some extent, if not the general welfare. Victoria, moreover, was "a free port *in the strictest sense of that term*," with no duties assessed on imports and exports, foreign or domestic. "No where," a visiting American merchant reported, "is business so little trammeled." The impact locally, however, was baneful, advised Governor Douglas. The free of charge import of food and goods from the United States and elsewhere frustrated the expansion of British agriculture and industry on Vancouver Island. Colonists, in turn, when selling their produce on Puget Sound and in California, paid tariff rates "ranging from 20 to 30 per centum," with predictable dire financial consequences.[20]

Prospective settlers at first expressed keen interest in emigrating to Vancouver's Island. Reports claiming that the soil was "fertile" and "in general rich" turned out, however, to be exaggerated. The island, admitted pioneer immigrant W. Colquhon Grant, was, in reality, "little better than a mass of Rock, with a few little garden patches…interspersed at intervals along the sea coast." The Crown, moreover, required that land be sold to settlers for £1 (about $5) an acre. "Although this would appear to many in England…a low price," reported Donald Fraser, the London *Times'* Pacific coast correspondent, "yet in fact it is far too high." In neighboring Washington Territory, purchasers paid $1.25 per acre under the federal preemption statute. "The advantages of the settler on American soil…being so obvious," Fraser pointed out, "emigrants…give a preference to the American territory on the mainland." Pointing to the price differential and the contrasting results, observers south of the 49th parallel contended that Vancouver's Island "would…have been settled and improved in much less time if it had been the property of the United States."[21]

Certain developments on Vancouver's Island and in New Caledonia during the late 1840s and early 1850s, to be sure, exhibited positive results. To "escape the actions of the United States Government," the New Caledonia brigade shifted from the Columbia to the Fraser after the 1846 boundary treaty, with Fort Victoria displacing Fort Vancouver as the main depot. A pack trail from Kamloops linked up with the Fraser River at Fort Yale for one season and ran thereafter to better-situated Fort Hope, avoiding the river's difficult canyons. British sea captains and merchants, meanwhile, had known since the late 18th century that "the timber with which this coast is covered…would compose a valuable addition to our trading." Beginning with Captain Cook's visit to Nootka Sound in 1778, mariners had cut spars for their own use and for sale in distant ports. The Hudson's Bay Company opened two sawmills early in the colonial period, and, on their own account, the firm's resident employees established a third. In 1853 alone, a dozen vessels carried Vancouver Island lumber to San Francisco.[22]

Exploitation of the region's coal deposits, too, brought genuine profit. The H.B.C. opened a mine at Fort Rupert in 1849, but abandoned the distant site after sinking several experimental shafts. The following year, a permanent operation commenced closer to hand at Nanaimo on the Gulf of Georgia. Three person crews, "one…picking and propping, and two shoveling and carrying the dirt…away," labored in six-foot high galleries "solidly lined and roofed with squared timber." One contingent of skilled miners from England deserted and the firm's vessels were the wrong size for truly efficient shipment. Still, the H.B.C. found a ready market in San Francisco, selling even with the burden of a U.S. tariff at a lower price than mercantile interests importing from the eastern United States. Vancouver Island's coal "proved," a California newspaper advised, "of a better quality than any yet discovered upon the coast." George Simpson personally concluded a contract with the Pacific Mail Steamship Company to supply steamers running between San Francisco and Oregon and Washington territories. British and American warships assigned to the North Pacific also regularly called at the mine for coal.[23]

Despite these achievements, Vancouver's Island otherwise appeared to be a distinct failure. By 1855, the colony had fewer than 800 non-Indian residents, a fifth of the figure in Washington Territory. Of 500 acres under cultivation, only 40 were in the hands of persons not connected with the Hudson's Bay Company. Though small in number, "free settlers" were vocal in their complaints, demanding reduced land prices, voting rights, and revocation of the H.B.C. charter. At Victoria, they argued, "the public business" was "made, as it were, a private matter" of the H.B.C. "Had the British Government thrown the island open to the exertions of individual enterprise," insisted W. Colquhon Grant, "the greater portion...ere this, would have been settled." Some of the complainants had connections in Parliament, where the firm was already unpopular as a discredited reminder of the mercantilist era. Recognizing a losing proposition, economically and politically, the H.B.C.'s directors opened talks in London for the surrender of Vancouver's Island. "We shall be well quit," George Simpson privately conceded in early 1858, of the "troublesome" place.[24]

Compared to the failing Crown colony at least, the American Pacific Northwest was vigorous and prosperous. A number of contemporaries made much of the supposedly vital distinction between British corporate inefficiency and Yankee private initiative. "Instead of *States*," wrote Asahel Bush, the influential editor of the *Oregon Statesman*, the H.B.C. "wanted but *trading posts*" reserved to "the Indians and themselves." In contrast, Oregonians and Washingtonians intended, according to Bush, to "reduce nature's wilds to the dominion of the white man, to *possess the country*, and rear in it the institutions of civilization."

The advertisement page from a single issue of the Olympia *Columbian*, Washington Territory's first newspaper, confirmed the unfettered energy and "Young America" entitlement implicit in Bush's formula. David Maynard, Seattle physician, Indian agent, and delegate to two territorial conventions, peddled dry goods and hardware "suitable for the wants of immigrants," and offered to have timber and piling "hauled out and ready for taking on board" California-bound vessels. Michael Simmons, Maynard's political superior in the Indian department, ran the Olympia post office, and sold "a full supply of molasses, pork," and other delicacies, and stood ready to "sell or purchase Real Estate" in the several "growing towns on Puget's Sound." Associated with Simmons in these endeavors, Hugh Goldsborough had time and energy left over to proffer "professional services to the public as a Civil Engineer."[25]

Washington was, in reality, nearly as backward as Vancouver's Island. "There is not a stage or steamboat in the territory," a visiting Treasury Department agent discovered in 1854, "and scarcely a road that amounts to more than a trail." The mail service was abominable, leading to the witticism that "the President's Message will be printed at Bombay…about as soon as the people of this portion of the Pacific will be permitted to give it a perusal." In Puget Sound, however, the Americans possessed as fine a "sheet of water…as eye ever rested upon," with safe anchorages by the score and stands of enormous Douglas fir growing down to the high-tide mark. The demand for lumber in gold-rush California produced a local economy based upon forest exploitation and a close relationship to San Francisco. The first federal officials on the scene counted close to 4,000 non-Indian inhabitants. Olympia, the territorial capital, was twice the size of Victoria, and two other settlements, Steilacoom and Seattle, were nearly as large as the rude British metropolis.[26]

Arriving in 1853, New England merchants—"the people all seem to be Yankees turned speculators," one correspondent informed a California newspaper—founded the first great lumbering operations at Port Gamble, Port Ludlow, and Port Madison. Outfitted with up-to-date mills, schooner fleets, San Francisco yards, and foreign sales connections, these firms easily bested their Vancouver Island competitors in production, profits, and the potential for sustained business. Outside American capital also financed a major challenge to the H.B.C. coaling trade. Opened at Bellingham Bay in 1853, Edmund Fitzhugh's pioneer coal mine was at first troubled by labor shortages and a lack of equipment. Fitzhugh returned from a trip to San Francisco in late 1854, however, with new partners, a reported $60,000 in financing, and a crew of skilled miners. "Upwards of six hundred tons a month," a Puget Sound newspaper noted, "will now be delivered on the wharf for exportation." Keeping a close eye on Bellingham affairs, James Douglas lamented about the American firm's freedom from tariff duties, and of the loss, under political pressure, of Nanaimo's U.S. naval contract.[27]

Be they farmers or townspeople, Americans shared a consuming ambition—the desire for gaining profit through the sale of land, services, and produce. Most also had a common commercial adversary, England in general, and the Hudson's Bay Company in particular. Memories of the American Revolution and the War of 1812 still were vivid, accounting in part for the unsettling fact, as John McLoughlin observed, that "immigrants arrive in this country strongly prejudiced against us." Continuing U.S.-British international incidents—the recent mid-1840s Oregon boundary dispute being one of the more dramatic crises—kept anti-John Bull sentiment alive. Irish miners and laborers, periodically exposed to the oratory of Thomas Meagher and other touring political exiles from the old country, added another volatile element to nativist American prejudice on the Pacific coast.[28]

Certain complaints of long standing had focused specifically on the H.B.C. and its supposed misdeeds in the old Oregon Country. During the 1830s, for example, U.S. naval observer William Slacum and settler propagandist Hall Kelley had accused the firm of grossly mistreating Indians and pursuing unfair trade practices. American Protestant missionaries, too, charged the company with masterminding a vast anti-U.S. conspiracy, a "three-fold chord" binding the English, the Pope, and the region's native tribes. Although the firm provided vital assistance to persons arriving via the Oregon Trail from 1842 onward, many Americans at the first opportunity turned on their benefactors. Antagonism focused, in particular, on the firm's treaty-protected properties south of the 49th parallel. The claims put forward by the H.B.C. and its "illegitimate offspring," the Puget's Sound Agricultural Company, were, as many settlers asserted, a reflection of "base, gross and inexcusable fraud."[29]

Within days of reaching Olympia in late 1853, Isaac I. Stevens, the first governor of newly-created Washington Territory, shrewdly made the H.B.C. a political foil. During public addresses and in messages to the territorial assembly, Stevens forthrightly endorsed the settlers' interpretations of the 1846 treaty. The British, he insisted, "had set up the most extravagant pretensions, the effect of which, if yielded to, would be…to transfer the sovereignty of the country…to the Hudson's Bay and Puget Sound Agricultural Companies." As a good Democrat and a loyal American, the governor promised to fight foreign monopoly on behalf of "the emigrant who has come here to carve out

"Indian family migrating." R. C. Mayne, *Four Years in British Columbia and Vancouver Island* (1862).

a home." Issuing an immediate challenge on the economic front, he prohibited the Victoria-based firm from trading with Washington's Indians, the ban to take effect on July 1, 1854.[30]

Though a transparent attempt to channel the lucrative Indian business into the hands of U.S. citizens, Stevens's trade decision was generally hailed in Washington Territory as an expression of the purest concern for the general welfare. "The Indians...are more under the influence of the British... [than] that of our American authorities," the Olympia *Pioneer and Democrat* pointed out when endorsing the pronouncement. Like the early missionaries, settlers blamed the H.B.C. for depredations committed by tribes south of the 49th parallel.

At the outset of the bitter Puget Sound Indian war in the fall of 1855, James Douglas sent weapons and ammunition to Americans across the line, assigned a steamer to patrol local waters as a gesture of sympathy, and instructed Nisqually factor William F. Tolmie to keep the territorial authorities informed regarding the movements of hostile bands. Over the next several months, while a combined force of American regulars, volunteers, and tribal allies engaged in a hit-and-miss conflict with 200 warriors, Fort Victoria provided supplies for a good part of the war effort, on credit. The U.S. government, later responding in a gross display of anglophobic ingratitude, postponed repayment of the debt owed the firm and rejected an indemnity claim for damages to property and trade. Visiting Washington City, George

Simpson learned that Governor Stevens had recommended summary abrogation of all British rights under the 1846 treaty, claiming the H.B.C. had
taken "an active part in the War on the side of the Indians."[31]

Before and after the war, well-armed northern Indians, traveling from
distant British and Russian possessions in seagoing canoes, paid regular visits
to the Sound, precipitating general trouble and perpetrating the occasional
revenge-motivated attack on isolated settlers. The visitors were "an intelli-
gent, bold and athletic race," reported Fayette McMullin, the successor to
Stevens as Washington's governor. Fearful Americans claimed "these Northern Indians are incited to hostilities by attaches of the British Government."
The accusation angered James Douglas: "No man in his right senses would
ever suppose that the Governor of a…Province would be guilty of the monstrous outrage of arming a horde of savages and letting them loose on the
defenceless frontier of a neighboring and friendly state." Much of the public
opinion south of the border ignored his plea of innocence and the fact that
the northerners were beyond the control of all white authorities, British or
American. When Indians from the north murdered a prominent pioneer,
Isaac Ebey, on Whidbey Island in August 1857, territorial officials threatened
Douglas with "border warfare" should he allow the outrages to continue.[32]

Meanwhile, the H.B.C. had its own complaints, which dealt mostly with
more prosaic concerns and activities. American squatters and trespassers on
H.B.C. property south of the border continued to operate free of effective
U.S. restraint, and American smugglers dealt liquor to Indians on Vancouver
Island and the lower Fraser. The Oregon boundary agreement also had transformed commercial connections between Victoria and U.S. ports into a
crabbed form of international trade. Despite the treaty guarantee of free navigation on the Columbia River, U.S. customs officials impounded company
vessels for nonpayment of import charges in 1849 and again in 1850. With
a "good deal of running to and fro," James Douglas resolved this dispute with
a generally amicable resolution. U.S. officials, however, still required that
H.B.C. vessels obtain permits when entering the river.

The Americans also initially insisted that company ships sailing between
Victoria and Fort Nisqually go through customs at Astoria on the Columbia,
which until 1851 was the only Yankee port of entry. The H.B.C.'s attorney
sensibly petitioned the Treasury Department about this gross inconvenience:
"This when you consider the geography of the country you will see to be a
great hardship." Briefly suspended, the proviso was reinstated when deserters

from the U.S. Army garrison at Steilacoom escaped to Vancouver Island aboard the schooner *Cadboro*.[33]

In 1851, Nisqually became a port of entry and Olympia the site of a new customs house, developments that at first were regarded in a positive light by H.B.C. management. In November, however, U.S. authorities seized the H.B.C. steamer *Beaver* and the sailing vessel *Mary Dare*, citing inconsistencies between the written manifests and actual cargoes. Examining the reports at a distance, George Simpson was furious. "They have acted within the rigid letter of the law," he complained of the Americans, "but entirely at variance with the spirit of the Oregon Treaty." Personally handling the dispute at Washington City, with assistance from the resident British foreign office representative, Simpson eventually secured the release of the vessels. Still vexed, he advocated a virtual shutdown at Nisqually—with H.B.C. vessels sent there only to transfer stock to Victoria—as the only sure means of avoiding trouble. James Douglas in Victoria felt continually frustrated over the cross-border trade problems. "I hardly know what course to advise," he confessed in April 1854, "in order to escape the exactions of the United States Revenue Laws."[34]

For Isaac Stevens, his political philosophy and personal ambitions dovetailed. His development of Washington Territory's governmental and commercial tapestry—his immediate task as governor and then congressional delegate—was his best means of attaining other new and elevated political influences. Stevens pointed out in speeches and writings that until his governorship, the Pacific Northwest had been "regarded as a *terra incognita*," an obscure and distant locale "lying somewhere under the arctic circle." Ignorance had given way to informed recognition, thanks in part to his own western explorations for railroad routes when first making the long trek to Olympia. Thinking persons the world over now knew of Puget Sound as "the most magnificent roadstead on the shores of all the oceans," bordered by an evergreen forest, "which will supply...all the ports of the Pacific with lumber." When a northern transcontinental railroad line was built in the future—a route he had already personally surveyed—Washington Territory would link the Atlantic seaboard with Asia, fulfilling the vision of Lewis and Clark. "The imagination of man," claimed Stevens, "can scarcely set bounds to the future grandeur of our Pacific empire."[35]

Vancouver's Island, in fact, already was part of a global colonial empire, boastfully on which the sun never set. But the Pacific colony was a sideshow, an afterthought, and viewed as a dreary hinterland—the policies of the home government guaranteed it depression and defeat. Few genuine settlers went there and those who did often regretted the decision. The Hudson's Bay Company, the island's current master, desired to surrender its colonial responsibility, so long as proper compensation was paid. One element alone—shining bits of precious metal—would transform inertia into energy, and dismissal into desirability.

Chapter Two

Our Peculiar Field of Operations

You will...take those measures for securing the trade...which you think most advisable before a rush of strangers to the "digging" takes place & we find ourselves jostled out of what should rightfully be our peculiar field of operations.
—H.B.C. Governor George Simpson[1]

JAMES MARSHALL'S DISCOVERY of gold in the California Sierra turned the Pacific coast upside down and inside out, with immediate and long-term consequences of stupendous import. Strike-it-rich prospectors and capital-shrewd merchants rushed south from Oregon Territory in 1848. Others in substantially greater numbers came from the Atlantic coast, Latin America, Europe, and Asia in 1849, creating an insatiable demand for food, timber, and tools, not to mention luxury items, from slippery fresh shellfish to prime Havana cigars. "Goods were sold at unprecedented prices," George Simpson exclaimed upon perusing the returns in the Fort Victoria ledgers. Lumber brought $60 and then, if only briefly, $300 per thousand feet. A single H.B.C. cargo earned a gross return of £70,000. The Californian trade was, to be sure, a troublesome enterprise. Sailors deserted for the gold fields upon reaching port, and the pay increases necessary to retain crews generated demands for higher wages elsewhere in the H.B.C. establishment. Traditional trade relationships were disrupted, especially connections with Hawaii when the inflated gold country market absorbed the islands' entire sugar crop.[2]

Despite these frustrations, California gold compensated in part for the ongoing decline of the company's fur business. With beaver-fur clothing falling out of fashion in urbane Europe and America, and with resource spoliation in Oregon and New Caledonia, the Pacific Northwest posts registered a combined £7,000 deficit in 1851. "With the exception of Fort Colvile…," a touring executive reported in 1852, "the establishments within the American territory were all carried on at a loss." Simpson responded with yet another self-sufficiency edict. "I would strongly advise that you examine into the state of our affairs," he wrote coastal traders in August 1852, "with a view to retrenchment in every possible way."

On a more positive note, H.B.C. managers thought that precious metals might be found just south of the 49th parallel. Reports reached Victoria of promising signs east of the Cascades in the Spokane country. Venturesome prospectors, too, returned from the Yakima River convinced "beyond doubt" that gold in paying quantities existed on that stream. It appeared that the future of the Hudson's Bay Company and the Vancouver's Island colony depended, to a considerable degree, upon a mineral discovery of 1848 dimensions somewhere in the northern mountains.[3]

The Queen Charlotte Islands, a wild sea-mountain range in the fogenshrouded ocean northwest of Vancouver Island, formerly had been a prime resort for well-armed European and American trading ships in the late 18th and early 19th centuries. In this harsh Pacific wilderness, "the rolls," a Spanish explorer recorded, "were tremendous and the darkness terrifying." In more recent decades, however, the resident Haida tribesmen—the same who were feared by Indians and settlers alike when making long excursions to southern Vancouver Island and Puget Sound waters—had rarely experienced intrusions by whites. The occasional outside visitor, relieved at escaping unharmed, reported that the Queen Charlotte villagers were "hostile towards the whites," and Americans in particular, and the vast islands amounted to nothing but "solid rock, with a little earth composed of decayed vegetation."

Rumors of gold here first reached the outside world in the summer of 1850, transforming this treacherous and generally unappealing place into the latest Pacific coast attraction for wealth seekers. In moving to insure British control of the reported deposits, Governor James Douglas had to overlook certain legal obstacles. The Queen Charlottes, for one thing, were not under the jurisdiction of the Vancouver's Island colony. Douglas therefore acted informally to exert control based on his dubious interpretation of the 1838 H.B.C. Indian trade grant. Although British sovereignty was recognized under international law (the local Haida alone disagreeing), no serious attempt had ever been made to hoist the Union Jack on this rocky shore.[4]

"Should the gold deposits prove as valuable as expected," the London directors wisely concluded upon receipt of the original reports, "[it] cannot fail to have a very serious effect…on the interests of the concern." In the fall of 1851, Douglas sent the H.B.C. brigantine *Una* to the Queen Charlottes. At Edgefield Bay, the expedition discovered a vein seven inches thick running inland from the beach. Lacking proper equipment, not to mention mining expertise, crew members resorted to using gunpowder, blowing exploratory holes several feet deep in the sand and rock outcroppings. The Indians, knowing the value of gold, soon contested the claim in direct man-against-man fashion. "They would lie concealed until the report was heard," commanding officer W. H. McNeill recalled, "and then make a rush for the Gold." In the "regular scramble," the Indians wound up with "at least one half of the Gold." Blows were exchanged, weapons displayed, and lives threatened. McNeill prudently avoided further beachfront melees by sailing for Victoria. Sixty ounces saved from the *Una*, which ran on the rocks off Cape Flattery on the way home, went into the H.B.C.'s coffers, enough of a return to stimulate serious interest in the islands.[5]

Rescued sailors from the *Una* also made their way with purloined nuggets in hand to Portland and San Francisco, spreading word of the discovery. "When they were obliged…to leave," one newspaper reported, "they could see the gold lying in large lumps at the bottom of the hole made by their last blast." Forty Portlanders promptly left the Columbia River by chartered vessel. A second company, taking adequate time to properly prepare itself, outfitted one hundred men for "the new El Dorado." All told, a dozen American ships sailed to the Queen Charlottes in 1852. Five hundred prospectors examined "Gold Harbor," the original site prospected by explosives, as well as other appealing beaches. Most of the organized parties, James Douglas noted, carried "brass field-pieces, for the purpose of coercing the natives." One party, at least, constructed a fort complete with mounted cannon to guard against Indian and British challenge.[6]

In examining the various expedition accounts, George Simpson expressed concern over the greater energy so far exhibited by the Americans, as compared to the British. "I fear we have not been sufficiently prompt in securing this promising field of labor," the governor wrote to his people in Victoria, "& that we shall either be forestalled or driven out of it by… interlopers." As the nearest British governmental official, James Douglas already had attempted to have the gold "left to the better directed…enterprise

of Her Majesty's subjects." In a series of messages to London, Douglas requested authority to prohibit foreign vessels from landing in the Queen
Charlotte Islands. He argued that the Yankee miners would, sooner no doubt
than later, cause "serious difficulties with the native tribes," and when
reinforced "from the floating population in California" they would fatally un-
dermine British sovereignty. Douglas's proposed ban, once in effect, also
would materially benefit Vancouver's Island, "as in that case a flourishing
trade would soon flow into this colony"—an exchange of gold for food and
implements that otherwise would come from "ports in Oregon and California." His arguments were sound, at least from a mercantilist point of view,
but the colonial office rejected the advice, fearing that the United States
would respond by expelling British miners from the Sierra Nevada.[7]

Nevertheless, the American miners failed to prosper under the free trade
arrangement. The first party to reach the Queen Charlottes had departed after a few days, driven off by the Haidas. After the second vessel was wrecked,
the "wretched" survivors endured semi-captivity in a native village until rescued by a relief expedition. Subsequent ventures, though better managed and
armed, enjoyed little success. "We had neither the proper tools or sufficient
force to contend with the Indians," a miner reported after returning to Puget
Sound empty handed in March 1852. "We made only one blast, and from
that we found we should have to fight for what we got." Fortune seekers
aboard the brig *Eagle* experienced "an entire failure, the company being able
to obtain no gold." U.S. involvement in the Queen Charlotte Islands ended
dramatically in September, when Indians burned the schooner *Susan Sturgis*,
and held the crew and passengers for ransom.[8]

British efforts centered on the H.B.C. brig *Recovery*, which was sent north
from Victoria in March 1852 with 45 sailors and miners, and supplies for six
months. The man-of-war *Thetis* covered the expedition by cruising off the islands
in blustery demonstration of the Crown's sovereign claim. According to a detailed
account in the London *Times*, the shore party worked the beach "with great
energy, but with indifferent results." Patrols sent inland to "explore the interior of the island," meantime, "discovered…very little surface gold." When company employees, who had been promised shares of what now appeared to be
a non-existent treasure trove, threatened to mutiny, the *Recovery*'s captain returned to Victoria with only a modest cargo of precious metal.[9]

Once expenses were deducted for the 1851 and 1852 voyages, the attempted H.B.C. exploitation of the Queen Charlotte Islands had resulted in

a loss of £1,000. Unlike the Americans, who were scared off for good by the *Susan Sturgis* fiasco, the British retained their hopes for extracting wealth in the area. "I trust we may yet find the gold veins," George Simpson wrote. Taking a long-term approach, Douglas promised to recruit "a geologist of competent attainment," and a skilled and loyal mining crew. He believed time and money properly applied to permanent shore installations would in the end produce sustained profit, if not exactly California style riches. And, in July 1852, Douglas was finally appointed governor of the distant islands. For the moment, the Queen Charlotte affair revealed the importance of gold in the H.B.C.'s thinking about the future. Americans, too, obviously stood ready to take advantage of reported gold strikes in the north, both near and far.[10]

"California," the San Francisco *Alta California* remarked in October 1854, "is certainly a great country." Two hundred thousand persons, American citizens and foreigners, had migrated to the Golden State in the aftermath of James Marshall's fateful discovery, their mere presence providing much of the energetic evidence for the newspaper's celebratory assertion. The population was overwhelmingly male—nine out of every ten individuals in one accounting—and substantially more cosmopolitan than in most of the rest of the United States as a whole. The gold rush also was a youthful and impatient affair. Half of the Californians listed in the 1850 federal census were under the age of 30. Most residents of the camps and boomtowns expected to get rich without delay or hardship. "He cannot think of waiting the slow and sure progress of events," the *Alta California* observed of the Forty-niner, "but must branch out in a manner that will leave him a nabob in a year or two."[11]

Undeniably great, California nonetheless confronted a poorly concealed crisis. Peaking at over $81,000,000 in 1852, annual gold output fell to four-fifths and then nearly to half that figure over the remainder of the decade. Serious problems—in particular, the declining availability of good claims and the increasing cost of operations—were evident even as early as 1850. "Mining is not what it was when it was first discovered," a disillusioned prospector wrote that year. "There are only one or 2 out of a hundred that make much more than their living," another miner reported. Persons seeking more secure employment alternatives to prospecting, meanwhile, were subjected to periodic wage cuts, and unemployment was endemic to a California economy subject to as many downs as ups. Local and visiting journalists alike detected obvious negative signs in the human "tombs" of the Forty-niners "walking the streets of San Francisco," and in the "idlers and vagabonds… hanging about the different mining towns."

A growing conviction for many held that initiative and hard work were of no account, but what mattered was being first on the ground of a new strike. The population might have been youthful in terms of chronological age, one observer noted, but "no where do young men look so old as in California." The 1851 and 1856 vigilante movements, promoted by merchant leaders as battles of good against evil, in reality often reflected hard times, societal upheaval, and nativist scapegoating of Irish immigrants and the Catholic faithful.[12]

Altogether, California taught a harsh lesson—most fortune seekers were bound, for one reason or another, to fail. While some unlucky Forty-niners returned to homes in the east or abroad, numerous others refused to go back to families and friends in defeat. These disappointed individuals, joined by many others who genuinely loved the freedom and adventure of life in the mountains, remained at hand—and ready at a moment's notice to charge after the latest rumored field of dreams. "We are a singularly impulsive people," the *Alta California* noted of the tendency of many to abandon even steady employment and decent pay for new prospecting opportunities. The Californian was a peculiar human being—"certainly the most migratory," according to a Sacramento newspaper, "on the whole face of the earth."[13]

With California's mines "giving out" and "used up," as a number of influential voices loudly proclaimed, attention turned to the Northwest Coast. The discovery of gold in southern Oregon in 1852 drew three to four thousand prospectors to the steep-walled Rogue River Valley and establishment of the rough boomtown of Jacksonville. Reports of precious metal finds also came the following year from the Port Orford vicinity on the southernmost Oregon coast. The beach there, over a distance of 30 miles, was said to be, "literally covered with black sand…richly impregnated with gold." Miners earned "over one dollar to the pan," subsisting in the absence of civilized provisions upon "muscles, clams, fish and game." Making their way inland through the dense forbidding forests, adventurers found promising sign along the Coquille River and other rushing streams.[14]

Farther north, following hard upon the U.S. government's conclusion of the Walla Walla treaties with Columbia Plateau tribes in June 1855, prospectors found a "new Ophir of the Pacific" in the mountainous region tributary to Fort Colvile, the venerable H.B.C. post on the upper Columbia in Washington Territory. The initial reports were, to say the least, encouraging. "The fact that men have washed out from $30 to $100 per day, with a common tin pan," an Oregon newspaper pointed out, "is enough to convince any man familiar with gold placers, that these mines are exceedingly rich." The original diggings actually were near the mouth of the Pend Oreille River just north of the unsurveyed 49th parallel line, a geographical fact unknown to, or at least ignored by, trespassing Americans. Other problematic aspects of the gold rush, however, became perfectly evident—the country was rough and unexplored, the Indians unfriendly, and capital and supplies difficult, when not impossible, to obtain. Two hundred wealth seekers decided anyway to spend the winter, relying upon uncertain connections with the outside world for provisions and reinforcement.[15]

In Oregon and Washington territories, some greedy and fearful miners shed Indian blood in the pursuit of gold. Three "Rogue River wars" broke out between 1851 and 1855, the violence ending only when Joel Palmer, the territorial superintendent of Indian affairs, evacuated the surviving natives from the region as the only practical alternative to extermination. For no apparent reason, saltwater prospectors attacked a Coquille River village in early 1854, killing 16 persons in cold blood and precipitating months of hit-and-run retaliation. Some miners reportedly molested women and stole horses on the way to Colvile in 1855, provoking revenge attacks upon the transgressors and innocent passers-by alike. A dozen or more whites perished, according to unreliable official accounts, culminating in the murder of Indian agent Andrew Bolon and the start of eastern Washington's Yakama war of 1855–56.[16]

⌐⌐⌐

Though cut off from the Willamette and Puget Sound settlements during the Columbia Basin's Yakama conflict, miners in the Fort Colvile region remained profitably employed. "That the country is full of gold," a Hudson's Bay employee reported from the Pend Oreille River, "there cannot be the least doubt." By 1857, H.B.C. interest in gold shifted, as well, to the New Caledonia interior well north of the 49th parallel. Thompson River Indians had for some time traded gold dust at Kamloops, and post trader Donald McLean discovered promising signs at several points during excursions in the area, in one instance digging a bit of metal out of a riverbank when stopping for lunch. Though in small amounts, the returns for early 1857 were "enough," James Douglas wrote, "to prove the auriferous character of that country."[17]

Some of the Colvile prospectors, hearing rumors from travelers, crossed the border to the Thompson River in mid-summer, joining local Indians in the first serious investigation of the Fraser River basin. One mixed white and native mining party reported earning $2,000 inside of a week. "I have traded 49 Ounces of Gold Dust," trader McLean advised Governor Douglas, "and could have obtained much more if I had been provided with the proper Goods required by the Diggers," namely California boots and corduroy trousers. Receiving this account, which took 10 days to reach Victoria on September 1, Douglas immediately dispatched the good news to London—"gold has been found in considerable quantities in the district of Thompson River." The prime placers, according to McLean, were along the stream's lowermost dozen miles, which in his view ought to be immediately preempted by construction of a fort.[18]

American prospectors explored the Thompson River throughout the summer and fall of 1857, a fact widely communicated by accounts and letters from the scene in Oregon and California newspapers. A returning party of miners reported averaging "three hundred dollars each" in a month's time. Another company claimed $20 a day to the man. The H.B.C., the only real source of manufactured items and other necessities in the new mining areas, prospered along with the fortune hunters. Fort Victoria's storehouse began shipping regular consignments of clothing, shovels, and pans to Fort Langley for transport into the interior. "A trading party with an excellent supply…of goods," Governor Douglas wrote, "is kept constantly running among the diggings, to pick up the Gold as fast as it is collected." Receipts increased from 62 ounces of dust in September—including "the largest nugget…yet found at Thompsons River"—to 152 ounces in October, and 209 ounces in November.[19]

Recognizing a significant money-making opportunity, H.B.C. officials intended to establish a monopoly over the mainland gold fields, with the Indians serving as the actual miners. "No effort should be spared," George Simpson instructed, "to secure for the Company a fair share"—in other words, complete control—"of the business which the late discoveries will cause to spring up in that district." The firm proposed, Douglas observed, "that the Indian population, alone should be employed in working gold." In planning to solely work the New Caledonia gold fields with native miners, the H.B.C. could legitimately defend its right to do so under the provisions of the 1838 grant. Politically, of course, the company could ill-afford to be identified in London or Washington City as encouraging acts of Indian opposition and aggression against white American miners. "It would be very wrong," Simpson pointed out with respect to the necessity of adhering to H.B.C. covert action in this regard, "either to connive at or assist their [the Indians] acts of violence towards the whites who wish to embark in the gold washing business," even in cases where "these whites may be American adventurers."[20]

In pursuing this subtle and undeniably cynical policy, the company relied upon the Americans' often in-bred fear of Indians, and on the unwillingness of the Thompson River people to share in the gold diggings, not to mention providing salmon and other provisions to the interlopers. "Inculcate upon the Indians the duty of being kind to all white men," Douglas instructed his field traders in a missive suited for publication in England. But, H.B.C. representatives must also, according to another official letter of instruction, "take care to inform…white strangers coming into the country that the Indians are dangerous and not to be trusted." Personal advice of this cautionary nature— proffered in a backwoods authoritative man-to-man fashion—was all but guaranteed to be effective, especially when extended in the context of the occasional genuine native assault. Writing to the home government as colonial governor, Douglas condemned the Indians' opposition to Americans as "high-handed" and "unwarrantable." In private as a chief factor, he thought otherwise, saying the Indians should be left "entirely to their own impulses."[21]

Douglas took necessary measures to incorporate the natives into the company's commercial gold network. "I have…sent a supply of shovels, washing pans and picks to the Indian diggers," he informed the London directors, "who will receive every encouragement at our hands to induce them to work the auriferous streams." As a means of speeding the upstream shipment of supplies and downward flow of gold, the governor after a good deal of calculation developed plans for improving transportation. Under this new scheme, H.B.C. employees proceeded in well-laden craft, specifically built for sailing on the Fraser, from Fort Langley up to Fort Hope, located at the foot of the lower canyon. There, a specially trained corps took over, carrying goods around the great gorge's obstructions by horseback and, when returning to the Fraser above, ascending to the mouth of the Thompson in a second set of boats. "Though the difficulties be great, and the River dangerous," Douglas asserted, "yet we hope and shall strive to succeed."[22]

Shortages of capital and skilled labor, combined with the usually difficult seasonal weather, prevented the full implementation of these plans during the winter of 1857–58. However, the increasing monthly returns recorded during the final quarter of 1857 suggested that matters were well on track. The Indians were "daily becoming more alive to the advantages of gold finding," Douglas remarked in optimistic reports to his superiors, and were "exceedingly desirous to employ themselves in digging gold."

Moving with customary ease between his roles as governor and chief factor, Douglas issued an official proclamation in December declaring that the New Caledonia deposits were Crown property and off-limits to unauthorized persons. The prospects of ultimate success depended, however, upon the news from Thompson River being kept quiet, or at least to a minimum, south of the 49th parallel. Despite Indian frights, though, Americans were maintaining an active, if so far limited, interest in the country. However, months later in the midst of the 1858 excitement Douglas would have to concede that it had been "impossible to keep the discovery of Gold… concealed from the public."[23]

Chapter Three

A Mad Crowd Thronging with Eager Steps

It is scarcely necessary to advert to the history of the Fraser River excitement; how...the people of California and of Oregon and Washington Territories were startled by rumors industriously circulated, of fabulous gold discoveries on Fraser River; how day after day steamers and sailing vessels left the port of San Francisco for Victoria, crowded to excess—many of them carrying three times the number of passengers allowed by law; how thousands, who were then in prosperous circumstances in California, dazzled by the prospect of immediately acquiring immense wealth, abandoned their occupations both professional and manual, and selling off their mining claims and other possessions at a great sacrifice, threw themselves into the mad crowd who were thronging with eager steps to the new gold fields.—John Nugent, U.S. State Department special agent[1]

WINTER EASED ITS BRUTAL HOLD on New Caledonia in late January 1858. With the Fraser again flowing free of ice, the Hudson's Bay Company prepared to fully implement its gold policy devised in the preceding months. "These arrangements," wrote James Douglas, his thoughts focusing in particular on constructing a new post near the Thompson's mouth, "will lead to a considerable outlay of capital in the outset, but the object is important and if gold is found to be abundant the trade will become highly remunerative." The chief factor had placed the steamer *Otter* in regular service to and from Fort Langley, ordered additional river craft constructed, and reinforced the transportation corps. Through regular correspondence with Donald McLean and other traders, he also was paying close attention to market conditions in the interior. "Tell me how you find the Indians...," Douglas instructed a subordinate departing for the Fraser, "if they have much gold among them; if they were pleased with the Picks[,] Pans & Shovels which you took up; if they want more tools, what kind of goods they like best, and wish us to send them."[2]

The current and prospective returns seemed to justify the expenditures and time spent on such details. In early February, a small mining party visiting Fort Langley to trade gold dust for clothing and supplies reported that they had found the Fraser River itself a "country…as rich as any part of California." The sojourners intended to return and make their fortune, once the snow melted and the stream fell to a workable level. "If even half of what they tell be true," Douglas noted, "it is certain we are on the eve of a great discovery." Personally inclined to note caution, however, the governor pointed out that total H.B.C. gold purchases to date barely exceeded 1,000 ounces.[3]

Outsiders bound for points north of the 49th parallel—either coming by way of Puget Sound, Bellingham Bay, and the Gulf of Georgia, or overland east of the Cascades—had remained the prime concern at Victoria. "A great number of people are preparing to visit the mines in course of the coming spring and summer," a worried Douglas had informed London in January 1858. Already, "excitement" among employees in New Caledonia and on Vancouver Island had compelled the company to "be a little more liberal in regard to pay[,] giving something extra over and above the…regular standard."

A disgruntled servant named Charles Adams soon claimed credit for releasing news about the gold strike—the supposed great secret of his H.B.C. masters—to the world. However, there was no James Marshall of the Fraser—no single individual was responsible for instigating the mad rush to the cold streams and snowy mountains. Numerous Americans already knew about the Thompson diggings from personal experience or especially from hearing accounts by returning pioneers. Regular steamboat connections between the Sound and the British colonial capital made for a porous international border and encouraged the exchange of news, gossip, and speculation.[4]

However, at the start of the new year, 1858, Washington and Oregon residents seemingly were preoccupied by other dramatic developments. Periodic eruptions of Mount St. Helens (dating back to mid-decade) continued to provoke mystification and dread. Unseasonable cold in late winter, followed by uncommon heat in early spring, interfered with sleep and comfort. A

10-year-old girl became the first white Oregonian known to die from a rattle-snake bite. The steamer *Traveler*, the mainstay for Puget Sound-Victoria passenger service, sank near Port Gamble, with only three survivors. Reports from the Sound also focused on the tragic final days of the Nisqually Indian leader, Leschi, who finally was executed after being convicted (upon perjured testimony) of murder in the 1855–56 Puget Sound Indian war. Governor Fayette McMullin, a former Virginia congressman, drew almost as much attention. In a series of truly edifying episodes, the slaveholding McMullin had procured a legislatively sanctioned divorce from his wife, caned a political opponent, and loudly demanded a recall of regular Army officers at Fort Steilacoom for asking him to pardon Leschi. In a final uplifting moment, McMullin engaged in a public quarrel with territorial secretary Charles H. Mason over the right to pocket proceeds from renting the capitol building to private parties.[5]

Except for a brief announcement in an early February issue of the *Alta California*, that "excitement" was "increasing" in the "new gold mines on Frazer's River," American newspapers on the West Coast were giving relatively little attention to developments north of the 49th parallel. The partially exploited southern Oregon mines appeared to be the likely new focal point for prospecting, especially with the local Indians now removed by federal fiat. The Rogue River "country," the *Alta California* pointed out, "…is of precisely a similar character to that of one of our [California] mining sections, and the bars, gullies, and banks are quite as rich in gold deposits as those of any of our own rivers." San Francisco residents also were considering investment opportunities, mainly in the Bellingham Bay and Nanaimo coal veins.

Then suddenly, by early March, word broke about the Fraser strike! "The news of extensive mines…came upon us unawares," the Olympia *Pioneer and Democrat* would recall after the fact, "at a time when the country was not prepared for this state of things." (As it turned out, Puget Sound merchants might have profited handsomely if they had correctly anticipated future events and laid in extra supplies and provisions.)[6]

Virtually overnight, the Fraser gold strike became, said James Douglas, "the great subject of conversation" up and down the West Coast. The Olympia *Pioneer and Democrat* proclaimed in the first week of March: "Much excitement exists on Vancouver's Island, in consequence of the alleged discovery of rich gold deposites [sic]." At several points on the Fraser between Fort Hope and the Thompson River, white prospectors reportedly had taken out

$25 per day and Indians between $10 and $12 to the man. "Obtained merely from surface diggings, without the aid of anything more than...pans and willow baskets," the Indian return alone was in the view of Washington Territory's other weekly newspaper, the *Puget Sound Herald*, ample proof of the riches to be found north of the boundary. Bellingham Bay pioneer R. W. Peabody returned from a hurried tour with graphic proof of his own in the form of bright golden flakes. "The question is settled beyond a doubt," the *Puget Sound Herald* enthused, "that gold can be found...in as large quantities as ever found in California."[7]

In private messages to H.B.C. directors in London, James Douglas confirmed the newspaper pronouncements. "People are rapidly gathering about here for a rush," he noted from Victoria on March 1. Then, a mid-month visit to Fort Langley provided him with an opportunity for first-hand consultation with traders and miners. "Gold is found in more or less abundance," the governor reported in passing along the latest intelligence, "on every part of Frasers River from Fort Yale to the Forks." According to an experienced prospector encountered in the course of this mainland tour, the rock formations and gravel accumulations along the main stream and its tributaries were "all characteristics of the gold districts of California." Within a month, Fort Langley's veteran factor, James Murray Yale, traded merchandise for $4,353.50 in dust, calculated at the rate of $16 to the ounce. The sight of "strangers proceeding up Frasers River...almost every day," Douglas admitted, was "unpleasant." The H.B.C. had prospered over many decades, however, by facing up to realities. Douglas now said that the company must "press onwards at all hazards" with improvements in the transportation system and shifting focus, reluctantly but inevitably, from the Indians to the newcomers.[8]

Many persons abandoned their normal occupations upon receipt of the first credible news from the Fraser. The Bellingham Bay coal mine closed after losing its crew of laborers to the rush. They were followed by deserters from the Bellingham Bay military post, recently established to counter the northern Indians. Other deserters from Fort Steilacoom, the regional army headquarters, also joined in the flight to the mines. Sailors abandoned ship at Port Gamble and other mill towns, preventing the export of lumber. "Already has the contagion infested the logging camps in this section," the *Puget Sound Herald* reported from Steilacoom, "and hands are leaving daily for the gold region."

Monument on the Fraser's south bank commemorating the H.B.C.'s Fort Hope; photograph by Asahel Curtis, June 13, 1930. Note the rugged mountainous terrain across the river. *UW Libraries, A. Curtis 57012*

Desertion also was a problem north of the 49th parallel. James Douglas struggled to man H.B.C. sailing vessels with adequate crews and stationed armed guards at the Victoria dock to intimidate would-be defectors. "Though a few of the riotous spirits on board made an attempt…to cause a strike," he wrote of a demand for higher wages on the company's *Princess Royal*, "it was speedily checked, and all hands repaired quietly to the windlass, and gave no further trouble." The Anglo-American boundary commission, which finally had begun surveying the 49th parallel, curtailed its work, due to the unavailability of workers.[9]

Oregon, as opposed to Washington, withheld its endorsement for a time. Portland currently was serving as the supply center for the Colvile mines and other points east of the Cascades, a profitable position sure to be challenged should rival diggings come to the fore closer to Puget Sound. "At present it is hard to ascertain what is mere rumor and what facts," an Olympia correspondent observed in a bit of cautionary advice that quickly was published by Asahel Bush in Salem's *Oregon Statesman*. "All reports from new gold mines…," another Oregon newspaper affirmed, "should be taken with a large margin closely cut down." Initially, at least, relatively fewer Oregonians joined in the Fraser rush. Those intent upon protecting the Columbia River as the Pacific Northwest's main commercial artery dismissed the Fraser gold talk as the latest example of "blowing" by "humbug" editors and land speculators who wanted to entice prosperous neighbors into "wandering after the *wild geese*" in the direction of Puget Sound and New Caledonia.[10]

Numerous Californians, however, were more than ready to put their hopes in any good tidings from the north. "San Francisco is, at this moment," the *Alta California* reported midway through the preceding hard winter, "crowded with more unemployed…in proportion to her population, than any other city in the Union." Expectations for many in the Golden State undeniably had been tarnished. Visiting California's interior towns, London *Times* reporter Donald Fraser was astonished to find "crowds of idle miners" with nothing to do but "eat, drink, read the papers, and discuss the 'big strikes' that other and luckier miners made."

Nevertheless, caution initially prevailed over hysteria regarding the earliest reports from the north. On the basis of "second thoughts," correspondent Fraser decided against forwarding the original New Caledonia accounts to London on the first available steamer, "because I have sufficient experience of the frequent fallacies of suddenly made 'rich discoveries,' and of the disappointments ensuing from the 'tremendous excitements' caused by them so often in this country [California], to make me cautious in reporting unconfirmed news." Persons contemplating immediate departure for New Caledonia, the *Alta California* repeatedly advised, ought to remember "past deceptions, intentional and unintentional" and use "a grain of caution."[11]

Publishing a detailed letter from Port Townsend on March 9, however, the *Alta California* had provided its readers with the first reasonably accurate "flattering accounts" from the Fraser. Three weeks passed, though, before a definitive announcement appeared in the San Francisco press, based upon intelligence from the passengers and crew of the Pacific Mail steamer *Columbia*. On April 4, headlines blared: "Gold Discovery Confirmed," and "Miners Making $8 to $50 a Day," and "People Abandoning Everything for the Mines"!

These facts were clarified over the next several days in personal correspondence and other pronouncements presented by returnees. "Every one who can possibly leave," a sea captain arriving from Washington Territory stated, "is wending his way to the diggings from every town on Puget Sound." Eight hundred prospectors reportedly were already at work earning an average of $15 a day, three times the prevailing rate in the California Sierra. "Gold, in paying quantities," another Port Townsend missive advised, "can be easily obtained, at almost any point." Carrying an actual sample of "thin, scaly gold," visiting Seattle storekeeper J. A. Chase drew widespread attention as the celebrity of the day. Arrivals from the north also warned against the Hudson's Bay Company, a concern enjoying, through its charter and control over supplies and prices, "complete command of the trade."[12]

A massive northward rush of California miners had been sparked. "Each succeeding arrival from Frazer River," the San Francisco *Herald* exclaimed, "seems to add to the already prevailing excitement." A *New York Times* correspondent, noting a return to "the halcyon days of 1849, " said San Francisco's streets were filled with "rough, stalwart fellows" carrying picks, shovels, and pans, and boarding vessels for the journey north. Others were proceeding overland up the coast or through the interior plains and deserts. Most observers remarked upon the reprise, at last, of good old Californian times. "You have no idea of the excitement," an acquaintance of Portland editor T. J. Dryer wrote. "Think of '49 and you have a faint idea." Donald Fraser confessed that he was unable to keep pace with the "astounding" chain of events, making it difficult for him to prepare comprehensive reports "for the mail to Europe" on departing vessels. Though still hesitant regarding the true nature of things on the Fraser, the *Alta California* predicted that 50,000 persons would depart for "the new gold region" by the end of spring.[13]

Remarkably, there were, as yet, only relatively small returns seen coming from the mines. "Only a very unconsiderable quantity of gold has come down to San Francisco in the regular channels of trade," Donald Fraser reported in mid-June; the "trifling consignments" carried to date by the express companies totaled less than 600 ounces. The London *Times* correspondent also pointed out, however, that gold rushes were sustained upon "stories of what was seen, and heard, and could be learned," rather than by the earliest statistics. Besides, the small number of people traveling on southward voyages from the Pacific Northwest amounted to a form of arithmetical validation—apparently people were staying in the north for good reason. Fraser also noted that passengers "brought a good deal more" gold concealed upon their persons. "No steamer has yet returned with more than a dozen or fifteen passengers," the *New York Times* representative noted two months into the excitement, again implying that most people were remaining in the Fraser gold fields because of good opportunities. Eventually, even those California observers previously inclined to skepticism began taking little notice of the minimal profit so far recorded. For example, the *Alta California* stated, "There can be no longer a doubt, that a second California is about to be opened up to the world, and one, too, that bids fair to equal her in every respect, as far as the richness of the gold deposits are concerned.[14]

For the third time in a decade, said the editors of the *Alta California* in harking back to 1849 and to more recent events in Australia, "the world is about to be turned topsy-turvy by an excited struggle to get to an *El Dorado*." The "mania," the *Times'* Donald Fraser observed, consumed everyone but the clerks at the docks, who were presumably too busy forwarding merchandise and issuing passenger tickets to consider leaving. "None are too poor and none too rich to go," wrote Fraser. "None too young and none too old." Some went for gold and some—including a merchant confessing that he "longed for a change"—for adventure. Others were escaping incarceration, such as the prominent vigilante target, Ned McGowan, who boarded an outbound steamer from a small boat just inside the Golden Gate. A number of black Californians also emigrated. Fed up with public and private acts of discrimination, 400 black men, women, and children eventually headed north on James Douglas's promise of protection and fair treatment. Chinese also departed in such numbers that the *Alta California* bemoaned an "exodus" of laborers who might otherwise have served as "a cheap and practical substitute for…white men."[15]

Two basic approaches to the diggings were available to Californians. One was by ocean-going vessel to Northwest waters and by smaller craft into the

Fraser's mouth, and then by struggling upstream through the rapids or taking difficult trails in the forested mountains.

The other, confirming British fears that Americans would attempt to "force a passage into the Gold District through their own territories," led up the Columbia River to The Dalles or Fort Walla Walla, then north overland via old Indian and H.B.C. trails. Heavily promoted in Portland—once Oregonians realized that money could be made from the Fraser rush—this was in many respects the superior choice. A $15 ticket took an expectant gold hunter by sea from San Francisco to the Willamette River. An additional $11—supposedly "a sum no man will complain of"—took him, in one day by steamboat and portage, to the east side of the Cascade Range. At The Dalles, he could choose among "thousands" of Indian horses offered for sale at between $25 and $70, purchase a saddle for $6, and stock up on provisions and mining tools at rates a mere 10 percent above Portland standards. Once in the Columbia basin, as a traveler pointed out, "you are in an open country clear to the mines, with an abundance of grass and water." Unresolved problems from the Yakama war, exacerbated by the renewed movement of prospectors to Fort Colvile, appeared at first to be of little consequence. "The rumor that the Indians are troublesome," an experienced wilderness hand assured migrants, "is all fudge."[16]

Despite this claim, the interior Columbia passage could be closed by untoward developments. Launched at The Dalles in May, the pioneer steamer *Venture* was promptly washed into rapids—along with prospects for comfortable and efficient travel—when the captain unwisely cast off the wharf lines without engaging the engine. In the same month, Lieutenant Colonel Edward Steptoe, gallantly marching with 164 U.S. Army regulars to show the flag in the Spokane and Fort Colvile areas, confronted a thousand discontented warriors in the Palouse Hills, and fled south in hasty and dramatic retreat with seven men lost. The resulting war, embracing the Palouse and Spokane country north of the Snake River, as well as the Yakima and Wenatchee valleys just east of the Cascades, tended to bar the trails to New Caledonia.

Oregonians insisted, however, that the danger was exaggerated and, even after the Steptoe debacle, the interior routes remained superior to the Puget Sound alternative. "The northern Indians have already murdered more persons…ten to one," a Portland newspaper maintained, "than have been killed on the Columbia river trail." On June 20, however, Yakama warriors routed a large prospecting party bound for the Fraser. Other reports indicated that another group of miners attempting to head north under the leadership of noted route finder and Indian agent Joel Palmer were much delayed with problems on the trail. Another reinforced party lost a half dozen men in the process of crossing the 49th parallel. Rather than face the wrath of Columbia Plateau tribesmen, many prospectors waiting at The Dalles turned about for Puget Sound, either going by sea or via the overland Cowlitz-Chehalis portage to the southern Sound.[17]

Whether heading for the Strait of Juan de Fuca or the Columbia's mouth, most Californians traveling by sea first left through San Francisco's Golden Gate. On a tour of California's upcountry settlements, Donald Fraser found "the masses…in commotion," with "squads of miners" and storekeepers, "who could manage to leave," all "making for San Francisco to ship themselves off." The fever, one gold camp newspaper announced, "extends alike to miners, mechanics, merchants, traders and gentlemen of 'elegant leisure.'" According to one of the *Alta California*'s Sierra Nevada correspondents, "you can scarcely speak to a miner…whose mind is not made up to go." The only persons remaining, another interior paper claimed, did so "from want of funds to reach the new El Dorado." Thousands of men and some women, too, deserted Sacramento and Stockton. The daily riverboats were packed to, and beyond, capacity.

Unlike the situation in 1849, however, the new rush failed to produce a significant migration from the eastern United States to the Pacific coast. Rather, the Fraser River rush mainly was a shift northward of California's population. San Francisco's residents and those of its hinterland, Donald Fraser astutely noted, "have merely changed their location."[18]

Californians of all social, economic, and ethnic classes joined in a "wild state of excitement" in San Francisco. "Here," a visitor from Oregon wrote home, "nothing is talked of, dreampt of, sung of, drunk of, read of or seen but Frazer's River." Miners and merchants, along with "preachers, hotel keepers, 'ladies of the pave[ment]' and…pretty near every body else is talking of going." Competing with one another for readership, the city's *Alta California*, *Herald*, and *Bulletin* issued extras and special steamer editions, featuring maps, letters from the north, and supposed expert advice. Hostelries had too few rooms and restaurants had insufficient food to accommodate the mass of fortune seekers. Boxes and crates in an amazing variety of sizes, all marked for delivery at Victoria, Bellingham Bay, or a Puget Sound port, overflowed the sidewalks and wharves. Police officers vainly tried to keep order, breaking up

"Ho! For Frazer River." Though rather whimsical, this drawing by California proponent J. Ross Browne nevertheless captures the full-blown excitement in San Francisco during 1858. *J. Ross Browne: A Peep at Washoe.*

fights among scufflers, who jostled for position in front of ticket offices and dockside boarding places. "It resembled a crowd at one of the London theatres on a 'Star' night," Donald Fraser reported after a visit to the waterfront.

"Clothed in the secular mining garb of coarse wollen [sic], or flannel shirts, with heavy boots," another observer of the wild scene wrote, men marched in groups through the streets, brandishing paid-up passage vouchers and loaded down with "blankets, canteens, tin pots, miners' wash-pans, picks, spades, shovels, firearms, and other articles."[19]

Previously limited to a twice-monthly mail boat and the irregular voyages of Northwest lumber company schooners, San Francisco's northbound commercial connections were hard-pressed by the sudden demand for sea transportation. Business interests quickly responded to the new opportunities, however, by pressing into service all available craft. Profit-seeking ship owners restored some long inactive vessels into service, supposedly in "thorough overhauled" condition, and also transferred vessels from the San Francisco-Los Angeles-San Diego runs. Rechristened as the *Commodore*, the mishap-prone *Brother Jonathan*, widely known on the coast as "a miserable old tub, no more seaworthy than the ordinary...coffin," took on new life. "A...steamer bursts her boiler, shatters to pieces plank, timber and human flesh," the *Alta California* complained of a distressingly common occurrence. Then, "she is put upon the beach...patched up again, another set of machinery put into her, and a new name painted upon her sides."[20]

Between April 20 and August 7, 81 ships (which includes those making repeat voyages) cleared San Francisco Bay for the Strait of Juan de Fuca and Vancouver Island, carrying 12,760 official paying individuals. When publishing these customs house statistics, however, the *Alta California* appended a significant disclaimer pointing out that the "books do not contain a full list of the vessels, and the number of passengers reported is considerably below the truth." Some ships evaded notice altogether and most packed as many people aboard as space allowed, regardless of maritime regulations or insurance limitations. "It is well known," the *New York Times* correspondent reported, "that at least one-fourth of those departing are not enumerated in the clearances." The *Cortes*, for instance, carried 500 passengers that were not recorded on the books, and the *Panama* 400. The recorded tally of 9,216 through the third week in June fell well below an actual figure thought to be "not less than fifteen thousand." A merchant traveling north on the *Sierra Nevada* confirmed this practice, recording in his diary a complement of fifteen hundred passengers for a voyage supposedly limited to no more than nine hundred.[21]

Steamships took four to five days, while sailing vessels required between ten and twelve days, to make the passage. The fare, using the language of the docks, was $60 to $65 for "nobs" and $30 to $35 for "roughs," the former with cabin accommodations and the latter without. The entire trip virtually took place within sight of the Pacific coastline, with captains using the massive headlands of northern California, Oregon, Washington, and Vancouver Island as guides. "The navigation," observed Donald Fraser, who departed for Victoria in early summer on assignment for the *Times*, "is so simple that a school-boy could sail a steamer." Passengers with an inclination for observing nature enjoyed themselves all the way north, provided they could find a good viewpoint from the crowded decks. "From the shore, where the trees dip into the sea," wrote Fraser, "back to the verge of the distant horizon, over hills, down valleys, across ravines, and on and around the sides and tops of the mountains, it is one great waving panorama of forest scenery."[22]

Of course, the trip to the diggings was hardly a vacation cruise. Northbound passengers, Donald Fraser noted, were "crowded 'like herrings packed in a barrel'" aboard "crazy old vessels, not one which is really seaworthy." Deck space was so confined, day and night, one wag observed, that "the waiters…have to fight their way when serving 'the quality.'" Those attempting a stroll or some other form of exercise had to do so with "the general forbearance and good humour of the crowd." The food was "so so" in first class and awful in steerage. "Nobs" endured association with uncouth Sierra miners—"the mud of their last diggings on their clothes and boots"—as well as the stench wafted on salt air from horses and mules carried on most vessels. Infamous San Francisco rowdies, like Bully Bill Carr, who spent his time on the *Commodore* physically abusing and robbing black and Chinese passengers, were another regular feature during the passage north. Relying on their numbers and threatening violence, street toughs forced their way aboard without paying and ate well, even when penniless, by extorting provisions from weaker shipmates and passengers.[23]

Saltwater bullies, however, were an insignificant hazard when compared to the prospect of drowning. Those persons taking passage north on the mail steamers, which stopped at Portland en route, endured inbound and outbound crossings over the treacherous bar at the Columbia's mouth. Navigation at sea was relatively safe from a technical point of view, but vessels often leaked and shipmasters tended to be incompetent. In mid-July, the grossly overloaded *Commodore*, just as prone to have a mishap under its new name as well as the old one (*Brother Jonathan*), nearly foundered in a storm three days out of San Francisco. The pumps failed, the starboard boiler went out, and, as a passenger later reported, the vessel "groaned, and creaked, and trembled." Working for their lives, all persons aboard, "nobs" included, threw the deck cargo overboard, then the horses, and finally most of the goods in the hold. The wind at last abating, the captain regained control, turned about, and slowly headed back to port. The same storm also came close to sinking the *Sierra Nevada*. For several days, the steamer made "but little Headway...," passenger Cyrus Olin Phillips recorded in his diary, "having been Struck by a Number of Heavy Seas." The pumps finally got "ahead of the leaks," saving the fifteen hundred persons from certain death, aside from one would-be miner washed over the side. Three weeks later, the *Oregon* ran on the Point Reyes rocks, north of San Francisco. Fifty terrified people intent on saving themselves leaped to the beach, only to be left behind when the crew somehow extricated the damaged vessel and, backing off to deep water, steamed away in the fog.[24]

With good reason, passengers were happy to round Cape Flattery and enter the broad Strait of Juan de Fuca. To the left, the view of Vancouver Island's rugged southwest coast alternated between dense forest and handsome prairie, with occasional Indian villages presenting the only sign of human habitation. On the right, the jumbled Olympic Mountains in Washington Territory, "their summits," one arrival noted, "clad in snow, and rivaling in whiteness the double banked clouds surrounding them," practically rose straight up from the timbered shoreline. At sunset, the peaks stood "in bold relief against a clear blue sky," illuminated by "mystic light" from the western horizon. At water's edge, lighthouses recently installed at Cape Flattery and Dungeness Spit by the federal government winked on, indicating the way to the gold. To the east, Mount Baker towered over the mainland, islands, and sea with such dramatic presence that newcomers invariably overestimated its height by thousands of feet.[25]

⌐⌐

Altogether the wealth seekers from California, Washington, and Oregon probably numbered between 25,000 and 30,000 in 1858, passing through Victoria, Bellingham Bay, and from other points on the mainland. "Crowds of people are coming in from all quarters," James Douglas exclaimed to his colleagues when reporting upon "the prodigious emigration." From mid-May through the end of June, according to H.B.C. figures, 19 steamers, 9 sailing ships, and 14 "decked boats" entered port at Victoria. Based upon his analysis of official manifests, Douglas estimated that Vancouver's Island and New Caledonia together "have gained an increase of 10,000 inhabitants within…six weeks, and the tide of immigration continues to roll onward without any prospect of abatement."[26]

Most of the adventurers, especially those from California, knew little about the actual location of the diggings or the best means of getting there from the sea. Some, relying on the *Alta California*'s claim that "the *great bend* of Frazer river comes down below the 49th parallel," were badly misinformed. For most Californians, Donald Fraser pointed out, the "real difficulties and hardships" began after reaching the Strait of Juan de Fuca and Victoria. Until then, their course had been obvious, a northbound heading with the coast in view—their main challenges had been to prepare an outfit and securing a ticket. Debarking passengers now had to make their way through a largely uncharted wilderness. When inquiring of "the news from the mines," they were answered with the rival claims of proponents and merchants from competing American and British settlements and towns. "The temptations, allurements and lies…were very hard to withstand," a new arrival wrote from Bellingham Bay. Faced with "conflicting and contradictory" advice, the Steilacoom *Puget Sound Herald* noted, fortune hunters "deem[ed] it about as well, perhaps, to trust to chance."[27]

Some things, at least, quickly became clear. Ocean-going ships could not enter the Fraser, forcing miners to transfer at some point to watercraft appropriate for river travel. Victoria was the only British port of entry in the vicinity, and it was there, after Governor Douglas's December 1857 proclamation, that mining licenses were issued. Except for a duty on liquor, a prime source of government revenue, the colonial capital was a free trade emporium. This factor was bound to prove increasingly advantageous to the British as the gold rush continued and many vessels avoided U.S. mainland harbors where high tariffs prevailed.

Though previously a "quietist little nook of a town," Victoria quickly was becoming a replica of San Francisco on the Northwest Coast as an obvious intermediate destination for persons bound for the mines. When the *Commodore* (the first arriving California steamer loaded with miners) had reached Victoria, a passenger aboard wrote: "The good people [of Victoria]…were at church." In capturing the sensational impact of this event, the writer noted that these churchgoers "were perfectly astounded when they came out, and beheld between 400 and 500 Yankees, armed with revolvers and bowie knives." Within a few weeks, Victoria had, according to one merchant, "near six thousand people," an eight-fold increase in population for the entire colony.[28]

Steamer captains, however, soon began avoiding Victoria's difficult harbor for a much safer moorage several miles away. Except for some vessels guided in by a few skilled pilots, and possibly by some foolhardy ones as well, ships would eventually stop entering Victoria Harbour (particularly in September after the *Pacific* ran aground, and when a rock punched a hole in the *Constitution*'s hull). The waterway "answer[ed] well enough" for Fraser River craft, a visiting journalist noted, but its "zigzag shape," the "long low sandspit" at the entrance, and a shallow anchorage made the place "hazardous for large vessels." Victoria might be a new San Francisco in terms of "dust and wind," a resident jokester pointed out, "but it has not that admirable bay."

Three miles to the west, however, Esquimalt Harbour offered some of the best anchorage on the Pacific coast. The unlighted Race and Fisgard rocks offshore had to be carefully avoided, the entry was difficult to locate even in daylight, and the channel was narrow, but, when once inside, ships found refuge in a vast circular basin. "We slid in through…two low, rocky promontories," Donald Fraser wrote of his arrival from California, "and found ourselves suddenly transported from the open sea…into a Highland lake, placid as the face of a mirror, in the recesses of the pine forest." Debarking passengers according to personal preference either walked to Victoria working off their sea legs, rented horses or wagons for the brief journey, or booked sailboat passage around to the capital.[29]

Despite Victoria's navigational limitations, new arrivals otherwise praised James Douglas's "sagacity and good taste" as a town builder. Victoria occupied only a portion of the well-watered bayside heights—there was space enough here "to build a Paris," said Fraser of the *Times*. "It is prettily laid out," a visiting *Alta California* editor reported, "and, overlooking its little harbor, stands on an extensive plateau…now verdant with grass, and…a variety of wild flowers." Most Californians, however, probably paid scant attention to the beautiful natural surroundings, or paused to contemplate the magnificent Olympic Mountains south across the Strait, or the distant blue Cascades in the east. Of 225 buildings constructed in the first six weeks of the rush,

200 were mercantile establishments, reflecting the entrepreneurial leanings of the new population. Operating in a trade that was "all cash," merchants imported lumber from American sawmills, and beef cattle from Oregon driven overland to the Sound and then north by steamer, to be "thrown overboard and compelled to swim ashore." At Victoria's H.B.C. fort, Roderick Finlayson and other overworked company employees sold goods and doubled as informal Crown officials, handling customs chores and dispensing licenses. "There is so much hurry[,] bustle and confusion here," Governor Douglas complained, "that our regular work is got through with great difficulty."[30]

Newcomers accustomed to the delights of San Francisco, civilized and otherwise, found conditions at Victoria primitive. The Hudson's Bay Company had never wasted money on such fancified improvements as municipal lighting and serviceable streets. Fashionably attired capitalists and bedraggled miners alike slogged about in mud and carried lanterns at night. Unlike the soft-palmed merchants, who already had reached their El Dorado in Victoria, prospectors tarried only briefly here, "waiting," in the favored saying of the day, "for something to turn up." Temporary residents made do with tents, either of the standard variety or makeshifts assembled from blankets, downed tree limbs, and discarded bits of lumber. "Hundreds of these miniature dwellings are scattered through our suburbs," the *Victoria Gazette* noted. Permanent residents walking in the woods came "suddenly here and there upon an isolated specimen." At night, the occupants sat by scrap-wood fires, contemplating and conversing about "the chances of the golden future."[31]

The horde of newcomers drove real estate prices to astronomical, even irrational, levels. Outside Victoria, a standard 1 Pound per acre rate prevailed. In town, the H.B.C. sold 60 by 80 feet lots, first at $50 and then, depending on location, at $75 to $100. "There is a rush from morning to night," Donald Fraser wrote of an early June visit to the land office. All-told, sales amounted to $1,700 for the first quarter of 1858, but increased to $11,700 between May 1 and June 11, when transactions were halted while more acreage was surveyed. When the land business resumed, the land office took in $63,000 in the first two days. Once in private hands, lots increased rapidly in market value, from an average of $150 to as much as $3,000 in a matter of weeks. Late arrivals could not afford to buy, while property holders, expecting further increases, declined in any event to sell. "To an old staid business man," a rare fiscally conservative observer noted, "all this looked like building up large prospective fortunes on *shadows*."[32]

San Francisco's influence was evident in many aspects. "The life…of the place is imparted to it by the Californians," *Times* representative Fraser pointed out. Letter writers reported regular sightings of well-known Golden State immigrants on Victoria's muddy streets. Familiar California mercantile establishments opened branch businesses in Victoria, complete with the same style signs used back home. Victorians, accustomed to relying on the California press for news, now had their own local paper, the *Victoria Gazette*, owned and edited by expatriate partners from the bay. "The place," one of the *Alta California*'s correspondents suggested of Victoria, "in some respects may be called San Francisco in miniature."[33]

British colonials had the Californians uppermost in mind when they complained of their town being overrun by "all the worst characters of the coast." Alfred Waddington, author of *The Fraser Mines Vindicated, or, The History of Four Months*—the first book published on Vancouver Island (1858)—condemned many of the newcomers as "speculators of every kind…bummers, bankrupts, and brokers," not to mention "gamblers, swindlers, thieves, drunkards, and jail birds…In short, the outscourings of a population containing…the outscourings of the world." Invective of this vivid sort captured a certain degree of reality. But as Waddington also admitted, most Americans behaved themselves most of the time. However, the bad conduct of some tended to darken the reputation of all. Robberies, often involving large sums of stolen cash or gold dust, were common. So too were street fights, often pitting old California vigilante combatants against one another. Some white fortune seekers openly protested the relatively tolerant racial climate in Victoria, where blacks served on the police force and even, according to an offended California reporter, sat "down to the same table with families." A number of Americans rioted in July, releasing a prisoner held by the authorities and then beating up the sheriff, before dispersing when British naval officers anchored the warship *Plumper* within two cables-length of shore and trained cannon on the mob.[34]

Good Yankee patriots, however, condemned "our lunatic Californians" for building up a city in British territory. "American capital and American energy," the *Alta California* exclaimed, ought to be expended "upon American soil," and on "some point on Puget Sound" selected as "the entrepot for trade with the back country." After all, as *Times* correspondent Fraser conceded in a survey of possible mainland alternatives to Victoria, U.S. citizens were "great adepts" at city making. Washington Territory's largest community, Olympia, was advantageously located at the terminus of the overland route from Oregon, but the territorial capital also was at the farthest southern point on the Sound from the 49th parallel. Steilacoom to the north, a place of some regional importance, occupied a prime spot near the tidewater end of the Naches Pass wagon road over the Cascades, opened in 1853 and connecting with the Columbia Basin trails to the Fraser. Seattle, again a little farther north, faced broad Elliott Bay with the best crossing of the Cascades, Snoqualmie Pass, at its back door. The crisis in Indian relations east of the mountains, however, prevented Steilacoom and Seattle from prospering in what otherwise would have been particularly viable connecting points between sea and land.[35]

The Olympic Peninsula's Port Townsend, located at the northwest entrance to Puget Sound, possessed some undoubted advantages. Built at the foot of a bluff fronting on Admiralty Inlet, leading from Juan de Fuca Strait into the Sound, the town was roughly equidistant between the Fraser and the mountain passes behind Seattle and Steilacoom, and therefore "the most central starting point." As the location of the U.S. customs house, Port Townsend prospered upon the complications produced by the 49th parallel boundary. All vessels sailing between Vancouver Island and any of the northwest American mainland points had to call here, no matter how inconvenient it was to do so. The community also prospered from the export of timber and

Port Townsend, Washington Territory, ca. 1862. *UW Libraries, 23139z*

piling, the Indian trade, and by selling supplies and services to nearby lumbering centers.[36]

Californians arriving here "saw Indians & clams a plenty" as they debarked into the thriving commercial emporium. "Every other house," an observer just off a ship reported, "in fact is a store." Pointing to the frame buildings under construction and the San Francisco-financed deep-water wharf, a visiting Puget Sounder compared Port Townsend to "a beehive." Newcomers with money and connections stayed at the Pioneer House, where the owner increased the weekly rate from $7 to $10, meals not included, when the first boat from Victoria entered port, and to $12 upon sight of the second. Others made do with "*impromptu* hotels," tents and scrapwood shanties thrown up on the beach or in brushy ravines. Enterprising merchants charged "four times the common price" for provisions and mining implements.[37]

Letter writers made the standard California comparisons. One exclaimed that Port Townsend reminded him of "Yerba Buena in '48," and another called the place "a second San Francisco in '49." Drinking and gambling became notable daily activities, exceeding the community's already renowned episodes of liquor induced conviviality. "There are two monte tables in full blast, with crowded audiences," one Californian wrote home, "whilst poker, etc. are in almost every corner." Unfortunately for Port Townsend, the good times did not last long. Though the customs authorities compelled shipmasters to call on a regular basis, miners themselves soon dismissed the town as too remote from the Fraser to be an acceptable resort for transportation, resupply, and gross misbehavior. The San Francisco *Bulletin*'s roving correspondent tarried in Port Townsend in late April, and again in early June, finding it in the second instance, "deserted." A dejected storekeeper charted the complete boom and bust story: "Building lots went up three hundred per cent and all thought that the day of prosperity had arrived, but alas…in a few days all our hopes were dashed to the ground."[38]

Seventy-five miles north by northeast from Port Townsend, Bellingham Bay was often termed the "finest natural harbor of the Puget Sound district," a vast refuge where "the fleets of the world might ride in safety and manoeuvre with ease." Only the great bay of San Francisco itself offered better and more extensive anchorage. Bellingham Bay also was strategically located close to the Fraser River, which was just across the border in New Caledonia. Undeniably enticing, Bellingham Bay had a singular flaw, however. The retreat of the tide uncovered an enormous mud flat, reaching out three-quarters of a mile or more to deep water where vessels had to drop anchor. Passengers went ashore in canoes, except at the lowest ebb, when they struggled through the mud or hired Indians to carry them piggyback to shore. At all stages of the tide, cattle, horses, and mules were dropped over the side to swim and wade to the beach.[39]

An *Alta California* correspondent pointed out that Bellingham Bay really was "a harbor within a harbor," featuring two gold-rush boomtowns—Sehome and Whatcom—on a bay front previously inhabited only by Indians and 20 or so shellfish-imbibing, tide-rat settlers. Laid out in early May next to the Fitzhugh coal mine, Sehome was the one place in local waters where steamers could safely anchor close to shore. Before the end of the month, investors from San Francisco sold forty lots, erected three substantial buildings, and commenced constructing a wharf. By mid-June, a dozen cabins and shanties, fashioned from rough timber and cedar bark, sat among smoking stumps on the bluff. A boarding house offered dry shelter to miners unwilling to make do with tents. Canvas-covered dining establishments dispensed salmon and venison meals for 50 cents, washed down with a shot of disreputable whiskey at a quarter extra.[40]

A mile and a half to the north, Whatcom had been founded in 1853 as a prospective sawmilling center, but almost immediately floundered. Returning from a quick inspection of the suddenly rejuvenated settlement in the spring of 1858, however, an Olympia resident wrote of seeing "houses going up in every direction, on lots, streets, alleys, and water flats." Acreage was even set aside for three churches. "The energy and perseverance of the old residents, together with the assistance of Californians," a merchant confided to associates in San Francisco, "have completely, as it were, revolutionized the place." Inhabited by 3,000 white persons as of late spring, Whatcom easily eventually displaced Olympia as Washington Territory's largest community.

A careful count revealed 80 houses on the beach or among the cedars on the sandy bluff, two dozen grocery stores, an equal number of saloons, eight restaurants—all featuring the usual 50 cent meals—and three hotels. Eight physicians, four attorneys, and two real estate agents comprised a tide-flat professional class. Intent upon repairing the principal local defect, mercantile interests formed a company capitalized at $25,000 to build a long wharf out to deep water. By late spring, with both Whatcom and Sehome growing rapidly, a visiting reporter noted that "the most sensible land holders...think of emerging [sic] the two into one...to be called Bellingham"[41]

Like Victoria, Whatcom was a miniature San Francisco—just as if it had been packed up in California and shipped by express to northwest waters. Its largest hotel, best store, and *Northern Light* newspaper were California owned. So many bay area politicians were on hand, one observer quipped, that they probably would hold an election out of habit. Whatcom's founders had once, in a futile inducement to settlement, offered free building tracts. In the first weeks of the Fraser excitement, however, prices rose to $1,000 for lots above high tide and to $300 for those subjected to tidal flow. In late June, latecomers revolted, contending that old-timer "land sharks" held "no title except possession." Organizing a Settler's League, immigrants redistributed the choicer bits of real estate in hundred square foot dimensions, the recipients agreeing to pay "certain reasonable assessments" for the vital wharf project.[42]

Thousands of miners waited at Whatcom, "living," said a veteran Puget Sounder, "in idleness at an exhorbitant [sic] rate of subsistence." No one of adult mind and experience was surprised "that the promptings of the first law of nature should lead to acts of dishonesty and crime." The saltwater camp, another sojourner remarked, was "as near like the city of Sodom of old as ever a town could well become in this advanced day of the world." Faro, monte, and poker, not to mention soiled-dove pleasure emporiums direct from the Barbary Coast, ran "full blast" in brick fronted buildings and in tents standing from the sand to the forest. Doors and canvas flaps were left wide open to all comers from dawn to dusk, and beyond into the darkest imaginable night. Horrified British visitors from Victoria fled at the first thankful opportunity, convinced that the depraved inhabitants were dominated by "the riffraff of San Francisco of both sexes," and "gamblers, pickpockets, swindlers, and men of broken down fortunes."[43]

In addition to Bellingham Bay's short connection by water to the Fraser's mouth, Whatcom and Sehome expected to prosper from the construction of a pack trail, and then a wagon road, northeast across the 49th parallel to intersect with the Fort Hope-Kamloops brigade route to the mines. Beyond the broken-forested country immediately behind Bellingham Bay, prospective travelers anticipated little difficulty in traversing the Nooksack prairie lands and crossing the Nooksack River, before entering the steep forests of the Cascades and New Caledonia. Miners not only looked forward to avoiding the Fraser's navigational hazards, but also the exactions of H.B.C. officials. "They can go by thousands," Whatcom boosters enthused, "and no delay need be feared." Californians took the lead in organizing the project in mid-April. Under the direction of Oscar Smith, formerly assistant engineer of the San Francisco fire department, two dozen men had cleared the first 25 miles by early May.[44]

For the wealth seeking masses gathering at Victoria, Bellingham Bay, and Puget Sound, the final stage of their journey to the New Caledonia gold fields posed a difficult and dangerous challenge. For now, adequate trails were primitive or non-existent. "People will find their way up there somehow or other," a confident, if somewhat naïve, newcomer wrote from Port Townsend. The physically fit might follow in the wake of the Bellingham road builders. A shortage of pack animals, the uncertain distance, and the difficult terrain, however, meant that overland travelers could hardly expect to carry enough provisions on their backs to get across the Cascades, much less to survive on when they finally reached the gold fields.

According to varied reports and rumors, one or more alternative water routes to the interior existed north of the Fraser. A Victoria informant noted of Howe Sound, for instance, that, "it is said this gulf extends inward to a great distance, and that vessels of the largest class can be taken up to a point in the mountains, from which there is an Indian trail through a good country." The only remotely reliable knowledge regarding such places, though, was derived from dimly remembered readings of the George Vancouver journals. Until detailed explorations could be undertaken, the mainland above the Fraser's mouth could only be regarded, and avoided, as "a strong and iron bound coast."[45]

Miners tried to spend as little time as possible in Victoria, since every dollar expended on room, board, and entertainment reduced the funds available to them in the diggings. The 400 men arriving by the *Commodore* on April 25, Governor Douglas reported two days later, "have either gone or are preparing to leave this place for Fraser's River with canoes and any other conveyance they can procure." Less than two hours after coming ashore at the end of the month, the *Bulletin*'s special correspondent formed a company with three other Californians, purchased a boat for $50, and departed for the mainland. According to Donald Fraser of the *Times*, a thousand canoes, each one an "ugly cradle…built impromptu by some Yankee carpenter," left Victoria between May 1 and mid-June.[46]

Parties traveling the 90 miles from Victoria to the Fraser in canoes and small boats thought more of gold than of their own safety. Their course lay around the southeast tip of Vancouver Island, then northeast through the San Juan archipelago. Under ideal conditions, the trip took three days, with nighttime stops on one of the islands where wood and water were plentiful. Tidal surges and hidden rocks posed regular hazards, and sudden storms were not uncommon. The official Royal Navy sailing instructions—geared to the speed and maneuverability of steamers—misled many unwary amateur mariners into danger. Four hundred men in a "lilliputian fleet" of canoes departing Victoria in early July attempted to stay together in the interest of mutual protection against the elements. The *Bulletin* reporter admitted to good fortune after completing the final leg, a 25-mile paddle in open water to Point Roberts: "We were rather anxious…as our canoe was deep, and if a sea had sprung up, we would have been in no enviable situation."[47]

Impatient men at Whatcom also busied themselves, constructing rude canoes and repairing any available old boats. Writing to associates in San Francisco at the end of June, a merchant reported, "at least 100 canoes have been built since I have been here." Another Californian advised that a dozen parties departed daily, the paddlers shoving off in early morning to be sure of making Point Roberts by nightfall. The close-to-shore journey was relatively safe and easy in terms of navigation. However, miners formed convoys from fear of native attack. Northern Indians supposedly lurked about in the islands, ready to pick off Americans in the brutal head-hunting, Isaac Ebey manner.[48]

People in the small boats coming from Victoria and Bellingham Bay camped overnight at Point Roberts, prior to entering the Fraser the next day when tidal conditions were optimal. The main channel through the mudflats always had enough water for canoe travel, but the route was unmarked, crooked, and prone to changing its position. Inexperienced whites wisely hired Indians—for a dollar and provisions for "morning, noon and night"— to guide and handle the boats up the Fraser to Fort Langley. Paddling into the river, newcomers were welcomed by the monstrous, mangled roots of ruined fir trees, washed down by great freshets and now protruding from the mud. Numerous channels with banks covered by coarse scrub merged with the main stream. On the north, east, and west horizon, close to the coast and in the distance, mountains rose in broken and snowy magnificence. "The change from Vancouver's Island is at once manifest," wrote Donald Fraser of the London *Times*. "Everything on the continent is on a grand scale."[49]

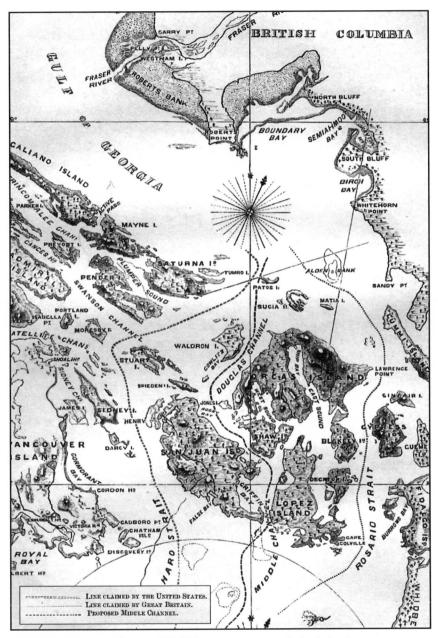

Disputed waters—on July 27, 1858, U.S. troops unexpectedly landed and soon were entrenching on the south end of San Juan Island. British naval forces arrived shortly thereafter, and eventually fortified the northern part of the island. R. C. Mayne, *Four Years in British Columbia and Vancouver Island* (1862).

Practically overnight, extensive urban growth expanded beyond the H.B.C.'s Fort Victoria stockade. *Illustrated News of the World, 1858.*

From a comfortable vantage point while riding on a passing river steamer, a Californian heading for the mines observed his less-fortunate brethren in small boats, "pulling like galley slaves" against the current on their two day trip to Fort Langley. Except for sweat and blistered palms, however, the lowermost Fraser was relatively free of trouble for paddlers. The river gradually contracted to "about the width of the Thames at Greenwich," according to Donald Fraser, then widened to a placid lake before narrowing again beneath forbidding peaks. Towering firs laden with mossy strands grew down to the riverbanks and stood on islands. Newcomers also passed large Indian villages with mat and cedar plank dwellings adjacent to which were numerous canoes lined up in orderly file on gravel beaches. That snowy "monarch of the north," Mount Baker— sometimes with wisps of volcanic smoke hanging above the summit—could be viewed to the south, the "landmark for all this region."[50]

The H.B.C.'s venerable Fort Langley was "quaint and primitive," wrote roving *Alta California* correspondent W. A. Wallace. Built on a rise above a sluggish stretch of the river, its main part was enclosed within a stockade of pickets 15 feet high, with loopholed corner bastions. The two dozen or so buildings—offices, warehouses, shops, and residences—were constructed of logs, now blackened from smoke and age. The fort's cedar roofs, too, suffered from impregnating moss. Outside the post's walls stood the salmon house, where fish supplied by the Indians were salted and packed for export. A few miles away, beyond a burnt-over district, the Langley farm produced grain, hay, and potatoes, and lush pasturage was available for cattle and horses. In its various self-sufficient features, the place perfectly reflected the H.B.C.'s traditional parsimonious management philosophy. "All the arrangements are with a view to business," Donald Fraser pointed out, "and great order and regularity reigns throughout."[51]

Prospectors were leaving Victoria despite repeated warnings from James Douglas about scant provisions in the Fraser country. The governor also pointed out that American vessels could not, in any event, legally enter the river. Under the exclusive grant to trade with the Indians, he asserted, New Caledonia was "made over by statute to the Hudson's Bay Company." Non-company watercraft attempting to navigate the stream were, therefore, "liable to seizure and forfeiture." The wealth seekers, of course, ignored this declaration, which was not supported, initially at least, by any real semblance of an official British constabulary or other governmental administrative force. "Canoes and other small craft," Douglas reported in a series of messages to London, "stealthily…ascended Fraser's River" in direct violation of British law and H.B.C. rights.

Once in the mines, of course, the Americans indeed complained that the "stock of provisions" was "utterly inadequate." As the population burgeoned in the gold districts, Douglas realized that his firm could never truly claim the continent without providing proper provisions—and correspondingly, meeting other of the miners' commercial, social, and legal needs. Vancouver's Island, however, had few supplies and the H.B.C. no shipping, except for the decrepit *Otter*, available to handle the emergency.[52]

Outraged U.S. citizens charged the H.B.C. with attempting to perfect an illegal monopoly—i.e., a foreign British monopoly dedicated to preventing legitimate free enterprise from crossing the border to fulfill the miners' needs. Printing the company's charter on its front page, the *Alta California* noted correctly that the document "does not say anything about exclusive privileges of navigation." The Spirit of 1776, too, lived on again in some Pacific coast editorial pages. "There are a few *Bunkerhillites* left," the Portland *Oregonian* blustered, "and some of them have an idea that they have the 'inalienable' right…to go where they please, without the pass-port of Gov. Douglass [sic]." Should the Hudson's Bay management actually allow miners to starve, Donald Fraser warned, "the British possessions will fall to American rule without fail."[53]

Even though his Vancouver's Island governmental responsibilities did not extend to the mainland, James Douglas nevertheless concluded that he must "act…without delay, and without distinct legal authority." The governor hoped that a distant and appreciative home government would endorse his decisions after the fact. "In consequence of the unexpected force of the immigration from the United States…," he argued in retrospect, "we were compelled in the emergency, by a stern necessity, either to take the initiative…or to submit to their dictation." Americans could not be kept out of the country and must, one way or another, be transported, fed, and governed, Douglas also privately explained to the H.B.C. directorate. "Sound policy" required that "all legal obstructions on trade" be removed in a manner at least technically consistent with the dignity of the H.B.C. and of Great Britain. In a missive to the colonial office, the governor specifically elaborated that he intended to "legalize the entrance of gold miners into Fraser's River on certain conditions, which at once assert the rights of the Crown, protect the interest of the Hudson's Bay Company, and…draw the whole trade of the Gold Districts through Fraser's River to this Colony."[54]

Taking on "an unusual amount of responsibility" in order to "keep pace with the extraordinary circumstances of the times," Douglas reiterated his earlier public statements. In a new proclamation issued on May 8, he declared unauthorized entries into the Fraser River "contrary to law," and warned that, after a grace period of 14 days, vessels navigating without H.B.C. "sufferance" would be "seized and condemned." After first upholding these governing principles, Douglas moved as a private businessperson to insure that the miners arrived in the diggings safely, and, once there, were maintained with supplies. The chief factor initially proposed that an agreement be concluded with the Pacific Mail Steamship Company, allowing that firm to run steamers between Victoria and the forts at Langley and Hope under the H.B.C. flag. Approved vessels were to carry only specified kinds of freight, and passengers holding valid mining licenses—this $2 per passenger "head money" had to be paid at Victoria. The "object," Douglas privately advised, also was "to afford facilities to miners for entering Fraser's River through Vancouver's Island, and thereby to prevent the trade of the gold region from being diverted into a foreign channel."[55]

The Pacific Mail Steamship line rejected the H.B.C. proposal, but other San Francisco navigational interests accepted the terms, including the proviso requiring that the vessels be both British registered and partially owned. John Wright sent the side-wheeler *Sea Bird*, recently running between Puget Sound ports after several years on the Sacramento River, to Victoria. The California Steam Navigation Company followed with another veteran of the Sacramento River, the *Surprise*. The latter, 180 feet long and drawing 9 feet of water, was "a beautiful Boat," said Douglas, with "powerful Engines." Renewed on a voyage-by-voyage basis, the agreements were highly "advantageous" to the H.B.C., the chief factor reported, securing "all the existing interest, connected with Fraser's River, without risk or outlay on the part of the Company."[56]

Both vessels went into service in early June, the *Surprise* only three days after arriving from California. ("Any one can ship aboard a steamer in San Francisco," the *Bulletin* correspondent reported in pardonable exaggeration of the impact on transportation, "and get off on any [Fraser River] bar they may wish to stop at.") Carrying 400 passengers, the *Surprise* completed a round-trip from Victoria to Fort Hope, a hundred-plus miles from the sea, in three days—two going upstream, and one down. One-way fare was $25, plus $4.50 for 200 lbs. of personal supplies and $1 per meal.

The *Surprise* entered the Fraser in early afternoon, paused briefly at Fort Langley to take aboard an Indian pilot, and then steamed against the current until dark, anchoring next to the bank at night. Casting off at daybreak, the *Surprise* arrived at Fort Hope around noon, after negotiating the rocks and raging water just below the post, the only real hazard of the lower river. "We came to the rapids…," wrote W. A. Wallace of the *Alta California*, "where they opened the doors of the fires for more draft, put on all the steam, and with even that the *Surprise* trembled and faltered; but she made a brave effort, spouting the air full of the blackest smoke, and coming into the eddy at the landing most beautifully." When stemming a particularly strong current, coal was supplemented with wood to power the engines, as crewmembers and passengers ashore cut up trees for extra fuel. Until replaced in mid-August, the *Surprise* made 15 complete trips from Victoria up the Fraser River. (A full navigational circuit in Northwest waters often could consume nearly a week, with a vessel sailing first from Victoria to Bellingham Bay for additional passengers, then to Port Townsend to clear U.S. customs, and finally to Victoria again to satisfy British regulations before heading to the Fraser.)[57]

Underpowered and weighing 450 tons, which was too heavy for efficient use on the Fraser, the *Sea Bird* failed to match the record of its early consort. Its deep draft and lack of maneuverability forced the *Sea Bird* to keep to the middle of the channel—thus, a pilot could not take advantage of eddies close to shore. The vessel never did make it all of the way to Fort Hope. "We…bucked away for ten hours," a passenger on the steamer's first trip wrote of the final 18 mile stretch, "until we got within a mile of Fort Hope, where there is a very strong rapid, which we could not make headway against, and were compelled to turn back." The *Sea Bird* ran aground at a river bend on a subsequent trip and, with the water falling, remained stuck in the mud for weeks. Finally dug out by a 20 man crew and then repaired, the boat caught fire soon after leaving Victoria on its next run and burned to the waterline on a nearby Vancouver Island beach.[58]

Side-wheelers—such as the stricken *Sea Bird* and even the stalwart *Surprise*—really were not suited to the Fraser's swift, sometimes shallow waters. Light, limber sternwheelers, on the other hand, were more powerful, had less draft, and were better able to avoid snags and overhanging branches close to the bank. Their superiority was demonstrated by the *Umatilla*, which arrived with the Columbia's Captain John Ainsworth at the wheel in the third week of July. In a genuine feat of navigation, the *Umatilla* steamed all the way to Fort Yale on its inaugural voyage. (The *Umatilla* was actually the repaired *Venture*, the vessel swept into the falls at The Dalles on the Columbia River earlier in the year.) "The boat stopped—went back—gathered again—advanced a few feet, and fell back again, where she held herself," W. A. Wallace reported of the effort required to overcome the last obstacles below Fort Yale. Captain Ainsworth then built up steam to the maximum, sending up huge clouds of smoke, and the *Umatilla* "slowly moved on," covering the final "100 rods" in 50 minutes.

Other vessels soon followed the *Umatilla* to the Fraser according to the terms laid down by the H.B.C. By September, the "steamboat interest" was "pretty well represented in these waters," with 20 craft in service, including the *Enterprise*, which had been lined over the Oregon City falls from the upper Willamette River, and the equally-famed, at least among passengers, *Wilson G. Hunt*. The most unique was the tiny *Ranger*, outfitted with a "coffee-mill of an engine and tea-kettle boiler," and steered north from San Francisco in a six week port-to-port odyssey hailed as "perhaps the most notable instance of marine audacity on record."[59]

Unfortunately, at the height of the gold rush in early summer, the side-paddler *Surprise* was for a time the only available steamer on the Fraser, and it could handle only a portion of the transportation demand. Persons unable, or not wishing, to secure accommodations on the *Surprise* therefore had to rely on muscle power to proceed upstream. During a July voyage, the *Surprise* passed 92 canoes carrying from 6 to 15 men each between forts Langley and Hope. During the next trip, 113 were counted. Mountains—"great round mounds, long serrated ridges, and snowy peaks," noted Donald Fraser, "none of them bald, all covered with timber"—rose up on each side and mammoth piles of bleached driftwood lined the shores. The Fraser swelled with water from tributaries, the Sumas and Chilliwack from the south, and the Harrison, brilliant blue in coloration, on the north. Paddlers probably paid little notice to the scenery, of course, for they were too busy laboring and cursing. "We have arrived…," a Puget Sounder wrote from the diggings, "after one of the hardest trips on record." Miners conceded that reports regarding mileage on the Fraser were suspect, since the zigzag efforts involved in getting from point to point inevitably made for an actual greater distance traveled.[60]

A canoe trip from Fort Langley to Fort Hope took four days or more with time allowed for brief prospecting, and, when necessary, a regathering of nerve. Safety necessitated a stout boat, some river experience on the part of the occupants, a willingness to engage in "hard pulling," and a capacity to endure "myriads of mosquitoes." One Californian wrote of "polling and sometimes swimming" up the Fraser. With ropes, men towed canoes through rapids while they stumbled on rocks and wallowed in the frigid water. "God knows what we have suffered," an Oregonian observed at the end of the journey. "From morning till night, we were dragging our canoes, waist deep in water cold as ice, and constantly in danger of being washed under and carried to hell." Some individuals turned back on the very verge of reaching the diggings, giving up from fatigue and fear.[61]

Prospectors willing to hire native help fared best on the upstream trip. "The secret of successfully ascending…is in knowing the place to go," a traveler pointed out. "They know every foot and every eddy…," the *Bulletin* correspondent reported of the local Indians after reaching Fort Hope without mishap, "and would take us five miles where we would have been puzzled to

"Prospectors at work." Matthew Macfie, *Vancouver Island and British Columbia* (1865).

have made one." Although the native villagers were inclined to thievery when not closely watched, the most common and common-sensical bit of advice offered to newcomers by old hands was to hire an Indian guide at Fort Langley, paying the going rate of a dollar a day in trade goods. Miners "should never interfere with their Indians," another experienced person wrote, "but permit them to go by any route they see fit to select, and to load the canoes as they please."[62]

Fort Hope, where the diggings for all practical purposes finally began, was recognized even within the H.B.C. as a shabby example of the company's parsimonious approach to style and comfort. Situated among pine trees on partially cleared flatland above the river, the post amounted to little more than "a square lot fenced in with high stakes," said an unimpressed Californian. The several buildings within the enclosure—one contained a bakery producing what Donald Fraser called "the best bread…I have tasted since I was in Paris"—were built of bark-covered logs. The place had no wharf, despite its sudden importance as a riverboat terminus—passengers and freight came ashore via a plank thrown out from a steamer's deck. On a more sublime note—at least for the few arrivals interested in scenic attractions—mountains, heavily timbered and usually crowned in snow, surrounded the post.[63]

Fort Hope generally was considered the interior gateway to the mines rather than as a final destination. Farther upriver, reactivated Fort Yale was "necessarily" the better located of the two upstream posts, James Douglas observed. Except for the single dramatic voyage of the *Umatilla*, unfortunately, no steamer was able to get that far up the Fraser in 1858. Again, miners faced foaming rapids and deadly boulders, risking all in the quest for gold to be found ahead. "The stream…is full of rocks and rocky islets," Donald Fraser wrote of the Fort Hope-to-Fort Yale stretch, "which render the navigation of it impracticable to anything but boats and canoes, and even these have to be drawn in places with tracking lines." Errors and bad luck on this final segment sometimes resulted in drownings. As originally constituted, Fort Yale was little more than a storehouse at a bend in the river. There, immigrants beached their vessels in a primitive El Dorado that many later would feel was unworthy of the penitence that they had just endured in the rapids below.[64]

There was more than ample evidence, all observers agreed by the spring of 1858, of gold in extraordinary amounts on the Fraser River. "But it would seem," a Puget Sound newspaper noted in stressing the obstacles to be surmounted, "that nature, miser-like, and as if jealous of having her hoarded coffers ruthlessly assailed, has so carefully locked up her precious treasures along fluted rivers, in canions [sic], ravines, and mountain fastnesses."

Even with the frightening canoe voyages factored in, however, the trip to the diggings failed to measure up, in a number of respects, to the legendary 1849 California experiences. Then, fortune seekers had spent months crossing the continent on foot or horseback, or risking jungle fevers when portaging over the Panamanian isthmus, or when rounding foul Cape Horn in storm beaten vessels. Now, in a lesser version of the olden days, California miners had reached the Fraser approaches to the diggings in a little more than a week from San Francisco, with many even sleeping between clean sheets and dining on hot kitchen meals much of the way.

Meanwhile, the H.B.C., through its customary rights and manipulation of British law, had thus far succeeded in directing the gold rush traffic and business toward Victoria. Assuming that the mining excitement continued, the thousands of Americans at hand, and those on the way, nonetheless would render the company's long-term prospects doubtful. "We will continue to guard…privileges of trade and transportation with the most scrupulous care," James Douglas glumly wrote of his lifelong private employer, "but all our efforts will fail in preserving them for any length of time."[65]

Chapter Four

Gold is King

The future history of California, and Oregon and Washington Territories, will demonstrate the truth of the assertion that "Gold is King."—San Francisco *Alta California*[1]

Aᴄᴄᴏʀᴅɪɴɢ ᴛᴏ ᴛʀᴀᴅɪᴛɪᴏɴᴀʟ ᴇsᴛɪᴍᴀᴛᴇs, perhaps as many as 30,000 persons, most of them madly intent upon prospecting for gold, rambled across the Pacific Northwest by mid-summer 1858. Most arrived too late—many, indeed, never advanced beyond tidewater—to actually engage in any profitable mining activity. Rumors "as thick as hail stones in a storm" rather than established facts, mass hysteria instead of rational calculation, helped propel the rush to the Fraser River.

When the *Republic*, steaming from northern waters, docked in San Francisco on June 19, accounts from the passengers and crew were broadcast within the hour on every street corner, courtesy of newspaper special editions. "At once," the resident *New York Times* correspondent reported, "assurance became doubly sure—and those who had hitherto hesitated, and held back, hauled down their colors, and went in, *pell mell*, with all the enthusiasm of fresh converts." The "best evidence," positive thinkers claimed, of riches yet to be found came from the fact that Fraser miners were visiting Victoria or the Golden Gate for supplies and returning as fast as possible to the diggings. "The only difficulty there seems to be," an overly-sanguine Puget Sound editorialist reflected in an otherwise enthusiastic commentary, "is to get there and to live afterwards."[2]

Californians absorbed in getting to New Caledonia—the popular wisdom after 1849 held, after all, that those first on the scene garnered the most wealth—often ignored factual information and cautionary advice. Early on, James Douglas had noted, "the yield has not been large; or at all proportioned to the number of hands employed in the diggings." The relatively small amount of gold dust exported in the spring of 1858 seemed to confirm this intelligence. The first miners to reach the Fraser, in fact, had offered a variety of warnings in letters sent home. "No craft that was ever built" could survive the Fraser's mighty current at its high water stages, one prospector advised. Rains were incessant, another unhappy individual noted. Also, some bona fide Pacific Northwest residents, American and British alike, exhibited intolerant attitudes toward California migrants.

Since the venture's hardest segment was in traveling into the New Caledonia wilderness, miners who were stalled in Victoria or Whatcom were, for all practical purposes, hardly any closer to their goal than if they had waited in San Francisco for the development of better interior transportation routes. And, in the definitive Fraser River lament, those prospectors who did journey upstream found that they consumed most of their provisions in just reaching Hope and Yale.[3]

Reports from the field, Governor Douglas advised the home government in mid-May, indicated that miners currently earned "probably from one to two dollars a man per day." When touring the Fraser at the end of the month, he found the average take to be only slightly above this rather disappointing figure. The returns were nonetheless "sufficiently promising," Douglas pointed out, "to nourish the prevailing mania for gold." Besides, to the enthusiastic gold seekers any accounts undermining the El Dorado ethos were bound to be suspect as the cynical work of special interests with ulterior motives. Some California business interests, for one thing, sought to dissuade their low paid workers from heading north. Oregonians, too, contended against any diversion from their Columbia Basin routes to New Caledonia. And, the Hudson's Bay Company would just as soon keep Americans out of the territory north of the 49th parallel. "There are many writing this, that and the other thing about the mines," a transplanted merchant observed in dismissing supposed expert accounts, "who have never been there, and, in my opinion, haven't spunk enough to go." Rejecting all words of caution, however, the 1,500 miners active as of May 1 became 10,000 by early June.[4]

Alta California correspondent W. A. Wallace stressed two points in his regular Fraser River letters to San Francisco. "There never was a gold field that offered so rich a harvest as this," he noted, "nor was ever treasure guarded…

by such fierce monsters." Aside from those miners smart enough to consult veteran H.B.C. traders regarding the latter, few comprehended the true significance that climatic factors played in turning dreams into nightmares. Beginning in April and continuing through July, massive snow melting in the upper elevations, augmented by frequent springtime downpours, produced a rapid and truly astonishing rise in the river—by as much as 80 feet in constricted places, such as in the canyons above Fort Yale. Commencing in early October, too, the autumn rainy season held the Fraser at high stage until December, when the onset of winter brought snow and froze the interior streams. Then, in an entirely unhappy coincidence, the optimum period for mining efforts at low water coincided with an "extreme cold," a prospector lamented, that "freezes up all active out-door operations."[5]

When the water fell, the Fraser's exposed bed actually was an ideal, naturally created, prospecting environment. At bends in the river where the main current ran along the outside banks, sediments and smaller detritus were deposited on the inner shores. When exposed at low water stages, these "bars," as the miners called the exposed gravelly beaches, often extended well out into the streambed. Mixed with the gravel, gold "in thin bright scales or minute particles"—washed down from distant mountains, and eroded and polished—was ready for exploitation. Based on their California experience, prospectors expected to find increasingly larger bits of precious metal, even actual nuggets, the further they went up the Fraser.[6]

Early arriving Californians—as yet with "no reliable or definite information…as to the location of the…diggings"—paused at likely river bars on their way upstream from Fort Langley. A British naval officer, James Prevost, reported that "a pan of dirt taken indiscriminately" by newcomers "at almost any position along the banks" was bound to "yield gold." A returnee to San Francisco recalled finding "two bits to the pan" at several overnight camping spots. "In two out of three pans of dirt washed," another prospector wrote, "we found gold, though in too small quantities to pay for working." The search for significant wealth—not just enough to make a modest living— kept people moving upriver. Anything "under six dollars a day," Governor Douglas dryly noted, "is not considered wages by the California Miner."[7]

Genuine Sierra-like returns finally were obtained from just below Fort Hope and upstream to Fort Yale. "Most of the available spots along the banks of the River are studded with miners," Captain Prevost observed after accompanying Douglas to the Fraser in late May, "all of whom, to use their own expression, are 'earning wages.'" Between Murderer's or Cornish Bar and up to Fort Yale, the sometimes humorous names for the river bars—Mosquito, Fifty-four Forty, Union, Puget Sound, Yankee Doodle, Sacramento, Texas, and Emory's—often reflected American origins and a stick-it-in-the-eye attitude toward the British.

The furthest upriver, Hill's Bar, a 50-yard wide expanse of moss-slimy rock and gravel, quickly became the rush's focal point. Located in early April by an advance party from the San Francisco fire department, the place soon had a varying population of between 200 and 400 miners. In a notable rarity—the maximum white female population of New Caledonia during 1858 was six—Hill's boasted a white woman resident, who operated a canvas-tent dining establishment identified by a sign made from a strip of "nether garment." Prospectors at Hill's Bar averaged $30 a day, with a lucky minority making twice that amount.[8]

Believing that "further up the 'big chunks' were in abundance," the braver prospectors passed through the canyons. Some proceeded in canoes, although in ever-present danger even at low water stages. Numerous portages were required, including one of four miles on a narrow ledge beneath towering cliffs alongside the raging current. Other miners went by land, their lives only marginally less at risk, and were all but suspended hundreds of feet above the Fraser on a trail so treacherous that mules could not be used. Safely arrived at Sailor's Bar, 20 hard miles above Fort Yale, prospectors deemed the risk—at least in retrospect—entirely worthwhile. Sailor's Bar recorded, Governor Douglas wrote in mid-June, "the greatest instance of mining success" in the spring rush. One party took 48 ounces of dust, valued at $16 to the ounce in Victoria, during the first week. A single miner estimated his earnings for a half month at $3,000. The least successful man on the spot, according to an informant, made $10 a day.[9]

Mining operations were primitive in nature and confined to the bars, reflecting the fact that only pans, shovels, and other rudimentary implements could be taken into the backcountry under the prevailing conditions. Miners dug holes in the gravel, usually down a foot-and-a-half, to the "pay streak," a layer of yellow clay containing pieces of gold. "You can see the… glitter in it before it is washed," one observer enthused. Prospectors needed little skill and the amount of physical labor involved was significantly less than in the California Sierra. "The work is not heavy," Donald Fraser of the *Times* reported, "any ordinary man can do it." Recognizing that teamwork

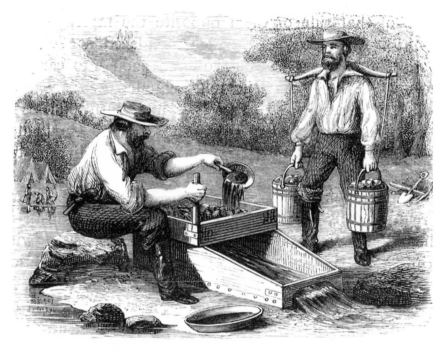

"Working with the rocker." Matthew Macfie, *Vancouver Island and British Columbia* (1865).

increased efficiency, most fortune hunters used rockers or cradles, with one man shoveling "dirt" at the rate of 200 buckets a day and his partner operating one of the crude devices, separating precious metal from the sand and gravel. A single miner could process a yard of dirt per day, compared to three to five yards for two men with a rocker.[10]

Overall productivity, however, was compromised by the nature of the deposits excavated from the bars. "The river…holds the gold, almost in solution," *Alta California* correspondent W. A. Wallace wrote from the Fraser, "and nearly all of it is water-worn and abraded, by its long journey from its yet undiscovered sources." Prospectors used quicksilver (mercury) to amalgamate the fragments. Quicksilver, though, was in short supply and thus extremely expensive, and even when properly used was only partially effective. "The mode of saving the fine gold is imperfect, and the miners are very careless," Wallace pointed out. "They all admit that they do not save half the…particles."[11]

The miners first on the scene saw no point, in a vast and obviously rich country, in legally organizing their activities. "The bars are very large, and pay from the top down," one prospector noted, "presenting a field for mining for all that get here without interfering with one another." There was, another informant confided, "room for everybody that is not afraid of blisters in his hands." The continuing influx from California, however, soon produced a demand for regulation. Replicating the methods earlier devised in the Sierra, occupants of the various bars formulated local mining codes. Claims, according to these rules, were defined as embracing a 25 foot water frontage extending inland as far as the high-water mark. Tracts so claimed had to be posted and actively worked, at a minimum of one day out of five, except during flooding. The mining codes usually limited an individual to ownership of two claims. Updated lists of claimants and locally devised laws were displayed at most bars. Individuals actively bought and sold locations on the river, although the practice was illegal—"a man who sells a claim," said Donald Fraser, "sells 'what isn't his'n.'" Douglas's proclamation held that all mineral deposits belonged to the Crown and were to be exploited only under its specific authorization.[12]

Relatively few newcomers went to the distant Thompson River, the central point of pre-1858 interest in New Caledonia. The H.B.C. succeeded, to a considerable extent, in dissuading Americans from entering that far away country. Falling victim to "Thompson river fever," an occasional party would set out on the traditional brigade route—otherwise known to Californians as "one of the worst trails in the world." At Fort Yale, the H.B.C. grudgingly sold supplies in quantities only barely sufficient for a two to three week trip. Reaching their destination, hungry miners found scrawny Kamloops cattle, selling at $40 a head, constituting practically the entire supply of available food. Before turning back, travelers wound up subsisting on rank horseflesh and gaseous berries. The Indians, meanwhile, refused to share their provisions, and, using superiority of numbers to good effect, frightened unwanted visitors into retreating from the best mining areas. A number of returning prospectors contended that this aggressive behavior was a sure indication of gold on the Thompson, but cited the "inhospitality" as more than ample reason for avoiding the region.[13]

Indians also interfered with white parties venturing past the Thompson's mouth to the upper Fraser. Miners penetrated as far as 60 miles beyond the Fraser-Thompson "Forks," finding gold in substantially larger fragments than on the bars between Hope and Yale. "*Reliable accounts*" received in Victoria, James Douglas noted, indicated that the upper diggings were "exceedingly prolific, yielding from 55 to 60 dollars a day, to the Rocker and two men." The inhospitable Indian villagers compelled miners to form armed camps, however, and give up isolated operations in favor of mutual security. The main difficulty in the upriver country, though, was the shortage of provisions, as only limited amounts of supplies could be packed into such remote locations. After a few days on the scene, prospectors had no choice but to undertake the arduous journey back to Fort Yale for supplies—and then a good portion of these new provisions would be consumed in just returning upriver to the diggings. "They all point to the one glittering object," W. A. Wallace reported after encountering several individuals willing to abide by this near-illogical regime, "gold—gold—gold."[14]

Opened in April, the principal Fraser mines all but closed in May due to the annual spring flooding. Most newcomers had no idea that the surge of immigration coincided, almost exactly, with the onset of the melting mountain snow pack. This proved both dramatic and traumatic for the roving population. "The water has risen about four feet since my arrival," a prospector wrote in early June after two weeks at Fort Hope, "and is still going up, and God only knows when it will stop, for there is no one else that does." A San Francisco returnee described the stream, "steadily rising, sometimes as high as three feet in a night." With the Fraser swollen and the bars inundated, only miners able to exploit "dry diggings" on the upper banks continued to work. Spirits remained high, though, with most persons expecting the flooding to be a short-lived phenomenon. Some self-styled experts thought the river would fall by mid-June. Others predicted, with equal confidence, early July. The most pessimistic analysts anticipated a return to normal conditions no later than the start of August.[15]

Though overall morale remained high, the first truly informed words of caution started spreading from the Fraser to the outside world. "At present," a Californian warned from Fort Hope at the end of May, "the river is entirely too high to work, therefore I would not advise anyone to come here yet." Writing from the same camp, a Puget Sounder recommended that "the boys…" back home "hold on for two months, and it will be just as well."

With the water high, provisions low, and "five times as many people here as should have come," practical considerations became paramount for some level heads. "To come here and *wait*," a San Franciscan pointed out, "costs twice as much as to remain in California and *wait*." Recommending that his friends "wait awhile," another flooded-out prospector sagely noted that the "gold wont run away." The sodden fact that "thousands of men are now along the banks of Fraser River, doing nothing," the *Alta California* asserted, demonstrated "the absurdity of rushing…at present" to the north.[16]

Coming up the Fraser in early May, the *Bulletin*'s reporter passed a few downstream canoes carrying miners with "black eyes, disfigured faces, and a decidedly disgusted look about them," who were returning to the sea and distant homes. For a number of people, the accounts of rising water actually increased their frenzy to get up the river, as indicated by a would-be miner writing from Victoria: "every hour's delay here…is only breeding future trouble." Governor Douglas observed in a series of July reports that the Fraser was still "all the rage," with 9,000 to 10,000 miners currently on the stream by H.B.C. estimate, "and hundreds of other persons…preparing to join them." The diggings might be flooded and the food running out, another Vancouver Island resident noted, yet the steamer *Surprise* "still continues her trips and goes full every time."[17]

One of the more telling aspects of the rush at this stage was the relatively small amount of time that many miners had actually spent in working the bars. One of the first Californians to reach the Fraser earned $10 a day, better than a good laboring wage, but left after less than a month "for the want of provisions." Another Golden State immigrant remained in the diggings only four days, after a capsized canoe left him with only a sack of flour for subsistence. Another terminated his stay at two weeks, after digging between $20 and $25 daily, when Hill's Bar succumbed to the aforementioned flooding. A former San Francisco hotel owner returned home in less than three weeks, desperately homesick for his family. Governor Douglas reported that three parties had to abandon their claims above the Forks after, respectively, just 12, 8, and 5 days of mining.[18]

With these problems, overall returns so far from the diggings continued to be somewhat disappointing. "It does not appear that there has been a large production of gold," Douglas noted in late July, "as most of the river bars are still inundated." Total official exports from the Fraser over the preceding two months barely amounted to 5,000 ounces, according to the governor, while "as much as half that quantity" had been privately carried to San Francisco in the pockets and baggage of returning Californians. Actual output, to be sure, was higher, as many prospectors still on the river were "hoarding up their gold dust" to pay for food and other necessities during the lull in operations. Meanwhile, a significant transfer of this wealth to the Hudson's Bay Company was occurring. Fort Langley alone took in $1,500 a day in payment for flour, beans, tools, clothing, and blankets. After digging an average of $12 a day for over a month, a disgusted miner returned to California in June with less than $100, blaming it on the "rascally high prices demanded for provisions."[19]

However, enough had been accomplished to date—even with the setbacks and disappointments—to convince most participants that their visions of El Dorado would be validated when the river fell to lower stages. "All who have visited the mines," Donald Fraser wrote from Victoria in mid-June, "are impressed with the conviction that their richness far exceeds that of California in its palmiest days." Nearly all proffered the same favorable comparison. "The miners," Governor Douglas advised London, "generally assert that Fraser's River is richer than any 'three rivers' in California." Returning from a tour of the diggings, Captain Prevost reported that "all of the old Californian miners I...met with declare they expect the Country will far exceed in auriferous deposit the wealth of California."[20]

Unfortunately, "waiting for the waters of Jordan to fall," as the saying went, turned out to be long-term. Early July reports that the Fraser was starting to recede generated new optimism among miners. "Hundreds of men...were pitching in, in right good earnest," the *Victoria Gazette* informed its readers upon the arrival of good tidings via the *Surprise*. "New comers," said Governor Douglas, took claims "wherever a bit of dry beach could be found." Warming temperatures, however, melted snow in the highest mountains and, with frequent rains factored in, the river soon reverted to "a whirling, raging flood." A regular up-and-down phase ensued, dependent upon the rate of precipitation. "The water fell a foot or two last week," a prospector wrote from Puget Sound Bar in August, "but is now slowly gaining ground again, which makes it about what may be termed 'on a stand.'"[21]

Disappointed at this soggy course of events, many miners finally faced up to the uncertainty. "When the water will abate, no one can tell," Wallace of the *Alta California* reflected, "but it must first cease flowing into the river." Some worried, on the basis of climatological intelligence belatedly provided by H.B.C. traders, that an entire mining season had been lost to the weather. Pending the uncertain resumption of operations, prospectors somehow had to survive on the limited rations carried upriver by canoe and steamer. "A large number of the gold seekers are laying in camp eating up their provisions," a concerned observer noted in advising friends on the Sound of the potential for problems. The issue pointed out by Governor Douglas in April—"what will become of this crowd...after their stock of food is expended, I cannot pretend to say"—remained to be addressed.[22]

Hungry prospectors, Donald Fraser pointed out, "cannot eat gold." There were, unhappily, few readily available provisions in the country to consume. Men stranded at tidewater complained of having to dig clams for subsistence, but they were better off than colleagues upriver in a country strangely short of game. Fighting off hordes of mosquitoes and flies, most miners saw few if any deer, elk, or waterfowl. "I have seen more animal life on the Cocomungo Desert," W. A. Wallace remarked, "than is to be found in all these grand old woods." Although the Fraser abounded in annually migrating salmon, Indians expressed little willingness to sell or otherwise part with their vital, preserved, winter supply. White newcomers lacked the inclination and implements to fish for themselves. Berries and fruit were abundant, but it seemed the immigrants, according to Wallace, "would rather lay upon the ground and growl at their hard fate...than to reach out their hands and gather the luscious harvest."[23]

Public and private assessments agreed on the basic dimensions of the supply problem. "There are now about 10,000 foreign miners in Frazer's River," James Douglas informed the colonial office in August, "and upwards of" only "3,000 of that number are profitably engaged" to pay for provisions. Of 7,000 persons supposedly camped between Yale and Hope, an American miner submitted, "not more than two hundred are making more than enough to pay expenses." Traveling downriver, the *Alta California*'s Wallace concluded, "the proportion of the workers and no workers, is one to ten." For the first time a significant reversal in the course of immigration began. Cursing "the country, and their own folly in visiting it" and thanking heaven to "have escaped the grand humbug with life and health," substantial numbers of hungry Californians started heading for home. "I see more men going down the river now than I see coming up," a miner from Puget Sound observed, "which is all well enough, for there are too many here already." A sudden drop in persons traveling from San Francisco to Victoria, meanwhile, reflected the impact of negative accounts coming out of New Caledonia.[24]

Lack of options—"there are many," one visitor reported from the mines, "who have neither means to go or stay"—and downright stubbornness caused most to hold fast, determined to see the river finally fall to a workable stage. The real "folly and 'humbug,'" contended Henry DeGroot, a newly arrived *Alta California* correspondent, "is not that there is no gold, but there is no patience." The low production of gold to date, advocates of toughing things out argued, meant nothing more than that wealth was not to be secured at high water.

In a series of articles, W. A. Wallace denounced returnees as "the weak, disheartened ones who always go off in the crowd," the same "men who never could find gold in California, and were always met *going down* by those going up." Having carelessly rushed north, these men went back to San Francisco unreflective and inexperienced—"not one fourth have been above this place," Wallace sarcastically wrote from Fort Hope. Possessed of "iron will," genuine prospectors, in contrast, "*know* there is gold, and they will not leave the country till they get it."[25]

Even the most iron willed miners, however, required a periodic ingestion of food; hence they tended to concentrate during the high water period near places supplied by the steamers. Fort Yale, previously a crude storehouse with the primitive quarters of H.B.C. trader Ovid Allard attached, became an "improvised" community with 2,000 temporary residents. Canvas tents and log cabins lined the Fraser for a mile and more, affording some comfort and good views of the nearby flooded bars and arriving boats. Prices initially were high with flour selling for 75 cents and sugar for 50 cents per lb. A meal of "old fish" and "undrinkable coffee" at the American Restaurant cost a reported "several dollars." Improved freight service, combined with the disposal of goods by persons departing for California, soon drove living charges down to a manageable level for all but the truly busted miner. The place even briefly had a certain orderly aspect, with a saloon being held in universal contempt for selling liquor to Indians. Except for individuals able to prospect dry diggings or profitably occupying themselves by manufacturing rockers, men idled away the days and then the weeks. W. A. Wallace noted Yale's unemployed inhabitants "gathering in knots, talking, eating, smoking, sleeping, hoping, watching the river, wishing—quietly enjoying their own thoughts, or listening to the *if* and *buts* of others."[26]

By late summer, in fact, Yale had taken on the appearance of "a considerable town," in the view of a visitor from Victoria. A sawmill produced lumber for constructing proper buildings. Streets were laid out, named, and squatted on by persons hoping to profit from urban development. "Everybody locates where he pleases," one observer reported, "and those who secured the first and best sites have made quite a pretty thing of it." Speculators bought and sold lots, although the absence of government surveys made such transactions informal and dangerously insecure. A population with nothing to do, meanwhile, made an inviting target for purveyors of the various social pleasures. Four gambling houses and as many drinking establishments ran "full blast" according to accounts, staffed by the usual immoral California immigrants. Rather than associate with such criminal types, the touring British-expatriate journalist Donald Fraser camped on a sandbar, removing himself from the "filthy and unsavory...ruffianism of the town."[27]

Downstream, Fort Hope was another "half-made town," the idle population varying between 200 and 1,000 souls. Taking a careful census, W. A. Wallace counted 232 tents and cabins within a mile of the H.B.C. post, as well as two restaurants, a combination gambling and drinking den, and, reflecting the importance of sound footwear for mining and traveling, a pair of boot repair establishments. After dark, at least, Hope was genuinely appealing. "The whole plateau was illuminated with camp fires," the *Bulletin* correspondent recalled of his early evening arrival, "showing the white tents in

A post-gold rush view of Yale at the head of navigation, looking upstream. Grolier Society, *The Book of History, Vol. 15.*

"Ground sluicing." Matthew Macfie, *Vancouver Island and British Columbia* (1865).

all directions, with the miners moving to and fro in the light." Prices constantly drew attention back to the harsh realities of everyday subsistence. Residents paid 50 cents for a cup of coffee and $1 for a meal of beans. "Just think," an unemployed prospector lamented, "of a poor fellow strapped and unable to get work…where bacon is sold at 75 cents a pound."[28]

Supposedly, the best place to wait out the high water doldrums was in Victoria. Yet the Vancouver's Island capital was, in some respects, barely civilized in its own right. Donald Fraser slept on "a trestle" in a tiny room "you would not think too good for a dog." He washed "*al fresco*…in an open meadow," and dined at a table fashioned of "rough, unplanned deal boards," sharing a mug of coffee made from "burnt beans and pease" with three uncouth Frenchmen. British free trade policies, of course, had attracted San Francisco merchants, and provisions were abundant and prices lower than at Hope and Yale. Between persons coming down the river and individuals yet to give the mines a try, 4,000 Californians—"some cheerful and…others completely broken down and discouraged"—assembled for the duration. "The streets are crowded with people," a storekeeper observed, "wandering aimlessly about, listening to the various rumors." Beggars were a regular sight outside restaurants and hotels, for the penniless prospector could afford neither a meal nor a bed. Violent crime increased, a sure sign of desperate men without means.[29]

Ironically, suffering of a peculiar pecuniary nature was acute among the mercantilist class—storekeepers had overstocked shelves and speculators had overvalued land, as the lull in the rush deprived both of sufficient cash carrying customers. "Half frightened" capitalists warned of "a strong reaction, when everything will go down…almost as rapidly as it has gone up." Merchants financing their operations on short-term credit were forced to sell goods either below cost or at auction, in order to raise funds to pay off their unsympathetic San Francisco bankers. "A term of quiet"—the expression favored by optimists for what pessimists preferred to think of as a depression— was bound to last, said students of Victoria's economy, "until the first gold begins to come down the river." The citizenry, with businessmen to the forefront, gathered on the wharf whenever a steamer chugged in, eager to hear if the Fraser had at last fallen and the diggings were reopened.[30]

Meanwhile at Whatcom, 3,000 prospectors waited for the Fraser trail to be constructed, which supposedly would provide the best year-round access to the diggings. "This is the route," a geography-challenged booster enthused, that would extend "all the way on American soil, without any British toll-gatherer to intercept your progress." James Douglas vowed to "prevent the success of their design, by seizing any goods that may be sent in." Bellingham Bay promoters nonetheless insisted that travelers, merchants included, would be able to cross the border "scott free," without "paying an ungodly tribute to the Hudson['s] Bay Company."

Misplaced confidence led to the belief that Whatcom, temporarily the Washington Territory community with the largest population, was about to become the "big town" of the gold rush, and the true successor to San Francisco in more than just drinking, gambling, and whoring. "Houses [are] going up as fast as lumber can be procured," an early summer visitor reported, "and everything raging, ripping and roaring." A hundred stores sold essentials from beans to cigars at prices half the going rate in Seattle and Olympia. The only topics "spoken of," advised a merchant relocating from the southern Sound, were "lots, land, lumber, gold mines, and the prospect of getting to them." Prospectors and effete real estate promoters alike dressed in stiff, fresh-from-the-box mining garb—gray shirts, wool pants, and heavy knee-high boots—and exuded unflagging round-the-clock energy. "On every side," wrote a touring California journalist, "is heard the rattle of hammers, the noise of sawing and planing, and now and then…the sharp crack of a rifle to add a dash of the romantic to the scene."[31]

All expectations for personal wealth and Whatcom's future depended on the trail. Commenced in April, the route was supposed to have been constructed across the 49th parallel no later than the end of May. At the earliest possible date thereafter, it was to be connected into the Fraser-Kamloops brigade route, linked one way to Fort Hope and another to the Thompson River. Unfortunately, the project sponsors possessed neither sufficient technical expertise nor an adequate knowledge of the natural obstacles to be overcome. Informing Washington Territory officials that the laborers had forded the Nooksack, the principal stream between tidewater and the border, a Whatcom merchant contended, "the portion yet to be opened is plainly marked by a well-beaten Indian foot trail, requiring no work save the removal of the fallen timber."

Increasing in number from 25 to 80, and finally 100 strong, the trail builders proceeded well into the Cascades by June 1, but then became lost and were unable to find a pass across to more open country and the mines. Repeated delays made the project something of a regional joke. A rival community's newspaper, for instance, announced "for the twentieth time" the completion of the "great institution."[32]

Reasoning that the failure had more to do with incompetent engineering than the difficult environment, the promoters hired a new contractor, W. W. DeLacy, an Olympia resident previously involved in military road construction. Leaving behind Whatcom, DeLacy soon found that he had been "somewhat deceived, not only as to the distance to the open country, but the obstacles to be surmounted before reaching it." Surveying parties under his leadership trekked, a participant wrote, "through…dense forest and over terrible mountains." Cresting likely summits, the explorers invariably became disconsolate when staring at another "three or four different ranges beyond." In the third week of July, DeLacy at last stumbled upon "a practicable pass" from where he could see, 20 miles away, campfires on the Hope-Thompson route. Reprovisioned for a final push, his laborers reached the brigade trail on August 17.[33]

Informed of this blessed event by a damn-the-horseflesh express rider, Whatcom's relieved and appropriately inebriated citizens fired a 100-gun salute from the bluff above the tideflats. "The news is perfectly reliable," the *Northern Light* pronounced. "We have waited for it long and patiently, and it has come at last, in such a form as to cause a thrill of joy to awaken in every American bosom." Chests swelled with Yankee pride, but hardheaded persons realized that the news had come too late, because the introduction of river steamers permanently had diverted passengers and freight to the all-Fraser alternative. Why climb mountains, the sensible traveler now reasoned, when one need only ascend a gangplank? The small number of persons attempting to reach the diggings learned to their dismay that neither horses nor mules could be utilized over most of the trail. At Fort Hope, W. A. Wallace witnessed the arrival of a lone adventurer, who had been forced to wade "through a swamp, with water up to his armpits," in the process losing "all he had except what he stood in." Over the next several days, a number of exhausted persons came in "nearly naked," declaring the trail "as bad a road as a man could ever get over alive."[34]

Sehome fell back on its coal mine, which continued to operate into the late 1870s, but Whatcom collapsed upon the failure of the trail to become a viable pathway to the gold fields. Many dejected merchants and miners took the first available steamers to San Francisco. Whatcom became a semi-comatose saltwater ghost town of sorts, inhabited by clam eating diehards unwilling, or unable, to give up blasted visions of wealth and urban glory. Victoria residents claimed that most of Whatcom's buildings were taken apart and shipped to Vancouver Island for reassembly.

"The *bubble has at last burst*," announced the Portland *Oregonian*, which was always more than happy to celebrate over calamities occurring in Washington Territory. "'Whatcome?' can now be answered, *nothing*," the editor of another unsympathetic Oregon paper quipped, while adding "'Sehome' has contained many an hombre who cursed the hour he ever *left home*." The *Northern Light*, which only weeks before had printed 100 extra copies in honor of the trail's completion, ceased publication in September, its owner joining the exodus to California. Ending his own sojourn in the north, W. A. Wallace paid a brief visit, wading ashore past the partially driven piling of the abandoned wharf project. The bored journalist "exhausted" exactly "sixty-four minutes" trodding the once lively sand-covered streets, restlessly consulting his timepiece and conversing only with Indians in Chinook jargon.[35]

Other locations on American soil drew brief attention as possible successors to ruined Whatcom. Point Roberts was an obvious, if strangely and fatally isolated, option. Ten persons resided at Point Roberts as of the spring of 1859. A very short distance east and also barely south of the 49th parallel, Semiahmoo Spit and Drayton Harbor, the headquarters for U.S. personnel serving on the joint boundary survey, possessed notable advantages. The three-mile-wide bay was "commodious, deep, completely land-locked, and accessible to vessels of any size at low tide," and a "well defined" Indian trail connected the site with Fort Langley. An American officer hiked to the H.B.C. post in a single day, despite having to negotiate a stretch of heavy forest—"we walked on fallen trees, and we jumped fallen trees, and, in fact, it was little else but fallen trees." Ignoring the legally inconvenient point that the harborside acreage already had been declared a U.S. military reserve, speculators laid out a short-lived town, Semiahmoo City, and began selling lots. Donald Fraser also noted that Semiahmoo was ideally located for smuggling purposes.[36]

Many of the miners and merchants stranded in Victoria, or on the Fraser's bleak river bars, or within Whatcom's battered remnants found a convenient scapegoat for their frustrations and disappointments—the Hudson's Bay Company. Americans complained that H.B.C. men, on the basis of nothing more substantive than their *"license to trade with the Indians,"* had "marked out for themselves the total and exclusive monopoly" of New Caledonia's commerce. U.S. citizens claimed that their right to seek mercantile riches rested upon the same reciprocal principle of non-interference as the U.S. government had assumed toward the many British nationals active in the Sierra Nevada. Some San Francisco observers, however, admitted that they too would have pursued "precisely the same course" as the H.B.C. if holding the same legal instrument of authorization. Relatively few conceded, though, that the English company's argument might actually have substance.[37]

Washington Territory's hard-driving U.S. congressional delegate, Isaac Stevens, charged the H.B.C. with essentially running a protection-style racket over the American firms that it allowed to operate north of the border. Adding to the dissension, moreover, it was obvious that the company was disinclined to enthusiastically assist newcomers in the British possessions. "The officers at the different forts...," a returning prospector noted, "are not disposed to look upon Americans with any friendship, rather looking upon them as interlopers." Friendly assistance might have been of limited value, though, for another complaint held that these emperors of the wilderness were supposedly ignorant of their own possessions. Some H.B.C. employees "know less about the geography or resources of this northern coast," a Yankee citizen claimed, "than any of the Oregonians...here for ten or fifteen years." Governor Douglas and the British traders, at least those able to read, supposedly relied on San Francisco newspapers for even the most basic information about developments in New Caledonia.[38]

At bottom, many Americans considered the Hudson's Bay Company to be unwilling to let others supply the mines, yet unable itself to adequately handle this responsibility. From a critic's point of view, the H.B.C. was a rather incompetent corporate entity and was "exceedingly oldfogy-ish" in regard to exploiting the diggings. "The old English and Scotch employees...," the *Bulletin's* Fraser River correspondent advised, "seem like so many Rip Van Winkles." According to a Victoria-based Californian merchant, the firm's servants, having been "brought up...from youth in the service of the Company," recognized "no other duty than to do as they were bid, and ask no questions." Unable to exercise initiative, the H.B.C. was, the *Alta California* charged in a series of hostile commentaries, "an incubus upon the development" of the country, and an institution moving "with precision and without impulse." In contrast to "the rush of Yankee enterprise," the stodgy British "system" sought merely "to preserve the wilderness in all its silence, and to let the birds and beasts multiply and increase."[39]

Critics to the contrary, James Douglas actually manifested considerable energy and ingenuity despite representing a rather somnolent private institution and a very distant imperial regime. The Vancouver's Island colonial administration was supported entirely by excise taxes, a source of "revenue so ridiculously small," Donald Fraser reported, "that the bare mention of it raises a smile." The governor was therefore without a real staff and was long accustomed, though hardly reconciled, to acting "alone" in public affairs. For lack of any other alternatives, he had to rely upon family and business connections to run affairs in the north. Fourteen of the colony's nineteen officers, in fact, were members of this family-company compact. Sons-in-law served as the assembly speaker and chief justice. John Work, Roderick Finlayson, and other H.B.C. veterans composed a majority in the legislature.

The firm's local land agent doubled as the Crown's surveyor. Douglas defended this situation, arguing that the qualities required for government service—"integrity, sobriety, firmness, zeal, industry, implicit obedience to orders, and a practical acquaintance with the nature of the duties to be performed"—coincided perfectly with the habits instilled by long association with the Hudson's Bay Company.[40]

On the mainland, of course, there initially was no colonial government and the H.B.C.'s claim to governing this area rested upon a questionable legal argument. Douglas, however, barely hesitated before instituting governmental control. The situation in New Caledonia was, the governor regularly pointed out, "very peculiar." At the commencement of the gold rush, Americans had freely entered the Fraser carrying in addition to provisions and tools, "spirits, arms, ammunition, and other prohibited and noxious articles." They also were ignoring warnings that their movements and activities were outside the law. Unable to wait for orders under circumstances essentially amounting to a non-hostile invasion by foreigners, Douglas moved as best he could to protect the rights of the Crown and the H.B.C., and to generate financing for his necessarily extra-legal public actions. He had neither a constabulary nor, for the time being, a military force at his disposal. However, the commanders of the *Satellite* and *Plumper*, Royal Navy vessels currently assigned to the boundary commission, offered assistance provided that their expenses were covered.[41]

To a considerable extent, Douglas relied upon moral persuasion and his expertise garnered from decades of working with frontiersmen in the unforgiving western wilderness. "One of the qualifications of Mr. Douglas is that he lived among our good cousins long before he became Governor," Donald Fraser observed. Therefore, the H.B.C. factor knew his American antagonists not just "like a book," but "like a small *library*." Despite a tendency toward pomposity—"it is not the custom with Governors of British Provinces to address the public," he pronounced in an elitist preface to a Fort Yale speech—Douglas usually spoke in a straight-in-the-eye style bound to appeal to prospectors.

Donald Fraser watched in admiration while Douglas, in his best informal style, resolved a summertime dispute over claims at Emory's Bar, standing among the assembled crowd knee-deep in the cool waters of the river. In this instance, "such assertions, denials, arguments, explanations, and replications were never heard before," the journalist recounted. "One quoted Californian laws, another Australian, and a third the 'law of all creation.'" Enduring the clamor "like a stoic," Douglas at last issued a definitive ruling, sending all parties "away in good humour." Such encounters explained his personal appeal, to genuine miners at least, as a sort of gentrified British Daniel Boone.[42]

As the first line of defense on behalf of British rights—and for establishing a sound fiscal base for an expanding governing function—Douglas relied on the quarterly mining licenses assessed at $5 on all persons entering the Fraser. Both Vancouver's Island and New Caledonia utilized Yankee dollars as a circulating medium. Under the local exchange rate, £1 equaled $5, a slightly more favorable figure than the official international ratio.

Originally instituted in December 1857, when the governor had anticipated a substantially different kind of rush to the diggings, the mining charge was reaffirmed in May 1858. "Being in urgent want of money to meet the unavoidable increasing expenditure of Government, consequent on the influx of people," Douglas explained, "I considered it would be only proper to make them bear the cost of that expenditure." This reasoning made sense, especially with English sovereignty upheld in the bargain. The concept, moreover, was anything but revolutionary, as similar fees had been imposed in California and Australia. "It is but a trifle anyhow," one journalist remarked in dismissing the possibility of objections by prospectors expecting to get rich in El Dorado. Initially, the only drawback in the scheme was the inconvenient requirement that the first $5 payment be made in advance at Victoria. Scofflaws, however, simply bypassed Vancouver Island, going instead to one of Washington Territory's harbors and then to the Fraser, where the British initially lacked the means of collecting the fee (soon, this administrative function was extended to the mainland).[43]

Contending that "the British Frontier is now violated in the most open manner by American Vessels," in mid-May Governor Douglas requested immediate help from Captain James Prevost of the Royal Navy's *Satellite*. Pausing only briefly to consider the practical implications of the request, Prevost had agreed to anchor his ship at Point Roberts and to accompany Douglas to Fort Langley. This "exhibition," the captain reported, convinced the miners that a "determination exists to uphold the Laws." Even so, he continued, the "complete revolution in the existing state of affairs in this part of the world" necessitated a more direct approach to the maintenance of English rights. Accordingly, Prevost moved the *Satellite* into the mouth of the Fraser in the first week of June. Operating from the deck of the warship, customs officials enforced the $5 licensing regulation and prevented unauthorized craft and goods from passing upstream.[44]

Except when absent on other "necessary" duties, the *Satellite* remained on station for much of the summer, with its 22 mounted cannons imposing on the small boats plying the Fraser. When the vessel departed to look after the boundary commission, however, Douglas was left without a "force…for the protection of the Revenue laws." Addressing the problem on a permanent basis, the governor refitted the Hudson's Bay brigantine *Recovery* as a customs vessel. Operated by sailors on loan from Captain Prevost, the ship was anchored in midstream below Fort Langley. While taking in the collection of fees due the Crown and company, it served as a small, quasi-official, sub-headquarters of empire hidden away amidst mountains and forest. "Without the little *Recovery*," the London *Times*' Donald Fraser reflected at the end of the year, "we should not have been allowed, I believe, to call the Fraser River our own."[45]

Despite Californian and Australian precedents, the mining license requirement drew immediate scorn from Americans, many of whom experienced difficulty in remembering that the Fraser was British-owned. Congressional delegate Isaac Stevens denounced the "enormity and absolute illegality of the impositions placed upon the citizens of the United States by…British authorities." The Portland *Oregonian* condemned the "arrogant assumption." San Francisco merchants in Victoria charged Douglas with a "usurpation of authority," designed to drain "a large amount of money…illegally into the coffers of a company whose headquarters are in London." The fees and shipping restrictions supposedly amounted to an embargo, since only individuals and interests acceptable to the H.B.C. were granted access to the gold fields. Smugglers, whose goods had been seized, vowed "retribution," and demanded that the U.S. send a warship to the Fraser to counter the *Satellite*.

Tales about brave Yankee prospectors brazenly paddling past the *Satellite*, daring an ashamed Captain Prevost to open fire, were, if apocryphal, well-calculated to stir up emotions. Reporting the bombastic gist heard in his conversations with miners at Fort Langley, Donald Fraser concluded that jingoistic bullying was at work: "What! Stop a free and independent Yankee in the exercise of trading in what, where, and with whom he pleased, subject only to the impulses of his own sovereign will and pleasure?" Given the facts, the anti-John Bull grousing was largely out of bounds.[46]

By the end of June, 2,221 licenses had been issued at Victoria. An additional 304 were disbursed from the deck of the *Satellite*. All told, $12,625 in revenue had gone into the British treasury up to that point. Though hardly an insignificant amount, these figures reveal that only a minority of the immigrant population complied in purchasing licenses. Although exaggerated, Donald Fraser's claim that "not one in 50 miners" procured licenses conveyed a sense of an administrative failure. Always a realist, Douglas was inclined, in any event, to follow the *Alta California*'s advice that he "make virtue of necessity," and be flexible when implementing his proclamations. Douglas's representatives, for example, made no serious attempt to collect the second and third quarterly installments of the licensing fees from miners. The governor also suspended tax gathering altogether during August, conceding that many immigrants would have no spare funds until work began again in the diggings at low water. Despite reports in San Francisco that the H.B.C. confiscated unauthorized goods at the Fraser's mouth, Douglas allowed individual miners to take enough supplies upstream to sustain them there for three months.[47]

Many fortune seekers had little trouble avoiding the British "gauntlet." When the *Satellite* was away in early and mid summer, prospectors entered the Fraser unchallenged. Even with the *Recovery* on permanent duty, small vessels could easily avoid detection. The British were "not very particular about the matter," a newcomer from Puget Sound wrote, "and if a canoe goes quietly on up the river, it will seldom be molested, or overhauled." Tax paying was virtually a voluntary gesture for persons traveling on their own accord. "I have no doubt that if we had introduced ourselves…that the demand would have been made," an American observed of his stop at Fort Langley, "but we passed on without saying anything, and consequently nothing was said to us." Although operators of the river steamers did cooperate with the revenue collectors under the contractual arrangements with Governor Douglas, evasion still was commonplace. For instance, the merchant Cyrus Phillips and a partner took 3,000 lbs. of goods to the diggings by the simple expedient of purchasing nine mining licenses and passenger tickets. One *Alta California* correspondent succinctly portrayed a fact of life in New Caledonia: "The old laws are not rescinded, but their violation is winked at."[48]

Some newspaper accounts of widespread suffering in the mines, even suggesting that starving prospectors had committed suicide, misled much of the American public into condemning the British. Douglas reported, however, after his first Fraser inspection tour, "there was really no actual distress for want of provisions among the mining population in all the accessible parts of the country." The governor's subsequent claim that the diggings had been "adequately supplied, both in respect to food and the other necessaries of life" came close to the truth. Business and political dictates, Douglas pointed out, demanded that the H.B.C. "make every effort to enable the miner to reach the field of his labors and to furnish him with supplies while there, at rates that will at once remunerate the Company and leave him a fair reward for his toil." This approach, of course, conformed to the firm's traditional policy of providing good service at a sustained profit, while at the same time shoring up its monopoly rights.

Bolstered by the heavy importation of California foodstuffs and by authorizing steamboat traffic, the H.B.C. largely met its self-imposed goal. "We are loading, selling and shipping Goods incessantly," the chief factor noted in an early June missive from Fort Victoria (The governor would later note after an early fall trip up the Fraser, "I was much struck with the healthy robust appearance of the Miners.") Some prospectors suffered, to be sure, but their travail had more to do with a lack of personal funds or by straying too far from Fort Yale than with corporate incompetence or duplicity.[49]

Indeed, the governor's principal antagonists were Yankee merchants, not American prospectors, a fact partially obscured by the publicity about miners' complaints. At the gold stampede's outset, San Francisco capitalists had hurried north to make money in record time, selling goods and services at the highest possible prices. Douglas, however, limited the presence of independent wholesalers and retailers on the river bars, while also introducing measures to dampen an unrestrained marketplace. Those merchants getting past the *Satellite* and the *Recovery*, for example, discovered that post traders at Hope and Yale sold supplies at comparatively low rates, and consequently garnered most of the business of exchanging food and implements for gold dust. Although free trade prevailed in Victoria, even here H.B.C. actions affected local commerce. The small lots mandated by the company's sales policy, for instance, prevented the construction of large California-style wharves and warehouses. A respected man among most miners, James Douglas nevertheless was often vilified in Victoria as a petty tyrant and stooge of distant London interests.[50]

When pressed by mercantile elements to throw open the river to unrestricted trade, Douglas continued to refuse to do so, citing his interpretation of the H.B.C. grant. In Victoria he made use of the firm's storehouse reserves to hold down the cost of living, support the unemployed, and thwart Californian ambitions. "Flour, which our speculators would have rushed up to starvation prices," W. A. Wallace reported, "has been kept at $20 to $25 per b[arre]l" through regular H.B.C. sales to consumers. As a general policy, the firm set rates for all basic commodities at prevailing San Francisco levels. "There would be no living here," a summertime denizen of the colonial capital wrote, "if it were not for the Hudson['s] Bay Company." At the governor's direction, the fort bakery also turned out bread for the indigent, and a rudimentary public works program set idle miners to work improving the town's streets. About all the storekeeping element could do in response was to sponsor a new anti-Douglas newspaper, the *British Colonist*, and organize occasional, deliberately offensive, pro-American parades.[51]

"Bothered to death by questions, and having so many to please," as an otherwise unsympathetic American observed, Douglas had acted responsibly on Vancouver Island and in New Caledonia. Bearing the "full weight" of the gold rush on his experienced shoulders—"he is an old hand at this sort of thing," said Donald Fraser of the London *Times*—the governor established a modest administrative apparatus on the mainland.

Returning from the diggings, he appointed apparently capable British subjects—or at least the most seemingly trustworthy of such individuals encountered in his tour—to revenue collecting positions. For example, Richard Hicks and O. T. Travaillot became commissioners at, respectively, Fort Yale and the Forks. They were charged with collecting quarterly license fees once the miners were back working the bars in low water. Douglas also appointed a collector at Langley and a justice of the peace at Hill's Bar, where white and Indian miners had quarreled. A new government postal service, too, linked Victoria with Fort Hope, with mail carried aboard the steamers. Authorities in London, however, declined to approve a regular gold convoy, the best means, according to Douglas, of protecting individuals against robbery and of diverting the maximum amount of the wealth to Vancouver's Island.[52]

Since New Caledonia originally had no formal governmental administration, obvious problems had developed at the more populated points like Hope and Yale where newcomers intended to establish themselves on a permanent basis. Without prompt action, Douglas warned, "the country will be filled with lawless crowds, the public lands unlawfully occupied by squatters...and the authority of the Government will ultimately be set at nought." Therefore, the entire gold bearing region must be "immediately thrown open for settlement," with surveyed acreage sold by the Crown "at a fixed rate."

While awaiting a decision from the colonial office, Douglas instituted on his own responsibility a *de facto* land tenure system. In late summer meetings at Hope and Yale, he proposed "a right of occupation," under which holders of town lots and adjacent agricultural tracts could make monthly rental payments, and "be allowed a pre-emptive right of purchase" upon the completion of official property surveys. Based on a positive response, Douglas commenced laying out townsites at the two camps and also at Fort Langley. Meanwhile, speculators had already laid out an illegal town, Prince Albert, at the mouth of the Fraser River. [53]

Fiscal concerns, of course, continued to preoccupy the governor's time, particularly in running an increasingly costly quasi-official government—a problem compounded by the limited success of the license fee system. The charge "will always be an unpopular tax," Douglas conceded, "besides being arduous and expensive to levy in a country so extensive and difficult of access as Fraser's River." Although the licensing proclamation remained in effect, collections were, as a practical matter, suspended until the diggings began generating more profitable earnings. As a substitute revenue-generating measure, Douglas instituted a 10 percent duty on all New Caledonian imports in September. The *Alta California* complained that the announcement from Victoria "out Herods all their former manifestos…and public notifications" This editorial rant apparently was drafted in amnesiac ignorance of longstanding American tariffs on foreign goods. Undeterred by the outrage expressed by San Franciscans, customs collectors took in, despite a troublesome shortage of coins, nearly $45,000 by the end of October. Douglas secured additional funds, meanwhile, by introducing $600 a year permits for saloons.[54]

A most pressing mainland need, also, was the development of good trails and roads. Above Fort Yale, gold was coarser and prospects were better there for finding considerable wealth, but this area was "for all practical purposes, nearly inaccessible." Proper exploitation of the upper Fraser depended on miners being adequately supplied, hence there was a need for "improvement of the internal communications of the country," Douglas pointed out. Partially addressing the problem, private interests set about upgrading the trails around the canyons during the summer—work that continued into the fall.

The more significant project, though, involved public development of the Harrison River route, long known to the H.B.C. and already used by some travelers. Harrison Lake, three dozen miles long, emptied via the Harrison River into the Fraser between Hope and Langley. Connected by a series of relatively easy portages between a string of lakes—Harrison, Lillooet, Anderson, and Seton—this northerly route eventually looped eastward to reach the Fraser again at a point well above the Forks. The latter three connecting lakes were, respectively, 13, 15, and 16 miles long. By opening a real trail, Governor Douglas expected to revolutionize transportation into the upper Fraser. The consequent increase in income generated by additional licenses and especially tariff duties, moreover, could well pay for the entire cost of construction.[55]

Running the sternwheeler *Umatilla* 15 miles up the "pure, cold and green" Harrison River and into Harrison Lake in July 1858, Captain John Ainsworth confirmed the scheme's practicality. The *Umatilla* had to tie up for the night to a convenient dead tree, because Harrison Lake was "too deep," reported the *Alta California*'s Henry DeGroot, one of the passengers, "for us to touch bottom with a sixty foot line." In the morning, Ainsworth steamed to the mouth of the Lillooet River at the lake's head, and then returned at flank speed to Victoria with the good news. Douglas quickly planned a large-scale construction project that also provided work relief for unemployed miners.

Five hundred men "proffered their services," Douglas wrote, "on terms so peculiar…and so advantageous for the country, that it would have been unwise of me to decline them." The men blazing the trail received no pay, only room and board, and posted $25 bonds as guarantees of good conduct. Formed into 25 construction crews, each with a British supervisor and Indian guide, the workers headed for the lakes district (men were segregated into white, Chinese, black, and Hawaiian crews). "Let every assistance in the way of…Interpreters, Boats and Canoes be given…," Douglas instructed company traders, "and pray give your immediate attention to any requisitions for stores, provisions, tools or other wantages." With cold autumn weather in the offing and prospectors again on their way to the upper Fraser, speed was essential. "I am exceedingly anxious," Douglas informed the colonial office, "to establish that communication thoroughly before the winter sets in, to remove all cause of complaint against the Government."[56]

Despite considerable trouble—a number of the laborers were inexperienced and the H.B.C. was unable to efficiently supply the scattered crews—

"the great work of the season" opened to pack trains in early November. The final cost, approximately $70,000, absorbed half the public revenue for the final quarter of 1858. From the head of navigation on Harrison Lake, the most "convenient communication with the interior of the country" extended 108 miles by portages, 62 bridges, and boat travel on lakes Lillooet, Anderson, and Seton. (Rapids in the Harrison River, however, posed problems when exposed at low water.) The substantial savings in time and transportation costs encouraged larger numbers of miners to travel via this route. Port Douglas, the principal construction town on Harrison Lake and afterward the transfer point for passengers and freight, emerged as a boomtown of sorts, featuring three log huts, an H.B.C. warehouse, and a wharf. Following the policy earlier adopted at Langley, Hope, and Yale, the governor laid out and informally distributed town lots at Port Douglas. [57]

While Douglas coped with affairs on the mainland, major developments were occurring in England. In early 1858, negotiations for renewal of the H.B.C. Indian trade monopoly had culminated in a draft agreement extending the grant for another 21 years, but transferring control of Vancouver's Island from the H.B.C. back to the Crown. The gold rush, however, had immediately complicated the London-based decision making process. And, at this time, a new government came to power—a ministry substantially less friendly to the H.B.C. than its predecessor. A new colonial secretary, Edward Bulwer Lytton, a second-rate popular novelist and politico-statesman, soon retroactively approved Douglas's emergency conduct of affairs in New Caledonia, including those actions that strictly speaking might have been illegal. On the other hand, Lytton expressly rejected much of his distant subordinate's interpretation of H.B.C.'s rights. Lytton also made clear the government's aversion to mining licenses, except when expressly, and solely, required for generating revenue. [58]

Two central premises determined Lytton's policy regarding New Caledonia. No actions must be taken, first of all, to unduly antagonize American immigrants, as Her Majesty's government had no desire to provoke a crisis in Anglo-U.S. relations. Lytton therefore ordered Douglas to convince Americans, through "personal influence and conciliatory communications," to "lay aside any feeling of prejudice or mistrust with which they may have entered the territory." At the same time, the colonial secretary prohibited "any act which directly or indirectly might be construed into an application of Imperial resources to the objects of the Hudson's Bay Company." Customs charges were appropriate, and indeed essential given the current need for revenue, so long as they were based upon the established principle that "the navigation of Fraser's River above the mouth is open in law to British vessels only," rather than, as in the present case, to those willing to operate in accordance with the H.B.C.'s exclusive use of the stream. While endorsing Douglas's decisions made since the commencement of the gold rush, Lytton at the same time in effect rejected much of the rationale for those decisions in Victoria.[59]

Conflicting impulses lay behind a series of actions taken in London. In mid-July, Lytton confidentially informed Douglas, by a letter reaching its destination approximately six weeks later, "a Bill is in progress through Parliament to get rid of certain legal obstacles which interpose to prevent the Crown from constituting a Government suited to the exigencies of so peculiar a case" as existed in western North America. Approved on August 2, the measure created the Colony of British Columbia, a name selected to avoid confusion with French-owned New Caledonia in the southwest Pacific. The legislation also terminated, as of May 1859, the Hudson's Bay Company role in administering the Vancouver's Island colony. Then, a month later, Queen Victoria formally revoked the exclusive H.B.C. right to the Indian trade of the two colonies. Lytton, meanwhile, ordered that British Columbia be a "self-supporting" dependency, relying primarily upon customs charges for revenue.[60]

The governing of both British Columbia and Vancouver's Island, according to another of Lytton's directives, had to "be intrusted to an officer...entirely unconnected with the Company." His choice for governor was, therefore, somewhat surprising. Lytton announced his readiness on the basis of private discussions with the H.B.C. directorate to appoint Douglas as governor of the new colony, provided the latter sever all connections with the H.B.C., including stock ownership, "within as short a time as may be practicable." Douglas also, in an added bonus, would be retained in office at Victoria, thereby filling dual gubernatorial chairs.

Unhappy at being asked to terminate a decades-long association, Douglas also was offended by the thinly veiled suggestion that neither he nor his H.B.C. comrades on the mainland could be trusted to honestly manage affairs. Moreover, Douglas's £5,000 combined salary would be entirely insufficient for running a government. Pressed by H.B.C. managers, however, who already had named a new chief factor, Douglas gave way in the end to the wishes of his past and present superiors. "I place my humble services unhesitatingly at the disposal of Her Majesty's Government," he wrote Lytton on October 4, "and I will take early means for withdrawing from the Company's service."[61]

Lytton instructed Douglas: "You will be empowered both to govern and to legislate of your own authority," at least until such time as a settled English population made the introduction of an assembly feasible. Thus, Lytton had virtually granted Douglas unlimited powers in British Columbia. Douglas was, of course, the individual best equipped to undertake this responsibility in terms of experience, demonstrated initiative, and by being present on the scene. In leaving the actual conduct of affairs up to Douglas's discretion, the colonial secretary observed, "Minute directions conveyed from this distance [London] and founded upon an imperfect knowledge, are very liable to error and misunderstanding." Consequently, Lytton left most everything in Douglas's hands (no wonder Douglas would complain about being underpaid and overworked). The insufficient funding and the prohibition against any actions favoring the H.B.C. would further add to Douglas's difficulties in colonial operations.[62]

By deciding to send "gentlemen" from England to the new colony, Lytton made clear his view that most H.B.C. personnel lacked the appropriate social station, training, and experience to serve in a colonial government. Matthew Begbie, a formidable London barrister, arrived with a commission as British Columbia's first judge. He also had authority to act as the governor's legal adviser. In November, a contingent of Royal Engineers—formal policy dictates aside, the H.B.C. paid the initial costs of settling these soldiers in — assumed a variety of mostly civilian tasks, including surveying, locating a capital, and road construction. "As little display as possible should...be made of it," Lytton instructed regarding forthright military exhibitions, since movements of this type likely would "irritate rather than appease" the American miners. Colonel Richard Moody, commander of the engineering detachment, soon became lieutenant governor, commissioner of public lands, and the official in charge, for all practical purposes, of day to day governance on the mainland. Moody had previously served an eight-year stint as governor of the Falkland Islands. Granted by Lytton with sole legislative and executive authority, Douglas nevertheless was at the same time held in check, while also being ably assisted, by Colonel Moody and Judge Begbie. Lytton also sent out a customs collector to replace the H.B.C. employees previously stationed aboard the *Recovery*.[63]

Eventually, on November 19, 1858, the governor, along with Begbie, a few naval officers, and a Royal Engineers detachment, would formally proclaim British Columbia's birth in a necessarily spartan ceremony at Fort Langley. For its administrative purposes, the colony at first possessed just a cabin purchased at Hope to serve as a court and jail; prisoners previously had been confined to the *Recovery*'s brig. Easily accessible by sea and already cleared of timber, Old Langley—the site of the original H.B.C. post on the lower Fraser—was selected as the capital. The 900-acre site previously had been surveyed into a 183-block grid, with 3,294 lots available for acquisition by settlers. Sales would commence on November 25, 1858, and the 350 lots initially sold brought in $65,000. With the colonial exchequer filled with the proceeds, Douglas could next prepare to construct proper governmental buildings.

In the meantime, while awaiting these public improvements, ever active Californians conceived of Langley as a potential northern replica of early day Sacramento. The dozen huts and rough-board shanties, plus a small assortment of restaurants, boarding places, and gambling dens, occupied a few muddy thoroughfares close to the river. That low-lying part of town was so obviously subject to overflow, a visitor warned, that all the structures would eventually "have to be raised up on stilts and well moored, or be washed away." As affairs stirred at Langley, Victoria in the meantime had been named port of entry for British Columbia, mollifying merchants there who feared their city's displacement by Langley as the gold rush's main commercial center. [64]

There were as many Indians on the Fraser River "as there are hairs on the back of your dog, " one prospector wrote to an absent friend. The native peoples, including the Nlaka' pamux between the Forks and the canyons, and the Tait from Fort Yale downstream to Fort Hope, could not easily be avoided. Whites with open, reflective minds tended to be impressed, at least in part, by these people. Noting that the males were "handsome" and "well-developed" and the women "fair to look upon," one miner contended that "the Indians here differ much from the red men of California, morally as well as physically." An immigrant from Olympia thought the local villagers "almost on a par with the Puget Sound Indians, and perhaps one or two percent in advance." On his first judicial circuit into the interior, Matthew Begbie discovered that the native populace possessed "far more natural intelligence, honesty, and good manners, than the lowest class…of any European country I ever visited, England included."[65]

When touring Hill's Bar in May, Governor Douglas tallied 190 immigrants and "probably double that number of native Indians, promiscuously engaged with the whites" in the quest for wealth. From Sailor's Bar downstream to Fort Hope, where native miners brought in two-thirds of the gold dust purchased by the Hudson's Bay post, racial intermingling was a commonplace feature. "The Indians all have money and are as much excited…as are the whites," a returnee to San Francisco advised. Digging with sticks and washing with wooden bowls, villagers earned according to various accounts, "from 8 to 15 cents per pan" and up to $10 a day. Writing that the Indians along the river "have plenty of gold," another prospector observed that they also "knew the value of it." Addicted to mining, many natives neglected traditional food-gathering chores, setting the stage for considerable suffering in the coming winter should the annual salmon runs fail.[66]

With the onslaught of the great 1858 rush, one of the governor's principal aims now was to "prevent collisions" between Indians and whites—protecting the latter from the former, and, "to the utmost extent of our means," the former from the latter as well. The H.B.C. had prospered for decades upon an effectual live and let live relationship with the coastal and interior tribes. In the mutually beneficial exchange of animal skins for manufactured items, traders established the primacy of profit over cultural differences. "We trade furs, [and] none can hunt fur bearing animals or afford to sell them cheaper, than Indians," John McLoughlin pointed out in a classic expression of wilderness mercantile philosophy. "It is therefore clearly our interest, as it is unquestionably our duty to be on good terms with them."[67]

Traditional H.B.C. attitudes remained obvious during the gold rush. Governor Douglas's family was part Indian, a situation presumably scorned by colonial secretary Lytton who preferred proper "gentlemen" in North American governmental service. The veteran traders Donald Walker and Ovid Allard, stationed respectively at Hope and Yale, also had mixed blood families. Furthermore, natives were essential to everyday company and colonial operations. Local native pilots guided canoes, boats, and steamers up the Fraser. At Fort Langley, often referred to as the "civilized" H.B.C. mainland post, Indians monopolized the skilled trades, and had supplied salmon packed for export until they abandoned that occupation to hunt for gold. Reasoning that the indigenous people best understood the river's characteristics, gold commissioner Richard Hicks employed village elders to survey water claims in the Fort Yale neighborhood, something of an outrage in popular American opinion.[68]

But Yankees, too, had long depended upon and routinely interacted with Indians. Puget Sound sawmill owners and pioneer farmers had routinely employed native laborers. Indian workers also loaded coal aboard California-bound vessels at Edmund Fitzhugh's Sehome mine. American settlers had learned Chinook jargon, the Northwest Coast's prime trade language and means of intercultural communication. On the Fraser in 1858, Californians

"Indian burial-ground." R. C. Mayne, *Four Years in British Columbia and Vancouver Island* (1862).

and Puget Sounders alike engaged native guides. When local people were willing to sell food supplies, immigrants purchased fish and potatoes, driving up prices for these basic commodities. A few miners married Indian women, adding to the maintenance of racial harmony. In a poignant episode witnessed by the *Alta California*'s W. A. Wallace, prospectors built coffins and assisted in the burial of two Indian men killed by a falling tree at Hope. "This evening," Wallace reported, "there was a grand council of chiefs in front of the fort, at which several very earnest and eloquent Chinook speeches were made by the old men, in which they thanked the Bostons for their kindness."[69]

Many Americans, though, were by no means reconciled to living in harmony with Indians for any protracted length of time. "They are a thieving, pilfering, slothful, disgusting dirty set," a prominent Puget Sound settler, Hugh Goldsborough—an adviser to Governor Isaac Stevens in treaty making—wrote of Washington Territory tribes. Many might consider native labor essential for the moment, due to the shortage of white workers, but in the long term Indians were considered detrimental to economic and social progress. From Port Townsend to Olympia, the "smoky, filthy huts of the savages" preempted fine sites "needed for building purposes." Between their "slender appliances" and "lazy and worthless habits," Indians were charged with failing to properly exploit rich commercial fishing opportunities. By entering settlers' houses uninvited and traipsing about largely unclothed in hot weather, they displayed contempt for private property and societal conventions. Vivid memories of the 1855–56 war, too, accentuated by the resumption of fighting east of the mountains in 1858, encouraged settlers on the Sound to believe themselves under extended siege, targeted by a relentless foe.[70]

On the American West Coast, paranoia and prejudice combined to imbue Indians with hardly any semblance of legal standing in white courts and government. Washington and Oregon prohibited natives from testifying against whites, except in cases involving liquor smuggling. Persons involved in illegal alcohol sales often operated freely, and settlers who engaged in physical abuse and other illegalities towards Indians had little fear of prosecution. Murder, too, usually went unpunished, the authorities exhibiting reluctance to take action in such cases and juries unlikely, in any event, to return guilty verdicts. Two Americans got away with lynching a Seattle Indian in 1854—one of the defendants was acquitted on the flimsiest of technicalities after thirty hours of deliberation, when sympathetic jurors realized that his name was misspelled in the indictment. When the brother of Nisqually leader Leschi was murdered while under guard in Governor Isaac Stevens' office, no action was taken against the perpetrator of the brazen deed. "Under the laws of Oregon," an army officer observed, Indians "must forever be deprived of justice."[71]

Many white miners arrived on the Fraser prepared to expect difficulties with the local tribes. "The Indians here can beat anything alive stealing," Seattle resident Franklin Matthias wrote in late April, "and if they continue to improve in that art, they will soon be able to steal a man's grub after he has eaten it." Next to complaints about theft, Americans groused most over the natives' supposed tendency to behave in a "somewhat saucy" manner. The San Francisco *Bulletin*'s special correspondent considered the Indians "the most infernal set of rascals I ever came across"; although absolutely essential to safe navigation, their "eternal cry" was "give to us." Whenever the journalist's traveling party stopped to dine or camp, "they would draw a crowd of their people around us, and would refuse to go on without our giving them a coat or something else." More than one prospector resorted to "drawn revolver" as the best means of countering such behavior.[72]

Tense encounters were common above the canyons where Indians held a large advantage in numbers and were determined to keep interlopers out of the best gold fields. In one early incident, natives disarmed a small party of miners and, stabbing two of the whites in the process, forced them to flee downstream. Throughout the spring and summer, prospectors were, according to reports from the river, "compelled to abandon their claims" and make for the "protection" available at Fort Yale. Along the Thompson River, outmanned and outgunned immigrants had no choice but to "submit" to provocation. Americans plotted revenge, organizing expeditions to open up access to the coarse-gold bearing river bars regardless of local objection. "There will be h_ll to pay after a while," Seattle's Frank Matthias predicted. The whites, another Puget Sounder advised, "will have to fight their way up there, and whip the Indians out before they will be allowed to mine in peace."[73]

Indians often had legitimate complaints and, at least in some cases, cause for retaliation. Some villagers, presumably those not engaged in any mining activity themselves, contended that prospectors endangered vital salmon harvests by upsetting the natural order of things and by preempting fishing places and canoe landing sites. Some individual whites, ignoring advice from experienced persons that the Indians "will not suffer abuse or harsh language, nor tampering with," perpetrated standard gold rush outrages, including sexual assault, beatings, and theft. Donald Fraser of the London *Times* claimed in anti-Yankee hyperbole that the typical American was a cowardly "wretch" who would shoot a native "in the back, when he finds one alone and unarmed," but ran to the nearest H.B.C. post at the slightest sign of genuine danger, "groaning out the doleful tune, protection against the red skins."[74]

At bottom, a fundamental disagreement over claim rights lay behind most of the troubles. The Indians considered the Fraser and its resources to be in their sole possession. Governor Douglas took their grievances seriously, and took ameliorative actions to the best extent possible under difficult circumstances. On the basis of experiences in California, Oregon, and Washington gold fields, on the other hand, Americans believed that natives had no right to impede the taking of gold. These opposing views naturally resulted in tensions. At Hill's Bar, for example, the first Californians on the scene set to work, according to their own account, at a previously deserted riverbank. Within days, 300 Indians supposedly arrived to contest the occupation by whites. Women "thronged around the rockers," men "threatened a war," and only the stream's sudden rise, sending all concerned to higher ground, perhaps prevented bloodshed.[75]

Manifesting a perverse interpretation of affairs, a number of prospectors concluded that their own noble actions were misperceived as weakness by the natives. "The Americans…have exercised the utmost forbearance towards the Indians," W. A. Wallace wrote from Yale, "being told that if they treat the savages with kindness, they will appreciate it." The unintended and exactly opposite result, claimed Wallace, was that the natives "are grown exorbitant in their demands, and insolent in their conduct." Whites attempting to act fairly supposedly garnered only "insults of every description" in return. Aggrieved Yankees held the H.B.C. ultimately to blame, accusing the firm's "Jesuitical" agents of teaching the Indians to "scorn the American nation, and the American people."[76]

Sometimes, rumors and isolated incidents were transformed into stories of wholesale conspiracy on the part of the natives. In early July, San Francisco newspapers reported falsely about Indian revenge killings near Fort Hope. Natives supposedly also attacked canoes below Fort Langley later in the same month, murdering eight men and a woman, and taking a second female prisoner. Upon investigation, the affair turned out to be a non-fatal drunken brawl precipitated by a liquor smuggler. Circulating near the end of August, accounts that more than 40 prospectors had been butchered also proved to be falsified.[77]

In the midst of the excitement over the supposed massacre, a pair of headless corpses of white men actually did wash out of the lower canyon. Over 200 miners formed military-style companies, including the Pike, Madison, and Italian guards, and the Rough and Ready Rangers, at Fort Yale in the final week of August. H.B.C. factor Ovid Allard refused to supply weapons or ammunition, but the indifferently armed warriors set off anyway, some by the upper brigade trail and others directly along the riverbank. Although accounts from the field were rather contradictory, the volunteers apparently killed several Indians and burned a number of dwellings. A self-appointed "captain," the San Franciscan Harry Snyder, finally concluded a "treaty" with the main body of natives. Camped for the night on the peace council grounds, the Americans suffered their only fatalities—two men accidentally shooting each other—when another group of Indians, happening upon the scene in ignorance of the agreement, momentarily opened fire.[78]

Governor Douglas belatedly reached Fort Yale with a Royal Engineer escort and found that the Americans had imposed their own resolution of the conflict. "As the whites had effected that desirable result themselves before his arrival," a Californian boasted, "his tardy assistance will not be required." Anticipating an eventual resumption of the so-called "Fraser River War," miners expected they would have to fight again without help from the British. Tension subsided, however, when the initial massacre story was exposed as a hoax—the person responsible for the story fleeing to the woods, never to be seen again. The presence of the Royal Engineers, moreover, represented an important advance in providing security for both Indians and whites. Most importantly, the Fraser's waters finally fell, ending long weeks of idleness and setting all parties to work again on the newly exposed bars.[79]

Writing to longtime Hudson's Bay Company associates in mid-August 1858, James Douglas reported "a lull in the emigration from California." The stories of flooded bars, drowned diggings, and discontented Indians finally had deflated much of the hysteria in San Francisco, stalling the rush. A mere 224 persons, according to official customs figures, sailed for Victoria in the first week of August, compared to 3,733 in the initial seven days of July. The steamer *Panama* carried a combined 1,070 passengers on a pair of June voyages, but only 173 on its next two sailings. Another vessel, the *Pacific*, departed on July 27 with 60 paying customers aboard, down from at least 500 on each of three previous trips. Trade figures also reflected San Francisco's declining interest, with exports to Vancouver Island falling from $669,000 in July to $52,000 in September.[80]

Meanwhile, disillusionment on the part of persons unwilling or unable to wait out the high water produced a significant abandonment of the mines. At Fort Yale, W. A. Wallace described defeated prospectors coming downstream, "all having the same ragged appearance—worn out shoes, torn pants, burnt faces, lean and hungry, looking penniless and miserable," and convinced by harsh circumstance that "hunger is more powerful than cupidity." Gathered about nighttime campfires, miners talked of "going home...to California." As one of those ready to give up on the Fraser diggings wrote, it was similar to what they once had done in California when disillusioned and speaking of returning to "the Atlantic States." Some of the disappointed, however, were remaining in the Fraser mining areas because they lacked the means to leave. Many others, too, still were convinced that their diggings, though presently flooded, eventually would prove to be rich, and they stayed to hold on and satisfy the legal requirement that claims be worked every five days.[81]

Previously, steamers returning from the Fraser had carried few passengers back to Victoria. Steamers also had run virtually empty when sailing to San Francisco. Large numbers of failed fortune hunters, however, now were booked on every voyage, bound for empty-handed reunions with friends and families to the south. During May and June, a total of only 141 persons had sailed from Victoria to San Francisco. From the first of July through August 6, however, the number increased to 2,187. At the end of July, the *Cortes* and the *Santa Cruz* each took home 600 individuals, all reported to be "highly disgusted with the gold region." Derelict prospectors, "utterly destitute of means" and unable to afford passage, made their sorry way to Puget Sound, too, to take jobs in lumbering and the fall harvest. "Not a day passes," the *Puget Sound Herald* noted in late August, "that does not bring to Steilacoom more or less miners...in canoes and small sailing craft."[82]

Even with the departures, however, approximately 10,000 foreigners still remained on the Fraser, but only a small number were actively working claims beyond the minimal make-believe labor required to maintain legal possession against would-be squatters. "They are like the tide," wrote W. A. Wallace, "going and coming always." James Douglas reported: "Nevertheless, the miners have unwavering faith in the richness of the country and are in great spirits in anticipation of an early fall in the river."

The miners at Hill's Bar had taken out $40,000 in gold prior to the stream's rise and expected to make at least that much on a weekly basis once the diggings opened again. Prospectors, though, were enduring dreary idleness, short rations, and uncomfortable living conditions. Describing the "day by day" routine at Fort Yale in a dispatch to the *Alta California*, Wallace wrote of miners eating "beans and bacon from tin plates," and drinking "bad ground coffee from tin cups," while watching "the glorious sun rise and rise in the heavens" and then "fade away." A unique display of sustained energy came from two decidedly uncouth prostitutes, who devoted fetid afternoons and evenings to paddling in a canoe between the camps, selling personal attention and rotgut whiskey.[83]

In tantalizing fashion, the Fraser sometimes fell overnight to partially expose rocky outcrops and sandy banks, a bleached harbinger of good times to come. When the long-awaited intelligence reached Victoria, it invariably set off "a violent reaction in the public pulse," and "a perfect stampede of boats and canoes." New freshets, however, combined with the last melting snows, quickly drove the water level back up, burying sand bars and the aspirations of prospectors and merchants alike. The one positive sign, confirming the wisdom of being patience, was that each cycle left the Fraser a bit lower. "I am still at Fort Hope lying on my oars…," a determined miner wrote of these mixed blessings in early August. "The river has fallen eighteen inches, but it must go down eighteen feet further before all hands can go to work."[84]

By about the first week in September, the Fraser at last dropped to, and remained at, a workable stage. In Victoria, reception of the first genuine accounts left the population "agog with joy." Though the Fraser's current remained strong—"at some points," according to Governor Douglas, "with a force and impetuosity almost insurmountable"—every steamer in port departed for the mainland, loaded down with passengers and freight. Once on the river, captains blew steam whistles and jubilant prospectors fired pistols into the air as vessels struggled against the downward flow "like…ant[s] in a cup of milk." At nightfall, boats tied up to shore, renewing the miners' wilderness domesticity: "A crowd of miners spring on shore, each with his blanket, his frying-pan and his little kit," observed Donald Fraser. "In a few minutes fires had been lit and the frying-pans brought into play to cook their bacon; coffee was preparing, and some of the fellows were actually asleep." The first returns from the reopened diggings justified the jovial optimism. "It is safe to say," a merchant informed associates in San Francisco, "that at present, about $4 per day is being realized to the hand from Fort Hope to the Big Canon."[85]

Detailing happy future prospects, another observer enthused, "bars which have never before been visible are now laid bare." Unfortunately for a number of miners, however, the Fraser also exposed beach claims that now were almost barren of gold. "To the chagrin of everybody…," one of the *Alta California*'s regular correspondents wrote on September 25, "so far from the diggings improving as the water falls, they grow less productive." The possibility that places briefly exploited at the commencement of the excitement, Hill's Bar included, were already "worked out" turned many optimists into pessimists. There appeared to be no chance for sustaining the original scale of the gold rush if it was to be limited to the original Fort Hope-Fort Yale area.[86]

Overnight disappointment—with visions of easily gained wealth now replaced by new torments and frustrations—drove prospectors to desperate measures. Fearful of squatters and even the danger of being murdered by claim jumpers and thieves, many individuals with good claims or knowledge about potentially valuable diggings kept such information to themselves. "Men are almost at times out of their cences [sic]," gold commissioner Richard Hicks advised from Yale, "and are determined to infringe on the privileges granted to others." Miners dug madly wherever rumor suggested that untapped deposits might be found. At Yale, Americans even excavated ground beneath Indian dwellings, directly in front of the H.B.C. gate, and under mercantile establishments. "Good diggings of coarse gold were found," Governor Douglas observed, "which caused so much excitement that the miners could hardly be restrained from opening works in the very heart of the little town." Commissioner Hicks ordered such operations shut down, contending that "otherwise Fort Yale Town would not exist," which antagonized the prospecting class.[87]

Three miles downstream, the first important dry diggings on the Fraser were opened at Prince Albert's Flat. According to early investigations, this extensive site contained gold enough for up to 4,000 miners, but it sat at least 60 feet above the river's highest-known stage, making the availability of water to work the deposits problematical. By late October, however, two government-approved companies were at work building water flumes down from the nearby mountains, a project expected to be completed by the onset of winter. Commissioner Hicks personally surveyed the claims, allowing extra footage to miners to compensate for the added costs of getting water from ditches. Miners able to work the dry diggings were more than happy to do so, in order to be free of the river's frustrating water levels, and to be able to use substantially more efficient equipment. Using larger sluice boxes, Governor Douglas pointed out, "a man can earn ten dollars a day, in places where with the rocker he could not save more than one dollar a day."[88]

Water companies went into business at other locations, too, including at or near old river diggings that no longer yielded living wages for miners. At Hill's Bar, for example, projects intended to allow exploitation of upland deposits behind the original claims and cabins were nearing completion at the end of October. Flume construction and ditch excavation proceeded, as well, on hillsides above American and Santa Clara bars. Miners at Emory's implemented a two-mile long ditching scheme and installed a wheel to draw water out of the Fraser. On Cornish Bar below Fort Hope, another place where claims were thought to be exhausted, commissioner Hicks reported that the inhabitants "will shortly be able to work to better advantage" through installation of water works.[89]

Returning to Victoria from a tour of the Fraser, Governor Douglas noted that of all his varied observations on the mainland he had been "particularly struck with the ingenious contrivances for distributing water." At all convenient points, he informed the colonial office, "small Streams had…been diverted from their course, and conveyed in skil[l]fully graded ditches…along the higher parts of the mining bars for sluice workings." These new developments caused fundamental changes in the gold fields. Persons with capital became investors, building ditches and flumes, selling water, and hiring workers for construction and maintenance, while the prospectors without money moved on or, like the men interviewed by Douglas who made $8 a day handling sluice boxes for a California boss, became employee miners. The cost of water also compelled miners to more efficiently exploit claims, sinking deep shafts in the dry riverbanks rather than merely scooping out shallow holes. As operations increased in cost, Governor Douglas all but abandoned attempts to collect license fees. "A considerable public revenue may be raised," he instead calculated, "from the grant of water privileges," especially in light of expectations that 2,000 sluices would be built over the winter.[90]

Although Douglas hailed the sluice box as "a wonderful labour saving Machine," many prospectors continued, from preference or lack of funds, to rely on shovels, rockers, and pans. Following the long established "Up" dictum—"higher and higher still," wrote Donald Fraser, "the nervous, unsettled miner trudges, in the hope of finding the real 'Dorado'"—the adventurous and penniless headed for the upriver country above the canyons, their security supposedly guaranteed by victory over the Indians in the recent conflict. "Numerous bodies of miners…," the governor noted of a new potential crisis, "have pushed, reckless of consequences, and badly provided with food and clothing, into the interior." Some parties went as far as 200 miles above

"Hydraulic mining." Matthew Macfie, *Vancouver Island and British Columbia* (1865).

the Forks, "as high up as white men have ever yet penetrated." The latest boomtown supply center, Lytton, on a windswept plateau at the mouth of the Thompson River, soon had 50 dwellings and a floating population of 900 dusty fortune hunters.[91]

Most of the water projects remained under construction in early November. The opening of the Harrison-Lillooet trail reduced freight costs, as anticipated, and enabled miners above the Forks to secure supplies. However, lowering water flows revealed navigational hazards in the Harrison River, preventing maximum utilization of the route.

Then, beginning with a prolonged spell of intense rain, winter fell upon the country at this moment of incompleted preparations. "We have not had a dry day now for upwards of a week," reported Richard Hicks, who was down with "a severe cold" from the "damp in the tent" in mid-November. Average temperatures dropped, soon turning precipitation into snow. Governor Douglas reported eight inches on the ground in Victoria on December 4 and, in a more important bit of meteorological news, the freezing of the Fraser. "The weather…has suddenly turned cold and stormy," a prospector wrote from one of the recently opened upstream diggings, with "ice forming on stagnant water to a considerable thickness" and snowfall covering the landscape "quite down to the river." Miners earlier had expected to work through the winter, with shortened daylight hours being the only anticipated obstacle to full-term production. Witless confidence on this score quickly gave way to dreaded apprehension. "The extreme cold weather, the white hill tops, [and] the chattering of teeth," a Yale-based Californian noted, "convinces even the most daring that it is time to leave this country for one more pleasanter."[92]

Winter shut the diggings down just as quickly as high water had in May and June. Concern was greatest and most warranted above the Forks, where prospectors toiled far beyond convenient resupply points. "Food of all kinds has been scarce and dear…," Douglas observed concerning the developing emergency on the upper Fraser. "The miners…therefore kept continually travel[l]ing to and fro to procure subsistence, thereby exhausting their money as well as their physical energies in extremely fatiguing journeys…carrying loads of from 80 to 100 pounds on their backs." Below zero temperatures and mounting snow, combined with expended funds and declining morale, forced a reconsideration of priorities. Given the disappointing performance to date of the Harrison-Lillooet road, starvation loomed as a distinct possibility. Working the gold deposits was impossible, too, with the river iced over and water in the flumes frozen.[93]

"It took all we could make to live," a miner recalled of the best of times at Foster's Bar, 30 miles above Lytton, where beans, bacon, and flour sold for $1 per lb. By late October, said Robert Frost, "there was none to be bought at any price." Genuine privation confirmed the governor's earlier warning that "the cost of transporting provisions to the interior will absorb the Miners whole earnings." Generally speaking, an often-similar pattern prevailed below the canyons as well, except for the fact that the region between Hope and Yale continued to be adequately supplied when river conditions allowed. However, prospectors who could not work because of the cold weather had little or no gold dust, and thus were often unable to purchase adequate provisions. On the lower river, a miner reported, no one "within fifty miles" was "making grub"—in other words, digging enough gold to pay for adequate living expenses. The Fort Hope market was so overstocked with food and supplies that merchants were forced to reduce prices in order to sell goods.[94]

As the subsequent "rush south" to California grew, one diehard thought it was just as "unwarranted" as the original "rush North" had been. Hundreds of "chagrined, discouraged, [and] destitute" miners crowded aboard riverboats bound for Victoria. "The number of returning disgusted adventurers increases," a local merchant reported in letters to San Francisco. The exodus was pitiful and in at least one case genuinely dramatic. When the steamer *Enterprise* became stuck in ice near the mouth of the Harrison River in mid-December, most of the passengers immediately set out on foot for Langley, many neglecting in their panic to take along sufficient food or protective gear. Although fifty men eventually got through, four froze to death. The remainder, huddled together in misery, were picked up by the *Enterprise*, which had been safely extricated by its captain and crew.[95]

The reversal in immigration—having commenced with the initial gold-finding disappointments during September's low water—accelerated rapidly after the first snowfalls. Washington and Oregon residents took to small boats and canoes at Fort Langley, heading toward their homes south of the 49th parallel. Along the route, their mere appearance proffered eloquent and collective testimony to their sufferings and failures. Reporting the arrival in one day of 15 to 20 "canoe loads of miners" at Steilacoom, the *Puget Sound Herald* noted that every man manifested "a truly poverty-stricken appearance, some being shoeless, others hatless, and all more or less ragged." The prevailing view among the "large numbers" of returnees passing through Portland, according to the *Oregonian*, was that the Fraser River mines had turned out to be "a swindle and a humbug."[96]

Weeks in advance of winter's official arrival, a thousand miners already had assembled on Vancouver Island, intent on taking passage to California. "The population of Victoria to-day," a merchant wrote in mid-October, "is mostly composed of men who have flocked down from the interior in every stage of destitution, clamorous to get back to a country where, at least, they can *live*." The pace picked up with the falling temperatures, as "a perfect stampede" broke out. "Dead heads" were unable to pay for the trip to Victoria, much less buy a ticket to San Francisco. Some shoveled coal at Nanaimo in return for passage, the remainder traveling on charity. These unfortunates, a sympathetic observer maintained, should not be regarded as "shiftless, worthless fellows." They were in fact "as fine specimens of Californians as I have ever met"—real men who "did not give up the fight until it was sheer folly to remain longer in a country barren of everything."[97]

Newspaper correspondent Henry DeGroot compared the Americans "hurrying back" from the diggings to "a routed army." Pacific Mail and other steamship concerns provided free steerage quarters for those defeated gold soldiers certified as being truly out of funds. The *Northerner*, which took 181 passengers down the coast in late September, listed twice that number on the official manifest of its next voyage. The *Pacific* brought 262 returnees into San Francisco Bay in November, and over 400 in December. The *Panama* and *Cortes* arrived at Thanksgiving time with a total of 680 paying and non-paying customers.

Well fed San Franciscans watched with "a pang of pity" as their bedraggled "fellow-citizens" debarked. "There were men with just sufficient garment…to cover their nakedness from the cold and from public exposure," the *Alta California* reported. Many had to cover their heads with handkerchiefs instead of hats, their feet with gunnysacks instead of shoes, and their bodies with blankets instead of coats. All, however, "were filled with joy" at being back in a "prosperous" land, "from which, in an ill-advised hour, they had been lured away by the baseless visions of wealth held up before them."[98]

One passenger returning in late November (comfortably quartered in a government-provided cabin suite rather than a dank steerage berth) was an improbable and thoroughly offensive temporary U.S. diplomat, John Nugent. A native of Ireland, Nugent was the publisher of the San Francisco

Herald and a tarnished veteran of Democratic and Irish-American politics. When the governor of California demanded that President James Buchanan protect American miners from the "tyrannic rule" of James Douglas, Nugent, one of the president's old partisan associates, was close at hand angling for political reward. To general astonishment, Buchanan promptly appointed this professional Irishman and anti-British publicist as a special state department agent to New Caledonia.[99]

Nugent arrived in Victoria at the end of September and quickly exceeded the bounds of his assignment, not to mention those of acceptable behavior, by protesting the incarceration of Americans for nonpayment of debts, which was entirely proper under English law. When Douglas, pressed for time by many demands, sent an informal letter over a secretary's signature, the envoy challenged this as a gross offense to the United States and he severed relations with the governor.

Nugent spent the remainder of his tour gathering data, primarily from merchants, for a lengthy indictment of British policies and practices. On the eve of departure, he deliberately insulted Douglas in an address to the American residents of Vancouver's Island. "Much was to be pardoned," Nugent said, "to the inexperience of an Executive hitherto dealing for the most part with savages." Newspapers that otherwise were prone to criticize colonial gubernatorial actions stated that this bit of oratory was "rather unfortunate." The British government agreed, filing an official protest with the U.S. State Department in Washington City. Nugent's subsequent report, falling far short of objectivity and reasoned analysis, at least provided comfort for those Californians convinced that their failure to find gold was due to Hudson's Bay Company villainy.[100]

In one of his last New Caledonia reports, W. A. Wallace made a fundamental observation about the nature of most gold rushes. "We hear always of a hundred fortunate ones," he wrote, "but the voice is silent concerning the thousands of unfortunates." This did not necessarily apply, however, in regard to the Fraser rush, for the multitudes heading south to California in November and December widely broadcast their reports of failure. The gold dug out of the British river, a disillusioned Californian asserted, amounted to "a poor trifle." Neatly capturing the prevailing perception, a San Francisco shopkeeper displayed in his window a skeleton labeled "Returned Fraser River Miner," and a pair of human skulls were marked, "Heads of Families returned from Bellingham Bay."

"Returned from Frazer River"—J. Ross Browne

The Golden State's view of the 1858 Fraser Gold Rush
by
J. Ross Browne—an Irish-American itinerant
journalist and California propagandist, 1861.

A faint cry was heard from afar—first low and uncertain, like a mysterious whisper, then full and sonorous, like the boom of glad tidings from the mouth of a cannon, the inspiring cry of Frazer River! Here was gold sure enough! a river of gold! a country that dazzled the eyes with its glitter of gold! There was no deception about it this time. New Caledonia was the land of Ophir. True, it was in the British possessions, but what of that? The people of California would develop the British possessions. Had our claim to 54° 40' been insisted upon, this immense treasure would now have been within our own boundaries; but no matter—it was ours by right of proximity. The problem of Solomon's Temple was now solved. Travelers, from Marco Polo down to the present era, who had attempted to find the true land of Ophir, had signally failed; but here it was, the exact locality, beyond peradventure. For where else in the world could the river-beds, creeks, and canons be lined with gold? Where else could the honest miner "pan out" $100 per day every day in the year? But if any who had been rendered incredulous by former excitements still doubted, they could no longer discredit the statements that were brought down by every steamer, accompanied by positive and palpable specimens of the ore, and by the assurances of captains, pursers, mates, cooks, and waiters, that

Frazer River was the country. To be sure, it was afterward hinted that the best part of the gold brought down from Frazer had made the round voyage from San Francisco; but I consider this a gross and unwarranted imputation upon the integrity of steam-boat owners, captains, and speculators. Did not the famous Commodore [John] Wright take the matter in hand; put his best steamers on the route; hoist his banners and placards in every direction, and give every man a chance of testing the question in person? This was establishing the existence of immense mineral wealth in that region upon a firm and practical basis. No man of judgement and experience, like the commodore, would undertake to run his steamers on "the baseless fabric of a vision." The cheapness and variety of his rates afforded every man an opportunity of making a fortune. For thirty, twenty, and even fifteen dollars, the ambitious aspirant for Frazer could be landed at Victoria.

I will not now undertake to give a detail of that memorable excitement; how the [California] stages, north, south, east, and, I had almost said, west, were crowded day and night with scores upon scores of sturdy adventurers; how farms were abandoned and crops lost for want of hands to work them; how rich claims in the old diggings were given away for a song; how the wharves of San Francisco groaned under the pressure of the human freight delivered upon them on every arrival of the Sacramento and Stockton boats; how it was often impracticable to get through the streets in that vicinity owing to the crowds gathered around the "runners," who cried aloud the merits and demerits of the rival steamers; and, strangest of all, how the head and front of the Frazerites were the very men who had enjoyed such pleasant experiences [in wild rushes] at Gold Bluff, Kern River, and other places famous in the history of California. No sensible man could doubt the richness of Frazer River when these veterans became leaders, and called upon the masses to follow. They were not a class of men likely to be deceived—they knew the signs of the times. And, in addition to all this, who could resist the judgement and experience of Commodore Wright, a man who had made an independent fortune in the steam-boat business? Who could be deaf when assayers, bankers, jobbers, and speculators cried aloud that it was all true?

Well, I am not going to moralize. Mr. [John] Nugent was appointed a commissioner, on the part of the United States, to settle the various difficulties which had grown up between the miners and Governor Douglass [sic]. He arrived at Victoria in time to perform signal service to his fellow-citizens; that is to say, he found many of them in a state of starvation, and sent them back to California at public expense. Frazer River, always too high

RETURNED FROM FRAZER RIVER.

for mining purposes, could not be prevailed upon to subside. Its banks were not banks of issue, nor were its beds stuffed with the feathers of the Golden Goose. Had it not been for this turn of affairs, it is difficult to say what would have been the result. The British Lion had been slumbering undisturbed at Victoria for half a century, and was very much astonished, upon waking up, to find thirty thousand semi-barbarous Californians scattered broadcast over the British Possessions. Governor Douglass [sic] issued manifestoes in vain. He evidently thought it no joke. The subject eventually became a matter of diplomatic correspondence, in which much ink was shed, but fortunately no blood, although the subsequent seizure of San Juan by General Harney came very near producing that result.

The steamers, in due course of time, began to return crowded with enterprising miners, who still believed there was gold there if the river would only fall. But generosity dictates that I should say no more on this point. It is enough to add, that the time arrived when it became a matter of personal offense to ask any spirited gentlemen if he had been to Frazer River.

Excerpt from *J. Ross Browne: A Peep at Washoe or, Sketch of Adventure in Virginia City* (New York: Harper & Brothers, 1875; Lewis Osborne: Palo Alto, 1968), pp. 28–32. Originally published in *Harper's New Monthly Magazine*, December 1861 and January and February 1862, and *Crusoe's Island* (Harper & Brothers), 1864.

The actual facts told a less ghoulish tale. The official estimated gold production for June through November, as submitted by Governor Douglas, was 106,305 ounces, or approximately $1,700,000 at the going H.B.C. valuation. This figure, though only a fraction of the annual output in the Sierra Nevada during the 1850s, was six times the value recorded by California in the first year after James Marshall's 1848 discovery. Considering that active mining operations were limited to a number of weeks, the initial return was more a positive than a negative development.[101]

The Californians' perception of a failure on the Fraser River, however, also justified an assertion for Golden State superiority. "Any one mining county" in California, a merchant temporarily located in Victoria contended, "would have yielded its millions under the magic touch of the…men who have for the most part fruitlessly expended their toil along the Fraser." Indeed, claimed Henry DeGroot, "there is hardly a county in that State, but is worth more than the whole of New Caledonia." The northern country turned out to be, at best, overrated, another commentator observed, but California "never appeared to better advantage to thousands of her sons…than at present."

Citizens of the golden commonwealth largely rejected accusations that they had gone north too soon, or that they were in any other way guilty of miscalculation. "The old fogy bump, which teaches men to wait for the gold before they go to new diggings," a San Franciscan domiciled in Olympia retorted, "is small in the crania of Californians." The fortune seekers had failed, many stated, because of unfair H.B.C. practices and treacherous natural conditions. The Fraser simply refused to "rise and fall" in the same familiar, and therefore proper, pattern as watercourses south of the 49th parallel. Moreover, the ungodly climate, forcing inherently energetic persons to endure long periods of idleness, seemed made to order to frustrate always-active migrants from California.[102]

Since the New Caledonia excitement primarily was viewed and recorded from a Golden State perspective, the Fraser rush came to be seen by many American commentators and historians as a phenomenon occurring in *1858 alone*. Californians would ignore, or be ignorant of, what came later in the north. However, as Donald Fraser reported in a London dispatch, even though "the great bulk of the California miners" had departed, at least 5,000 others remained, determined to see the bad weather through at Langley, Hope, Yale, Port Douglas, and Lytton.

Many of the "summer visitors," too, had vowed to come back in the spring of 1859, when digging again became practicable. Other prospectors, moreover, had been arriving from the Atlantic coast, Europe, Australia, and Asia. Individuals and organized parties had set sail from those distant places within weeks of hearing news of the strike. Many arrived in the summer when the water rose, or finally arrived as the mines closed again. They had little choice but to stay through the winter. With the Fraser frozen over and the mining population in transition, more definitive proof of British Columbia's prosperous gold fields was still to come in 1859.[103]

Chapter Five
A Gradually Augmenting Yield

It is a significant fact that while the gold yield of British Columbia, with her mere handful of miners, is gradually augmenting, that of California with her hundreds of thousands of active miners, is rapidly decreasing.—Victoria *British Colonist*[1]

WINTER CAME EARLY to Britain's Pacific coast colonies in 1858. The temperature dropped suddenly in early December, snow began falling on a regular basis, and the mouth of the Fraser, if only briefly, froze shut. Victoria settled uncomfortably into a prolonged period of harsh weather, "marked," according to Donald Fraser, "by sudden alternations of frost, thaw, snow, rain, sleet, hail, [and] heavy gales of wind." Far in the interior, the new supply center of Lytton, located in what H.B.C. veterans had always considered a rather temperate locale, also experienced wild climatic fluctuations. The thermometer fell to zero on December 10, climbed to 48 degrees on the thirteenth, held steady for several days, and again plummeted, this time for good. Ice formed sufficiently thick to support pack horses crossing over the rivers. From the Forks to the sea, miners, merchants, H.B.C. employees, and the new colonial government's officials complained about the difficult climatic conditions.[2]

Dismay if not downright disgust, due to the day-in and day-out discomfort, became universal. Low water limited the cruising range of the steamers, and vessels periodically grounded at points normally considered easily navigable. Colonel Richard Moody and Judge Matthew Begbie, on their first official joint visit to Hope and Yale, had to abandon the *Enterprise* and complete the journey by whaleboat, canoe, and finally afoot. Construction activities at Langley, the recently selected colonial capital, were halted due to the bad weather. Mining operations closed down, too, when snow covered over the diggings, water froze in ditches, and the bitter cold kept prospectors domiciled in the minimal shelter provided by tents and primitive cabins. "Many were frozen so as to be permanently crippled," an American wrote of

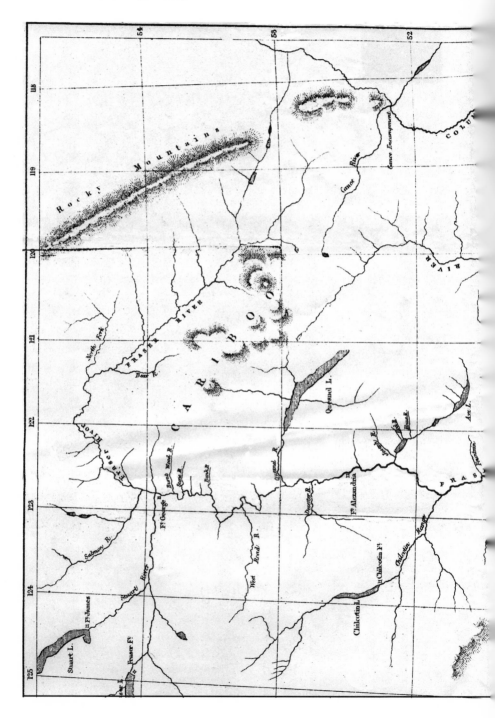

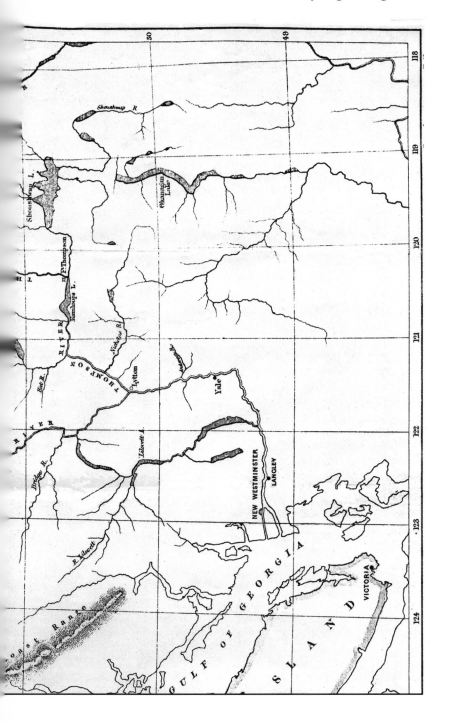

Modified from *The Handbook of British Columbia and Emigrant's Guide to the Gold Fields* ... (London, 1862).

his colleagues, an observation applicable to all of the river bar camps. Sufferers at least were spared the exactions of government administrators, since the Queen's agents refused to leave their warm quarters to collect license fees or otherwise perform their duties.[3]

Remarkably—considering winter's sudden onset and the departure of a majority of the miners—the Fraser country continued to produce gold in fairly decent quantities. English critics depicted the fleeing Californians as being unfit for the cold. "Those people…," said Governor Douglas, "appear physically disqualified by the enervating effects of a long residence in California for the more rigorous climate of British Columbia." Provisions might be low and costly, but persons with money and gold dust always could find adequate food stocks to purchase. The real problem downstream from the Forks, Police Inspector Chartres Brew pointed out, was the inability of quicksilver to "take up the Gold below a certain temperature."

Prospectors holding good claims still did well by expending a bit of extra labor on those days when the weather abated somewhat. "The persevering or needy miner may be seen," an *Alta California* correspondent noted, "panning out with warm water, or thawing the earth by means of a fire built on the surface." Pausing at several river bars on the way downstream in February, a traveler found that many inhabitants had "been able to make large wages throughout the winter, taking out from ten to twenty dollars a day to the hand." A man from Puget Sound Bar noted that miners on the lower Fraser were able to work "about one-fourth of the time."[4]

The coarse gold found above the Forks also could be easily mined, weather permitting. Just as winter settled in, rich dry diggings had been discovered near the mouth of the Bridge River, a stream flowing into the Fraser north of the Harrison-Lillooet trail terminus. Belying the view in California that prospectors had deserted the upper country, miners remained active there at several points, excavating ditches and taking, when able to work at the principal Bridge River site, $30 a day to the man. Gold also was found upstream on the Chilcotin River near Fort Alexandria, and downstream on a number of bars toward Lytton.

"Gold is coming down the river in large quantities," Chartres Brew wrote from Yale at the end of January. "The abundance of gold in that region," Donald Fraser noted in a dispatch to London, "is confirmed by the quantity of dust which comes to Victoria." Anxiety regarding food kept the population to a minimum and mandated a good deal of scurrying about for provisions, but the overall performance was impressive. In April, steamers carried $168,000 to San Francisco, most of this coming from the interior wintertime operations. (British Columbia's winter production, though noteworthy, failed to match California's performance. On the same day that the steamer *Foxwood* arrived in San Francisco with $25,000 in Fraser dust, the regular Sacramento riverboat brought in a half million dollars from the Sierra Nevada.)[5]

Miners were, of course, idle a good deal of the time, especially toward winter's end when the supply system partially collapsed. Repeating a previous pattern, many persons had retreated to Victoria where provisions always were abundant and prices relatively low. The days spent there, however, were dreary and the streets were buried in mud. Victoria's residents, wags insisted, were better-off slogging through in the darkness, because the outdoor exercise provided the best means of staying warm—"Buildings composed of thin walls of clapboards, not half thick enough for partitions even," Donald Fraser complained, "and innocent of fireplaces in most cases, afford an indifferent protection from cold and wind." The substantial reduction in demand for supplies from the mainland forced overstocked merchants to endure a "reign of dullness" until the arrival of spring.[6]

Along the Fraser, miners tended to congregate at the main gathering places, including Lytton, which had 20 trading establishments. Rough winter villages also had been established at the major river bars, with 500 residents at Emory's, and 400 quartered in 64 cabins at Hill's. Day-to-day living quickly broke down to carefully husbanding provisions saved from the 1858 digging seasons and the very prudent buying of additional supplies. Men often crowded into abandoned huts without bothering to inquire whether the owner had permanently departed or merely gone away on a brief excursion. "All you have to do…," a diarist recorded, "is to enter[,] spread your blankets[,] light the fire & make yourself at home." Prospectors ate fried bacon and potatoes from a common pan placed on a convenient stump. Denied barber services, an aspect of civilization more appropriate to the prim and proper confines of Victoria, the Fraser's wintertime inhabitants grew fabulous, chest-covering beards and great tangles of shoulder-length hair.[7]

With little to do and much time on their hands, miners often got into trouble. "Constant rows are by no means uncommon," Judge Begbie's clerk reported, "& as these fellows all carry revolvers in their drunken revels they are nasty customers." Several fatal shootings occurred, some comprehensible only as outright premeditated murder. Theft of personal items, gold dust, and canoes became so prevalent at Langley, along with gambling and the firing of pistols, that the *British Colonist* compared the scene to "the palmiest days of California." Police officials often declined to make arrests, fearing that if the miners' successfully resisted the constabulary, then all remaining respect for legal authority would be destroyed. Their sense of American patriotism enhanced by alcohol, a number of miners celebrated Washington's Birthday, but assaulted British subjects attempting to honor the Queen in a similar fashion.[8]

The wild state of affairs at Fort Yale, in particular, were comparable to 1849 California standards. The place "acquired," according to one observer, "a very bad reputation for gambling, drinking and violence of every kind." Abandoning Whatcom and other failing boomtowns south of the 49th parallel—"as rats desert a falling house," noted Donald Fraser—a number of American gamblers and other vice dealers had made Yale their new resort. Personally encouraged by Governor Douglas, respectable residents finally drove out a number of miscreants in a manner precisely reminiscent of San Francisco's old vigilante days. In fact, many participants, the righteous and criminal alike in earlier California law-and-order confrontations, had taken up residence in the Yale neighborhood.

Ned McGowan, the enforcer of California Senator David Broderick's Tammany-style political machine, held sway at nearby Hill's Bar, stirring up trouble against old Californian and new British adversaries. Since arriving the previous summer, McGowan had been involved in a series of scrapes with antagonists from San Francisco. And, in an incident regarded by the British as particularly offensive, he had rousted Governor Douglas, who had gone ashore for the night, from bed so that the steamer upon which both were passengers could promptly depart at dawn. The Crown's agents clearly anticipated bloodshed at Hill's Bar. "They have become habituated to violence…," Judge Matthew Begbie wrote of McGowan's faction, "and become their own avengers whenever and wherever they meet with any of their supposed oppressors."[9]

***

British Columbia, Edward Bulwer Lytton observed while presiding over the colony's gold-related birth, "stands on a very different footing from many of our early…Settlements." The statement certainly was true, if perhaps in ways not always fully comprehended by the secretary for the colonies. The semi-permanent white population consisted, once the original gold rush impetus was spent, of 5,000 men, "there being," as Governor Douglas reported, "with the exception of a few families, neither wives nor children to refine and soften…the cheariness and asperity of existence." Farmers, too, were scarce, in large part due to the interior's limited acreage suited for agriculture. Although Lytton authorized Douglas to sell farming tracts, the mandatory £1 per acre price had the same negative impact on the mainland as at Vancouver's Island. "There is nothing in this country but mines," a disgusted would-be settler observed in dismissing the colony's long-term prospects.[10]

Government also, of course, had to operate under extraordinary means. Colonists complained of "taxation by proclamation," and of "arbitrary and illegal exactions" designed to benefit Victoria "at the expense of British Columbia." The presence of so many foreigners compelled postponement of plans for an assembly and interfered with the orderly conduct of judicial affairs. For example, Judge Begbie had difficulty impaneling grand juries due to insufficient numbers of qualified British subjects.

Despite accusations that he was making "a traffic of the public service," Douglas had little choice but to rely, at the outset at least, upon inferior appointees. The original British magistrates that had been selected, noted a later arriving legal expert, were "generally…ignorant of the first principles of the law." Fort Yale's justice of the peace, P. B. Whannell, who had abandoned his family in Australia and fled to America with a mistress in tow, acted as if the main point of his position was personal aggrandizement. Vilified for assessing and pocketing excessive court costs—one wit suggested that the jurist ought to at least have the decency to refund his unneeded paycheck—Whannell was a prime example for the proposition, made by a visiting Englishman, that "law and justice have no existence in British Columbia." At Hill's Bar, magistrate Perrier, also generally was considered incompetent, and O. T. Travaillot, the Douglas-appointed gold commissioner at Lytton, wound up imprisoned for debt.[11]

Commissioner Richard Hicks, also stationed at Fort Yale, likewise ranked fairly high on the incompetency scale—to the extent that a popular witticism held that he best handled his Fraser River responsibilities when absent in Victoria. Improperly recorded leases compromised land titles at Yale, led to the illegal locating of cabins and stores, and raised the distinct possibility, as an appalled Matthew Begbie stated, that authorities might have to "recommence the town." Compounding his failure to make any genuine effort at collecting license fees (granted, under difficult field conditions), Hicks used the wrong forms to document the small amount actually secured. Recommending that "criminal proceedings" be undertaken against Hicks, Begbie pointed in particular to the commissioner's habit of extorting "unauthorized fees" for the granting of water rights. Ranged against such misbehavior, lurid allegations of Hick's addiction to alcohol and gambling seemed barely worth serious notice. Hicks somehow retained his office until March 1859, apparently because Douglas wished to avoid the appearance of giving in to American criticism of his appointees.[12]

Meanwhile, British Columbia's top-level positions fortunately had been filled by capable imported persons, such as Colonel Moody, Judge Begbie, and Police Inspector Chartres Brew. The latter had arrived in North America "with nothing but the clothes on my person" after his steamer sank in the Atlantic Ocean. Assisted by these newcomers, Governor Douglas intended to spend the winter lull reforming local administration on the Fraser.

Hicks and company were still in office, however, when a domestic insurrection broke out at Yale in early January. Acting on behalf of onetime San Francisco vigilantes, magistrate Whannell closed gambling establishments, invalidated the claims of political opponents, and jailed at least one protestor. In response, Hill's Bar magistrate Perrier deputized the notorious Ned McGowan, who organized a posse and then arrested and confined Whannell until the latter agreed to pay a $50 fine. According to the first reports reaching Langley and Victoria, McGowan and his followers—denounced by Douglas as "reckless desperadoes"—had shot Whannell and commenced a virtual uprising against British rule.[13]

Upon receipt of this alarming news at Langley, Colonel Moody and Judge Begbie departed for Yale, accompanied by whatever Royal Engineers and Marines were available to make the trip. Two hundred loyal volunteers were expected to join-in should fighting become necessary. On the second day upriver, however, an express canoe brought a reasonably accurate account of affairs. "There had been a squabble between the justices," Begbie summarized. Proceeding with a portion of their armed escort, the colonel and the judge attended a public indignation meeting as unofficial observers (but with Moody asking the red-shirted American orators to cease using "epithets"). Although the Hill's Bar group controlled the agenda and drafted the resolutions, the facts were easily divined. Ned McGowan might be a dastardly villain, but the rival magistrates were primarily to blame—Perrier from poor judgement and Whannell by acting "with quite illegal severity." The primary lesson taught was the need for making sound appointments in the first place.[14]

Cleaning up the muddle at Yale in a formal court session, Begbie allowed both sides to vent their opinions, and then dismissed all charges against the various defendants. Ned McGowan, who had enlivened the proceedings by beating a man within eyesight of Colonel Moody, pleaded guilty to assault and paid a $25 fine. Soon, McGowan's career in British Columbia would come to an ignominious bully's end. This occurred after the local Americans promised to behave themselves while celebrating Washington's Birthday and, as a good faith gesture, deposited their pistols with Police Inspector Brew. The celebration still broke down into a drunken brawl, ending in a mutual challenge to a duel with rifles between McGowan and one of his former co-horts. Before the fight to the death could take place, the scourge of the vigilantes sold his claim, crossed the border, and was last heard from planning to run for office in Oregon, a bastion of Irish-American politics.[15]

With Begbie keeping a stern eye on judicial matters and Chartres Brew supplanting Richard Hicks as gold commissioner at Yale, the quality of governance took an upward track. (The magistrates Perrier and Whannell, too, were dismissed from office, the former summarily, and the latter eventually.) Meanwhile, Douglas proclaimed a general plan for British Columbia's development. The colony, he argued, needed an official assay office and gold escort, institutions that would divert gold dust exports from going to San Francisco, and enable the colonial government to gather accurate statistics about mining production. Transportation, however, continued to be the key problem in the Fraser's exploitation. "There is a general outcry for better roads into the interior," Douglas exclaimed in a series of messages on the subject, "the difficulty of access still forming the great impediment to the development of its mineral resources." The substantial savings in freight costs already generated by opening the Harrison-Lillooet trail suggested the advantages to be gained elsewhere from similar improvements. Top on Douglas's to-do list, though, was additional work on the vital Harrison-Lillooet route itself so that wagons, in addition to pack mules, could reach the diggings above the Forks.[16]

Unfortunately, the home government dictated that British Columbia had to be self-supporting. Douglas sent regular protests to the colonial office regarding this frustrating mandate. "To accomplish this great object of opening up a very inaccessible country for settlement...," he pointed out, "and, in short, to create a great social organization, with all its civil, judicial, and military establishments, in a wilderness of forest and mountain is a herculean task," far beyond the "means of the country to defray." The high additional expense, too, of supervising a large foreign mining population near an undefended international border could only be covered by the home government.

As a necessary first step, the governor requested that Parliament grant, or at least loan, £200,000 to be used primarily for transportation improvements. "When the colony can do so," Douglas vowed, "the obligation will be faithfully repaid." Douglas also wanted lighthouses installed on the Strait of Juan de Fuca. Despite explicit official orders to the contrary, the governor continued to rely upon the Hudson's Bay Company as a sort of off the books administrative apparatus, providing personal services, transportation, and supplies.[17]

Douglas promised to "attend most carefully" to the self-support edict, but added that he was not at present "entertaining much hope of being immediately able" to pay even for the colony's minimal needs. "Like a nursling," he noted of British Columbia, "it must for a time be fed and clothed." Confirming the governor's pessimistic expectations, the colonial administration took in, during the first six months of its existence, £13,661 from mining licenses, customs duties, head taxes, and liquor permits. The initial land sales at Langley added £6,301 to the total. But due to heavy expenditures for the Harrison-Lillooet trail, an overall £2,000 deficit was recorded. Despite an increase in tariff rates, British Columbia continued to operate under a woeful shortcoming of funds.[18]

Everything depended upon improving the revenue flow. Mining license fees potentially were the largest source of income, but were collected with difficulty. Richard Hicks' failure in this regard seemed, in retrospect, more the fault of wintry conditions and prospector intransigence than of personal dereliction. Chartres Brew, the new commissioner, fared little better than his disgraced predecessor. "Two or three times symptoms of a thaw made me determine on an expedition down the river to collect gold licence duties," he reported in early March, "but frost and snow set in again and prevented me from carrying my intentions into execution." When the weather cleared, miners pled poverty (in some cases honestly) or simply refused to pay.[19]

Town lot sales at Langley, where original purchasers still owed over $40,000, represented the second most important revenue source. Governor Douglas earmarked the income, past and future, to the construction of government buildings and a church. Unfortunately, his plans along with the colony's finances became embroiled in an unexpected dispute. Exercising his professional military role, Colonel Moody concluded that Langley, on the south bank of the Fraser, was dangerously exposed to American attack from across the border. Therefore, acting upon the colonel's recommendation, the home government ordered the capital relocated to the far side of the river. The new site, named Queenborough in homely approximation of Victoria, occupied a well-watered prairie accessible by ocean-going vessels and crossed by a trail leading to Burrard Inlet.[20]

Governor Douglas was hardly overjoyed by the move, which threatened his closely figured revenue projections; Langley purchasers, after all, could not be expected to continue paying for their lots now that the capital, the prime reason for investing there in the first place, had been relocated. Deriding the new site as "Pineborough" and the "City of Stumps," speculators were, in fact, doubly outraged, for they had been cheated of both the wealth anticipated from Langley's growth and the funds already expended on holdings that now were virtually worthless. When Queenborough acreage went on sale in June, however, concessions were made granting credit to angry south bank investors toward their acquisitions at the new site. All but 8 of the 318 lots initially offered were sold within 24 hours at an average price of $290, adding close to $90,000 overall to the colonial income. Shortly thereafter, word arrived that the home government had renamed British Columbia's second capital; it now was New Westminster.[21]

Enfeebled by a chronic lack of funds, the colony nevertheless prepared for another, and presumably better, mining season in 1859. Winter lingered long, with snow still covering the river bars on April 1. Except toward the end, when supplies ran low and prices mounted, prospectors were sufficiently provisioned and thus withstood the cold weather with adequately filled bellies. In the closest thing to genuinely short rations, H.B.C. employees at Fort Alexandria, far up the Fraser, resorted to eating horseflesh.

The Indians, though, ran out of food due to the poor salmon runs of the previous year and their previous diverting of time and energy from food gathering to digging for gold. As a consequence of "neglecting their fishing," the veteran trader John Work reported to London, the Fraser River bands "are represented as suffering much for want and many of them [have] starved to death." Traveling from Fort Yale to Lytton as the snow melted, a pair of constables found the "poor natives" encountered along the way "in a state of fearful misery and want." Little could be done, beyond slim humanitarian efforts by the H.B.C. at the various interior posts, to alleviate these conditions. "Limmited [sic] as your means are," Work instructed company traders with respect to the Indians, "you may be able in some measure to alleviate their sufferings and save their lives no matter what the expense may be."[22]

Government initiative—though hamstrung by budget problems in general and the Langley-Queenborough fiasco in particular—focused upon improving the Harrison-Lillooet trail, the best means of getting freight to the region above the Forks in the shortest time possible. With revenue from the first Queenborough sales, Douglas finally concluded a contract for building a wagon road along this route. A hundred Royal Engineers and Marines also were assigned to the project. Private mercantile interests based at Hope and Yale on different trails, however, felt that their interests were threatened by this rival and generally superior route. They responded with their own transportation improvements. Installed at the worst rapid above Fort Yale, a primitive boatlift—locally known as "the 'Way'"—aided persons who wished to travel all the way to the upper diggings by water. In addition to further upgrades in the trail to Lytton, ferries facilitated river crossings by packers. Rude stores and restaurants opened at convenient points, supplying weary travelers with food, alcohol, and overnight lodging.[23]

The introduction of local agriculture production would be another positive change from 1858. The colonial government opened prairie land along the lower Fraser to "immediate occupation for the purpose of raising food and retaining a permanent population in the country," Douglas noted. One immigrant, too, prepared to cultivate soil on a plateau opposite to Yale, and another settler, occupying a site a day's travel below Lytton, enclosed 200 acres. At Lytton itself, a *British Colonist* correspondent wrote that with "gardening...being carried on extensively," pioneer farmers expected to supply the upstream market. On the Harrison-Lillooet route, meanwhile, a number of meadows between the lakes were converted to hay and barley production for subsistence for pack animals.[24]

Considering the winter's difficulties, prospectors who had stayed the course over the winter had relatively "done well," according to observers familiar with British Columbia affairs. Most everyone believed that the diggings finally would come into their own in the spring, in large part because the transportation and supply problems apparently were being resolved. "More good claims will be found and worked the coming season," a wintertime resident of Emory's Bar forecast, "than has been during the past." Citing the "deep confidence in the mines...exhibited by those who appear to know something about them," a Victoria merchant predicted "a very large immigration during the ensuing spring and summer." Even a number of Californians, convinced that "the whole thing...has, thus far, practically proved a delusion," expected the Fraser River to be vindicated, with "a considerable population taking up new claims." Heeding a lesson of 1858, however, veterans advised Californians against "a great and rapid rush" north in numbers that might overtax the logistical network, despite its marked improvements.[25]

A significant (though statistically unclear) number of miners did return to the Fraser River in the spring of 1859. Writing from Victoria in early April, Donald Fraser reported a "sudden increase of population, which continues to arrive in more or less numbers by every steamer." The composition of the new migration had changed somewhat, however, with a substantial portion being Chinese. Late in 1858, California newspaper reports had recounted how the "excitement" had taken hold in China, "stir[ing] the avaricious hearts of the Celestials." Consequently, a "general exodus" was in progress directly from Asia to British Columbia, or to San Francisco as an intermediate stop. "Batches of Chinamen...bound for the mines" departed Vancouver Island on every river steamer, Fraser noted in another of his springtime dispatches. Many went to the old diggings between Hope and Yale, where they became known for diligently and successfully reworking the supposedly played out bars. Even more remarkably, they paid the license fee without complaint. Other Chinese joined in the main object of the 1859 rush, proceeding upstream beyond the canyons and north of Lytton as far as the Bridge River.[26]

During the height of the British Columbia gold rush (1858–65), more than a score of mining guidebooks and descriptive travel logs were published in San Francisco, London, Victoria, and New Westminster.

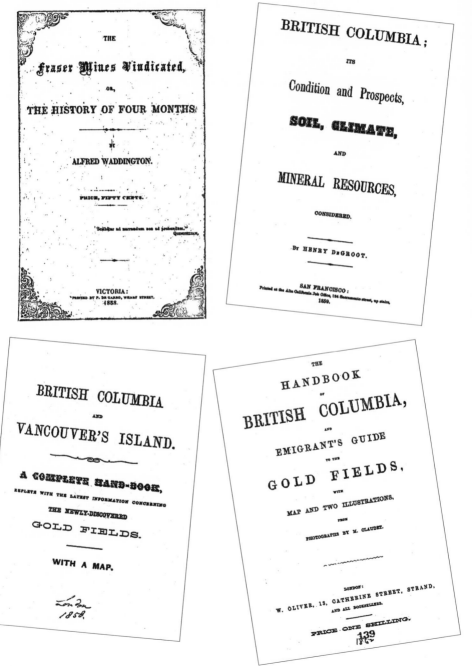

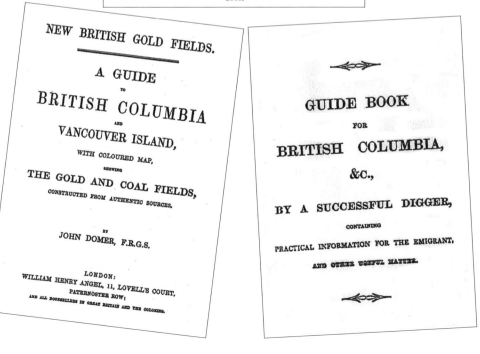

THE

GREAT GOLD FIELDS OF

CARIBOO;

WITH AN AUTHENTIC DESCRIPTION, BROUGHT DOWN
TO THE LATEST PERIOD,

OF

BRITISH COLUMBIA

AND

VANCOUVER ISLAND.

BY WILLIAM CAREW HAZLITT,
OF THE INNER TEMPLE, BARRISTER-AT-LAW.

WITH AN ACCURATE MAP.

LONDON:
ROUTLEDGE, WARNE, AND ROUTLEDGE,
FARRINGDON STREET.
NEW YORK: 56, WALKER STREET.
1862.

NEW BRITISH GOLD FIELDS.

A GUIDE
TO
BRITISH COLUMBIA
AND
VANCOUVER ISLAND,
WITH COLOURED MAP,
SHOWING
THE GOLD AND COAL FIELDS,
CONSTRUCTED FROM AUTHENTIC SOURCES.

BY
JOHN DOMER, F.R.G.S.

LONDON:
WILLIAM HENRY ANGEL, 11, LOVELL'S COURT,
PATERNOSTER ROW;
AND ALL BOOKSELLERS IN GREAT BRITAIN AND THE COLONIES.

GUIDE BOOK
FOR
BRITISH COLUMBIA,
&C.,
BY A SUCCESSFUL DIGGER,
CONTAINING
PRACTICAL INFORMATION FOR THE EMIGRANT,
AND OTHER USEFUL MATTER.

Despite heavy rains, early March signaled the beginning of the spring mining season. "Nearly all the able-bodied men" in Victoria left for the mainland, reported Donald Fraser. The Hope-to-Yale sector also was being deserted by white miners heading upstream (the white population of Emory's Bar declined from 500 to 30 in a matter of days), which opened up opportunities there for the Chinese newcomers. "Clusters of boats crowded with people are passing up the river," noted Chartres Brew from Fort Yale. Near the end of the month, Brew estimated that 300 canoes and small vessels, carrying an average of five prospectors and an Indian guide per craft, had already gone upstream to the Forks. "And I dare say," he added, "a greater number have passed up-country by trail." By April 1, 3,000 fortune seekers were actively digging for gold above Lytton. Aside from some miners that Donald Fraser had seen leaving "for California with their 'piles'" of gold, no one came downstream unless in need of supplies.[27]

The upriver migration proceeded through the difficult canyons, until the river level finally rose high enough to frighten off all but those inclined to risk suicidal dangers. An itinerant preacher named Ebenezer Robson remained present at the canyons—"paddling himself, as Saint Peter used to do." Even at its lower stages, the river was dangerous, and the drowned needed proper Christian burials. Four men, including one prospector coming down from the Forks with $2,000 in dust, drowned in late March. Two canoes capsized in the first week of April, with another four fatalities recorded.

News of such incidents naturally diverted travelers to the safer and more efficient Harrison-Lillooet trail. Portions of the route were undeniably dreary and the repeated land portages between the lakes grew tiresome. However, there were hostels every half dozen miles along the path, "where a hungry wayfayer might refresh the inner man with pork, beans, bread and coffee." A Californian wrote that packing was "not at all difficult, the country being open and the trails keeping along on the table lands, open for miles without interruption." Once on the Fraser again, travelers were "longitudinally, at the centre of the…mines, with at least one hundred and fifty miles of auriferous country to the north, and fully as far above the first diggings met with in ascending the river."[28]

Having been discovered in late 1858, the Bridge River diggings were the initial focus of the spring rush. In addition to being near the Harrison-Lillooet terminus, the Bridge mines also were accessible by a new trail from Lytton along the west bank of the river. The largest piece of gold yet unearthed in British Columbia—a nugget "weighing 3 ounces less 2 penny-weights"—was dug up there in April, sent to Victoria, and eventually shipped by Governor Douglas to the colonial office as a Fraser River souvenir. The usual collection of whiskey shops, card sharp tents, and grocery outlets opened for business in the neighborhood.

In addition, the Columbia Basin supply route from interior Washington Territory, too, helped shopkeepers stock their shelves. In the previous summer, the Indian obstacle to white travel east of the Cascades had been removed in two harsh U.S. Army campaigns. Colonel George Wright had defeated the Palouse and Spokane area tribes, while at the same time Major Robert Garnett successfully advanced northward against tribes along the Columbia's western tributaries, including the Yakima, Wenatchee, and Okanogan rivers. Joel Palmer of Oregon, taking advantage of the new commercial opportunity, guided two pack trains and cattle to the Thompson River and the Bridge mines, an 18-day trek from The Dalles.[29]

Many prospectors, following accepted wisdom, continued upstream expecting to find gold in ever increasing quantities and size. "The bed of the river," Matthew Begbie observed in the course of a judicial circuit above the mouth of the Bridge River, "pays the whole distance from $5 to $100 per hand per day." The Fountain—named after an early French *habitant*, La Fontaine, rather than, as many believed, a geological phenomenon—became another briefly famous digging ground.

Here and elsewhere on the upper Fraser, miners relied on rockers, "it being a work requiring too much time," a participant in the rush explained, "to get water for sluicing, even where it might be done without much difficulty or expense." Because the river had few tributaries and was bordered by benches hundreds of feet in height, Judge Begbie noted that eventually "considerable hydraulic works would have to be undertaken." But the 1858 experience had taught that time was of the essence—miners had to get into the country as fast as possible, quickly work as much ground as practical, and depart before the summer high water made the distribution of provisions problematical. The town of Fountain, high atop a terrace, was hardly built for permanence. The stores were of the "commonest sort," said Begbie, and, surprisingly, there were "no drinkable liquors, nor…any facilities for gambling."[30]

Springtime's best new mines, however, appeared to be in the Canoe country, centering upon the tributary stream of that name 120 miles northwest of the Forks and 40 miles above the Fountain. "A few pioneers…penetrated its wilds last fall, and meeting with good success, have made known their discoveries," the *British Colonist* reported, "and the result is an immense rush from all the mining camps on the Lower Fraser." The region was so remote that little actual information had penetrated to the outside world. The usual gold rush upriver reasoning nonetheless inspired confidence. Even though the diggings "extend nobody…knows how far," the *British Colonist* concluded that they were obviously rich. Donald Fraser of the *Times* was fully convinced, for "as the Fraser flows through it, and as we know the gold comes from 'above,' there can be no doubt that the country is auriferous." The first factual accounts from the Canoe—a four-person party had averaged $300 per day— apparently confirmed the wishful thinking.[31]

Returns from the first weeks of work at the Bridge, Fountain, and Canoe diggings seemingly justified the general optimism. Ocean steamers carried $195,000 in gold to San Francisco between April 11 and May 10. Also, informed sources estimated that an additional $75,000 went to California in private hands during the same period, plus $30,000 to Puget Sound ports.

Working from this total figure of $300,000, *Alta California* correspondent Henry DeGroot, who had wintered in the north, made a definitive calculation: "If we further suppose there were 3,000 men…at work in the mines…and that they labored twenty out of the thirty-one days in the month…Sundays and stormy weather being deducted, this would give an average of $5 a day, to the man," which compared favorably with the California mines. Other bits of evidence also seemed to confirm the basic point that the rush was off to a good start. The mostly Chinese labor force at Emory's Bar made, individually, "from 8 to 12 dollars per day with rockers." Prospectors using sluices in the Lytton vicinity claimed average daily finds of $7 to $12, although a water rights dispute threatened to reduce those earnings. The riverboat *Governor Douglas* brought down $48,600 in gold, passengers' personal holdings included, in the first week of June.[32]

Then unexpectedly, the rush began reversing course, turning back from upstream to down, where good diggings still remained. Doubts actually had begun as early as the end of April: "The news from the upper country is not very favorable," Chartes Brew wrote from Fort Yale. "Miners are wandering, prospecting in every direction, but as yet they have found no goldfields richer than those on the lower Frazer." The intelligence was not so much negative as it was mixed, with the lack of more good news becoming the same as bad tidings. "In this, as in all mining countries," a philosophical Californian reflected at Port Douglas, "there are the successful and the unsuccessful—the satisfied and the dissatisfied—some going, some returning; and accounts so extremely conflicting that one is at a loss to know what is the real state of the case."

As always, the gold fever psychology of the miners fluctuated between the positive and negative, accentuated by the potential problem of securing sufficient provisions. "Those who do not get rich claims at once," a Queenborough clergyman noted in sketching the stark alternatives, "are forced to return or starve." For the moment, the alarm was limited and the likelihood of a general collapse discounted. "The gold seeker is essentially a roving and unsettled being," the *British Colonist* observed. "Every day in California, more miners leave one central mining locality…for some other, where he [sic] believes he will have a better chance for lucky strikes, than are leaving our mines."[33]

Early returnees were, in fact, partly motivated by new excitement from an old quarter. A trading vessel arrived in Victoria at the end of March with a 14-ounce nugget procured from Indians in the Queen Charlotte Islands. Longtime residents remembered the earlier failed attempts to exploit the islands, and especially the opposition mounted by the Haidas. Californians and other newcomers on the Fraser knew little or nothing of those events, however, and expressed neither fear nor respect for the Indians. "When the news of this spreads," John Work wrote of the great nugget currently on public display, "very likely lots of miners will be pushing on there." A preliminary exploratory party set sail in June, heading for the problematic El Dorado. One hundred veterans of the Fraser, meanwhile, busied themselves organizing a follow-up expedition.[34]

Douglas thought that "the non-realization of extravagant expectations" caused these prospectors to abandon the Fraser in favor of new attractions in the Queen Charlottes, as well as south of the 49th parallel. The real problem, though, was neither irrationality nor impatience. British Columbia had enough gold to reward the 1859 rush, but the transportation network, despite the governor's efforts at road building, simply failed to keep up with the needs of the upriver migration.

"The remoteness of the Canoe Country," in particular, Donald Fraser reported, "carried the miners beyond the reach of supplies." Men had "incautiously flocked" to places hundreds of miles from the coast, the correspondent noted in a second letter on the subject—places where the cost of living "was so high as to consume the greater portion of their earnings." Passing on the gist of his conversations with returnees, Douglas made the same point. "All…admit that any industrious man can at any time make from four to five dollars a day," he wrote, "but owing to the high price of provisions that sum will scarcely maintain the miner in that part of the country." Bubble-like, the far-upriver spring rush collapsed, having expanded too fast and too far beyond a self-sustaining capacity.[35]

When not "cursing the country" and its environmental difficulties, miners often stressed their monetary complaints. "We have been making two, three and four dollars per day," a returning prospector informed friends in eastern Canada, "but it would not last more than two or three days; and so you would spend that before you would fine more." Californians delivered a similar "hard account of things up the river." Reminding *Alta California* readers that "in this climate men eat a great deal," a former San Francisco resident advised that there was "nothing to be bought for less than a dollar a pound" in the British Columbia interior. On the other hand, one of the relatively few individuals willing to spend the summer above the Forks noted that he had brought fishing gear, and therefore expected to "get along well" on salmon. A rather pessimistic observer proclaimed that the immediate construction of a wagon road along the Harrison-Lillooet route was "the *only means* of saving the upper portion from *utter depopulation*." Unfortunately delayed by budgetary problems, the wagon road project could not be completed until fall at the earliest.[36]

Commencing its normal late-spring/early-summer rise, the Fraser's waters increasingly interfered with digging. "It has risen here about twenty feet," a prospector wrote from the Fountain, "and rises or falls, more or less every day, getting, however, gradually higher." On the lower river, floodwater washed away cabins and stores at Yale. Many prospectors could only work on a sporadic basis. Between mid-May and early June, a thousand passengers departed Victoria for San Francisco. "The cry is 'still, they come!'" a merchant wrote of the continuing arrivals coming down from the Fraser River. "Every Steamer brings some 80 to 100 miners," John Work noted in a report to H.B.C. directors. Three boats arrived on May 21, carrying a total of 121 returning miners. The *Eliza Anderson* brought in 175 passengers, and the *Governor Douglas* docked with 65 more on May 23. Four hundred men from the interior came ashore at Vancouver Island over a three-day period in June.[37]

In a number of respects, merchants in Great Britain's Pacific coast colonies largely had been sustained through the long winter months by expectations of getting rich in the spring. The short duration of the initial 1859 rush, therefore, had a negative impact. In Victoria, confidence in a sustainable economic expansion had been great enough to justify the construction of the first brick buildings, including a branch of the British Bank of North America. Now, speculators and overextended shopkeepers again fell into gloom, which was made more burdensome by the apparent sense that their last hopes had been frustrated. "I can only repeat the same old story about business matters," a distressed merchant wrote, "with but the addition that they are duller than ever—indeed almost perfectly stagnant."

Revenue shortfalls forced Governor Douglas to fire the British Columbia civil service staff, with the exception of customs officers. Economic considerations determined the final stage of a shakeout in steamboat operations, which already was underway as a deliberate British policy to end reliance on American vessels. Steamers cut rates at the beginning of the downturn—the fare from Victoria to Hope falling to $10—in a largely futile attempt to sustain profits. Passenger and freight loads were so reduced by the end of June that the *Enterprise*'s owners towed their boat, a veteran of the 1858 glory days, down the Washington coast to Grays Harbor in anticipation of more profitable service on that isolated waterway.[38]

In California, defeated miners often blamed their fate on English villainy and H.B.C. greed, rather than on British Columbia's rising streams, unavoidably high food prices, and the great natural obstacles to building an adequate transportation system. Instead of assisting the immigrants, they claimed, British authorities had done nothing but "collect license and taxes," and had sent effete officials from England to live "on the exertions of the mining population." Governor Douglas was a mere "Indian trader," who "hated the American people" and "wished the Company…to monopolize the best portion of the country." They claimed the governor's discriminatory policy against Americans had backfired—if Californians could not find wealth on the Fraser, then the less-adept citizens of other nations (Great Britain included) would surely decline to even make the attempt.

British Columbia was, therefore, in the general San Francisco view, doomed without hope of attracting a sufficient population to properly exploit its colonial resources. In a moment of mock friendliness, the *Alta California* conceded that British Columbia actually was a moderately decent gold-bearing region, "but it were worse than absurd to think of comparing it to California." The "good people" of the north could only abandon their visions of "a magical empire," and in the future be "content to go slow."[39]

On July 4, 1859, a curious affair took place at Queenborough (not yet renamed New Westminster), reflecting the unusual circumstances generated by the presence of a substantial American population north of the 49th parallel. Workers imported from California to construct British government buildings laid down their tools for a makeshift Independence Day picnic, complete with ample food, strong drink, and modest attempts at Yankee Doodle oratory. The Royal Engineers and Marines stationed in the colonial capital joined in the festivities, forming ranks in front of their barracks, marching in best order to the riverside, and then firing a 101 gun salute in honor of the United States. "This is about the first time," a bemused observer told the editor of the *British Colonist*, when "English soldiers have celebrated their country's defeat."[40]

Barely three weeks later, American troops landed on San Juan Island, initiating a brief international crisis caused by rival boundary claims in the archipelago. An occupying British force, too, shortly arrived at the island. Due to vague language in the Oregon Treaty of 1846, London had claimed that the international border in the San Juan Islands ran through more easterly Rosario Strait, whereas the United States argued for more westerly Haro Strait. This left national ownership of Orcas, Lopez, San Juan, Shaw, and other islands in limbo. Consequently, San Juan Island was to remain in a state of prolonged, if reasonably amicable, joint possession.

Only recently the Anglo-American boundary commission had failed—prior to commencing the survey of the 49th parallel—to resolve the issue. Consequently, in July 1859 a minor dispute between resident citizens of the two nations, precipitated by an American killing a pig belonging to the Hudson's Bay Company farm, provided the pretext for a U.S. amphibious intervention. The true cause, however, was the desire of General William S. Harney, commanding regular army forces in Washington and Oregon, to address the continuing northern Indian threat by establishing a forward post on San Juan Island. The general, unfortunately, badly miscalculated the British response. Within a short time, both powers had soldiers ashore and war-ships patrolling adjacent waters.[41]

Local reaction on both sides of the border often reflected the traditional animosities between the Hudson's Bay Company and American settlers—a record of ill feeling recently exacerbated for some by developments on the Fraser River. In negatively referring to the H.B.C.'s San Juan agricultural op-eration, the Olympia *Pioneer and Democrat* praised General Harney for foil-ing a "diabolical scheme" by the company for "the planting of British Colo-nies upon American soil." The general's soldiers had come "like thieves in the night," the *British Colonist* noted in expressing the contrary Victoria perspec-tive, "to bully us out of our just rights."[42]

Fortunately, more rational views prevailed, however, and certainly so among the leaders of the contending governments. President James Buchanan reassigned a discredited General Harney, and Great Britain and the United States agreed to submit the boundary question to international arbitration, ending the prospect of a military conflict over an issue of little genuine importance. Perhaps, in another reflection of good fortune, the San Juan affair broke out just after, rather than before, the departure of most of the unhappy California miners for San Francisco. Possibly, if an overwhelm-ing American population still had resided nearby on the Fraser, the offshore dispute might have aroused further emotions, fomenting conflict over Brit-ish colonial authority.[43]

Chapter Six

Becoming a Business

Mining is no longer a speculation; it is becoming a business yielding an appreciable and certain return.—James Douglas[1]

T HE FARCICAL SAN JUAN AFFAIR, magnified into a military and naval confrontation, quickly "cooled down," as a Victoria merchant wrote with considerable relief. Though the immediate crisis had passed, tension remained for a time on both sides of the border. Many American settlers expressed admiration for General Harney's patriotic audacity in occupying the southern tip of San Juan Island. The H.B.C., meanwhile, complained that U.S. troops there were ruining pasturage and preempting watering places belonging to the firm's agricultural establishment. Governor Douglas worried that the transfer to San Juan Island of the Royal Marine detachment—men originally assigned to the Harrison-Lillooet wagon road—threatened completion of the latter project in time for winter. British subjects also expressed "outrage" when an American lieutenant, brazenly ignoring the 49th parallel, arrested two American deserters at Langley. These and other after-shocks failed, however, to circumvent a general trend toward the preservation of the cross-boundary peace. (A year later, when commemorating the anniversary of American troops landing on San Juan Island, U.S. Army Captain George Pickett would host, in a highly convivial manner, a party of excursionists from Vancouver Island.)[2]

Regardless of the disappointments and crises, gold rush activity on the Fraser resumed by late summer 1859. "For a period of two or three weeks people here were in a state of despondency," Donald Fraser had observed in a July letter from Victoria. Mineral production was down, numerous miners had departed, and "many persons…began to fancy that the mines had really 'caved in.'" In the midst of this incipient depression, however, "something…

turned up," the *Times* correspondent noted, "to allay the fears of the croakers."

The H.B.C.'s John Work took note of the resurgent popular mood, too, reporting that "but few are now leaving for San Francisco." To be sure, some momentary phantoms, such as stories about precious metal in the distant Bella Coola country, and rumors of silver in the Fort Hope vicinity, proved to be illusory. And, the Queen Charlotte expedition, supposedly the "last card…in the Fraser River game," eventually returned from the wild northern coasts to pronounce the reported island strike "the greatest humbug of the season."[3]

As attention reverted to the Fraser again, experienced prospectors argued that only individuals willing to endure "hard work, hard living and knocks," plus mosquitoes and dysentery, could properly exploit the stream's potential. Miners must persevere rather than complain. "There are many in this country who would not make a cent if the gold was as plentiful as the sand on the river banks," an Oregonian at the Fountain wrote to friends in Portland. "Some are always crying low water and some high water; while many…without ever doing a minute's work, pronounce the country a humbug." Levelheaded miners noted that good wages, rather than outrageous wealth, would be the return on their labor. "Two thirds" of the Californians, an old hand observed, gave up "in disgust" when they failed to immediately "procure what they came for, 'a pile' to throw into the laps of their dulcineas when they return home"; the other third knew instinctively that wealth still was to be gained in British Columbia.[4]

For example, miners claimed that the source of a substantial portion of the gold exported to date from Hill's Bar might still be profitably worked, According to expert prospectors, "a stream of pay dirt" lay buried beneath the original pits dug in the gravel. Better handling, moreover, would substantially reduce the loss of "rusty gold" in washing. "An experienced…ditch-owner" informed Governor Douglas that "he would have no hesitation in… work[ing] over again those parts of Hill's Bar which are suppose[d] to be exhausted, with a certainty of realizing from 6 dollars to 8 dollars a day for each man employed." Miners felt the same regarding other river bars opened in 1858. And, newer diggings, like those at the Fountain or in the Canoe country, likewise had been only partially exploited in the preceding spring. Recent geological investigations, as well, suggested that backcountry areas, far from any major streams, held rich deposits.[5]

"River operations on the North Pacific." Matthew Macfie, *Vancouver Island and British Columbia* (1865).

A hundred pack trains departed Port Douglas weekly, even before the full resurgence of prospecting activity in late summer. As many mules as could be obtained were pressed, too, into service carrying supplies from Yale to the upper Fraser. "Large orders have been filled by our merchants from all parts of the mining country," the *British Colonist* reported in mid-summer, announcing a business turnaround in Victoria. Firsthand accounts from the river claimed that the mines were "paying better than last year," primarily due to the expansion of hydraulic operations. The ditches, one of them five miles long, allowed 600 prospectors active between Hope and Yale to produce, according to Governor Douglas, a greater amount of gold than their more numerous predecessors of 1858. "The miners...are thus enabled to widen their field of labour by pushing shafts and other mining works into the banks far above the highest water levels of the river." Little sluicing was as yet being done beyond the Forks, however, but 2,000 men remained in the upper country excavating bars opened in the spring or seeking out new opportunities.[6]

New diggings, however, rather than the old fields, accounted in the main for Donald Fraser's pronouncement that now "all is hope, trust, and good spirits." Something, indeed, had "turned up" in the far distant interior of British Columbia. Continuing past Fort Alexandria in the search for the ultimate paydirt, miners went as far—and a few hearty, or perhaps foolhardy, individuals went even further—as the early century Hudson's Bay post at

Fort George. This was "the extreme point," wrote Governor Douglas, "to which they have…yet prospected." At practically every bar along the way, gold was found in paying quantities.[7]

Fifty miles above Fort Alexandria, a major find was made at the mouth of the Quesnel River, a tributary flowing in from the east. "For some time the discoverers kept the discovery quiet," Donald Fraser recalled. When the news eventually leaked out, the "Quesnel fever" brought 500 miners up from points below. Fortune hunters filed claims on the Quesnel (prospectors often calling it the "Canal") as far upstream as the lake of the same name, earning at the best locations $200 and more a day. Although east central British Columbia was far too remote to be adequately supplied year around, at least for the moment, enough was done here prior to the winter to whet appetites for the ensuing spring and summer mining seasons. "The extent of country over which the 'Blue Lead'…has been traced exceeds 300 square miles," Douglas informed his superiors in London, "and should it be continuous, as it has proved equally rich wherever struck, its wealth must be fabulous."[8]

In the opinion of a Victoria merchant, a true gold rush needed to be sustained by "a *furore*" [sic] as a stimulant. The Quesnel excitement provided the closest thing seen to a "furore" since the initial rush in the spring of 1858. By now, however, regional prospectors also knew from experience that they must be content with this preliminary investigation, and leave before the onslaught of severe winter weather. "The miners in the…district," Douglas observed, "will be compelled by the severity of the weather to abandon it in winter, the cold being then intense, often 20 degrees below zero…the rivers frozen, and the ground invariably covered with snow…between November and March."

Encouraged by the favorable prospects, however, the experienced wealth seekers now took the peculiarities of the changing seasons in stride, no longer reacting in panic to rising water or the first snows. "Many of the miners have done very well and mostly all very fair," John Work reported on winter's eve, "so that it is not the want of gold that makes them leave." They departed, rather, "chiefly on account of dread of the severity of the winter," fully intending to return in the spring. With an annual production now officially reckoned at $1,000,000, mining in the Fraser was becoming a regular seasonal enterprise, instead of the scene of mad dashes after instant wealth.[9]

While mining stabilized on a moderate, more practical basis, efforts to upgrade the quality of governance faltered. The basic obstacle to progress in this regard continued to be the requirement—renewed by a new colonial secretary, the Duke of Newcastle—that British Columbia support itself through local revenue. "My hands have been tied," Governor Douglas complained, "through the want of funds to undertake and carry out important and indispensable public works." Various fund raising gambits, such as duties on pack animals and canoes, generated widespread complaint that the governor's "sole aim and object" was to levy "tax after tax" on an overburdened citizenry.

The shortage of government buildings and suitable living quarters on the mainland meant that most British Columbia public employees resided in Victoria. "It is certainly an anomalous condition of things," one wag pointed out, "to live in one colony, and be paid for official services by another." Continuing to provide essential, if unauthorized assistance, the Hudson's Bay Company contributed financing to the construction of British Columbia governmental structures at New Westminster in 1860.[10]

London's refusal to provide funds for roads continued to retard development. "So essential are they as a means of settling and developing the resources of the country," James Douglas wrote of his schemes to open dependable communications with the interior, "that their importance can hardly be overrated." Forced to prioritize construction plans, the governor concentrated on finishing the Harrison-Lillooet improvements by year's end. When completed, "the great outlet of British Columbia" actually remained open to wagons throughout the winter. Private parties, meanwhile, placed small steamers in service on Anderson and Seton lakes, supplanting the whaleboats previously used on those portions of the route and speeding the overall pace of travel between the lower and upper Fraser. Public money, regrettably, was unavailable for other important transportation initiatives, to the chagrin of both the governor and his critics.[11]

Fortunately, a number of administrative reforms were implemented that generally entailed minimal expenses, and in some cases contributed to the public revenue. Instituted in August 1859, the Goldfields Act provided the first colony-wide system for registering and operating claims, while a government assay office was established in New Westminster to closely monitor mineral production.

Douglas still was troubled by the "dissimilar" nature of the colony's population (i.e., a large mining-focused population primarily consisting of unrooted foreigners). "I have given much anxious thought to the subject of settling British Columbia," he wrote, "and the conclusion is more than ever forced upon me that it cannot be successfully accomplished without adopting a very liberal land system." The traditional 1 Pound per acre price was finally and substantially reduced. Various bureaucratic requirements interfering with the timely transfer of titles were removed. Farming tracts still cost less on the American side of the line, however, minimizing the immediate impact of the changes. The governor's vision of "gorgeous forests" giving way to "cultivated fields and the other accessories of civilization" remained "a work of time."[12]

Dreams of civilized agricultural settlements aside, the present mining-oriented reality seemed promising enough. "An opinion is gaining ground among persons who have closely inspected and studied the phenomena of the gold fields," Douglas reported, "that there exists a zone or belt of country 50 or 60 miles in breadth, which is the matrix or depository of the gold found in British Columbia." Most observers, however, actually believed this "matrix" was much larger in extent. "The general character of the mining intelligence," the *British Colonist* asserted, "from the whole of that vast interior situated between the coast range on the west, the Rocky Mountains on the east, the United States line on the south, and the 54.40 parallel on the north, proves it to be beyond doubt rich in gold."

The same confidence prevailed below the international boundary, where rudimentary mines had been opened in the Yakima and Wenatchee watersheds. By 1861 in the Bitterroot Mountains farther east, thousands of prospectors would be driven by impossible-to-resist rumors, where they soon invaded the Nez Perce Indian Reservation. Californians, many who had been to British Columbia, would be in the vanguard of the series of rushes to the rich Idaho and Montana gold fields in the early 1860s.[13]

Compared to the previous year, the 1,000 miners wintering on the Fraser in 1859–60 fared well. Although sluicing operations halted in mid-November, weather conditions remained relatively mild, at least on the lower river. Between provisions brought by river steamers and vegetables prudently grown in local gardens, the wintertime residents avoided the "ravages of scurvy, by which," recalled Governor Douglas, "the health of many…men was seriously impaired in the winter of 1858." The Hope and Yale trails to the upper country, however, remained accessible only by Indian packers, and then were closed altogether by heavy snowfall. The improved Harrison-Lillooet route continued open, though, allowing the nearly 200 persons above the Forks to subsist on provisions at reduced prices. "The improvement in the condition of the miner is very great," Douglas reported, "as he can live substantially for 1 1/2 dollars per diem, instead of 3 or 4 dollars."[14]

For many observers, the mild winter was a fitting prelude to an anticipated profitable spring in 1860. "Five thousand seems to be the lowest estimate," a Yale-based miner wrote of the expected influx from San Francisco, "and from that figure to twenty thousand." Most Californians, however, were finding attractive opportunities closer to home in the Nevada mountains and other points in the American west, and did not join in the seasonal Fraser rush, at least not in large numbers. More persons probably migrated to British Columbia in 1860 than in 1859, though, but this was due to a preponderance of Chinese newcomers.[15]

On the far rim of the Pacific, "a perfect fever...in regard to Fraser river" continued in the Chinese ports open to emigration. Public opinion in Victoria—to the extent that the "leading men" represented popular views—favored "the introduction into British Columbia of a large Chinese population" as the best means of sustaining the population numbers previously dominated by American and European miners. "A detachment of thirty Chinese miners arrived yesterday," the governor reported in late January 1860, "being it is supposed the pioneers of a large immigration of that people."

There were 2,000 Asians on the Fraser by early spring 1860—"the 'Johns' are coming up...," a merchant noted, "in batches of forties and fifties, by almost every arrival"—and 4,000 at the onset of summer. The streets of Victoria were said to be "crowded with Celestials bound for the...mines," their purchases of mining supplies, implements, and boots accounting for a welcomed economic revival. "They are certainly not a desirable class of people, as a permanent population," Douglas reflected, "but are for the present useful as labourers, and, as consumers, of a revenue-paying character." Never forgetting the colony's need for population and funds, the governor therefore planned to help retain these newcomers by protecting them against the kinds of overt discrimination common in places like California.[16]

Chinese immigrants primarily went to the lower river bars where they quickly became a majority of the mining population. "At the present rate in which the Asiatics are flocking…," a white prospector observed, "it will not be long before the miners of British Columbia number in the proportion of one European or American to ten Chinamen!" A newspaper correspondent attributed the falloff in the volume of letters and news sent from Hope and Yale to the fact that most of the current residents could neither read nor write English. One quipster suggested that, as a tax-incentive, Douglas soon would apply a special "trifling" duty to "each and every 'tail.'" Douglas refused to adopt California-style discriminatory taxation, but nevertheless there was a lack of a sufficient constabulary to adequately protect the Chinese against other traditional mining-area injustices, or properly prosecute persons responsible for murder and assault against the newcomers.[17]

As they were being displaced on the lower river, most white miners in 1860 went to the upper country as soon as the weather allowed, particular to the Quesnel River. "The hopes of Victoria and of the whole country," the *British Colonist* asserted, were "based upon the presumed richness" of the partially exploited diggings in that sector. By late spring, 600 white miners were excavating gold there on a regular basis, their numbers restricted only by the continuing difficulty of getting provisions into the remote region. Indians, who traded gold dust at Fort Alexandria, and a few Chinese also were actively involved. A thorough investigation of two of the stream's substantial branches—the Muddy and the Horsefly—revealed more than enough wealth to go around, for the time being at least. Prospectors of all races earned by official report between $10 and $20 a day per individual. Private reports put the average at more like $50. "Dancing Bill's Company" claimed a daily output of $110 to each man. Four German miners carried $24,000 in gold dust out to Victoria, reporting that they had secured this amount in a five-week stay on the Quesnel.[18]

Miners remained active during the 1860 summer high water period by shifting from the river bars to dry diggings. And, in accordance with the more prudent behavior now common among the experienced mining population, they closed down for the winter in October. Just before the annual shutdown, however, the first prospectors entered the Cariboo country, 500 miles from the sea and four days of hard trekking northwest of the Quesnel River forks. "The whole distance, except in a few places, is one continual swamp," a traveler advised, "and in many places we had to walk to the knees in water for miles together." The journey, however, was more than worth the trouble. "In color it is a very dark yellow," a journalist observed of Cariboo gold, "and is much heavier than any we have heretofore seen." According to accounts from the scene, everyone undertaking the trip pried rich dust out of the ground with each turn of the shovel.[19]

∎⌐∎

In the next year, 1861, the Cariboo district emerged as the great wealth-producing center of British Columbia—the closest of anything on the Fraser to California standards. "The gold…is not confined to the rivers," Governor Douglas informed the colonial office. "It is found in the gullies and table land 300 and 400 yards from the rivers, and much beyond their highest levels." At least 1,500 prospectors, a "number…continually augmented by the arrival of fresh bodies of miners," were at hand by late spring earning $40 to $50 a day.

The region could only be partially supplied by routes from the sea, but it was accessible from the south by pack strings from Washington Territory using variants of the old Hudson's Bay Company trail network. American freighting interests brought in beans, bacon, bread, coffee, and cattle from The Dalles and Walla Walla. "The traveller who is prepared to encounter famine in its gauntest forms on his arrival at Cariboo," wrote Douglas, "is not a little astonished to find himself in the midst of luxury, sitting down every morning to fresh milk and eggs for breakfast, and to as good a dinner as can be seen in Victoria."[20]

New diggings also opened up farther south adjacent to, and overlapping, the 49th parallel. Douglas first learned from American newspapers that gold had been discovered on the Similkameen River, a border-straddling tributary on the west side of the Okanogan River. The region was, in a number of respects, the most attractive in all of British Columbia. "The whole of that district," Douglas pointed out, "is watered by running streams, possesses a great deal of arable land, and is diversified by woodland and meadows." Ideally suited to farming and grazing and possessing a mild climate, the Similkameen offered considerable "inducements to settlers" and might even be the right location for a new colonial capital. The gold first uncovered there during the winter of 1860, moreover, was "nuggety and…readily separated from the soil without the use of quicksilver," yielding from $6 to $50 a day to the miner.[21]

Further east along the British Columbia-Washington Territory line, but entirely within British jurisdiction, the Rock Creek mines also produced high

"Cairn, etc., on the boundary line, at East Kootenay." R. C. Mayne, *Four Years in British Columbia and Vancouver Island* (1862).

quality gold. First located by a Canadian prospector in late 1859, the diggings were not exploited until the following spring. The region was remote, bordered by high canyon walls and surrounded by mountains and rugged uplands. Despite the natural obstacles, 500 persons, most of them Americans, rushed to the scene upon the first verified news of the strike. By the time Governor Douglas passed through in the course of a late summer tour, the town of Rock Creek had 15 wooden structures, "chiefly shops and buildings intended for the supply and entertainment of miners." Returns for individuals with decent claims averaged between $8 and $16 a day.[22]

British Columbia's geographically widespread new diggings in the Cariboo, Similkameen, and Rock Creek districts significantly revived the interior H.B.C. trail system. It was with these routes that the earlier New Caledonia fur trade had been linked to the outside world, via the Columbia River rather than to the Fraser. Victoria and lower Fraser merchants, now losing much of the mining trade to American packers from The Dalles and Walla Walla, complained of suffering an additional illogical "injustice." All goods entering the lower Fraser, including those of British manufacture carried in English vessels, were subject to the colonial tariffs on imports. The same duties, of course, applied east of the Cascades along the 49th parallel. However, because of customs department inefficiencies and outright smuggling, most American pack-train goods entered eastern British Columbia virtually free of duty.

Residents of New Westminster, too, felt that the colony suffered economically because many Americans intentionally avoided customs payments. The Hudson's Bay Company, meanwhile, abandoned plans to shift livestock from old Fort Nisqually on Puget Sound to the Similkameen country when it discovered that Americans could supply cattle more cheaply from the Walla Walla Valley.[23]

Douglas stationed additional revenue collectors at the border crossings beyond the mountains in a futile effort to divert trade to British merchants on the west side. The geography of the 49th parallel was far too complex, however, to be easily dealt with to the advantage of either the British or Americans. "Smuggling across the boundary line…," the *British Colonist* conceded, "appears to have two sides." The straight-line international border devised by Washington City and London diplomats was poorly suited to local realities. A portion of the trail from Fort Hope to the Rock Creek district, for example, necessarily had to cross into U.S. territory. Packers bound from The Dalles to American mining camps in the Similkameen district encroached on British Columbia territory before reaching their several destinations. The principal Yankee diggings on that stream, American Bar, actually sat on the 49th parallel, extending north and south. "Men will buy in the cheapest markets," the Victoria newspaper noted in arguing that boundaries, to be truly honored by all parties, must be "marked out by the geography of the country."[24]

The Cariboo mining development of the early 1860s signaled the end of the Fraser rush as a prominent part of British and American cross-border history in the Far West. Henceforth, the search for precious metals far north of the 49th parallel was primarily of importance only to British Columbia and the soon-to-be-born Canadian nation. Americans began largely to ignore events north of the international border, with their attention diverted by the Civil War and to a series of spectacular new mineral discoveries in the western United States— along Idaho's wild rivers, in Nevada's desert mountains, and among crag-bordered valleys in Montana and Colorado.

Largely adopting the Californian perspective, Americans now tended to dismiss Fraser River mining as a failed phenomenon of 1858. The seasonal drive "up" British Columbia's great artery and the search for the ultimate source of coarse gold, however, was a failure only when compared to the original outlandish and over-inflated expectations. British Columbia, after all, did export $10,000,000 worth of gold between 1858 and 1863. When factoring in the relatively small mining population, the short seasons, harsh weather, and the difficulties of land and water travel, the figure becomes an indicator of a measured success, rather than a dismal humbuggery.[25]

After the Cariboo strikes, official actions ended some long-term diplomatic disputes and also resolved some lingering internal administrative difficulties in both the British and American spheres. In 1863, Great Britain and the United States concluded a treaty establishing a joint commission to dispose of Hudson's Bay Company and Puget's Sound Agricultural Company properties and claims south of the 49th parallel. In 1869, the tribunal awarded a total payment of $650,000 to the British concerns. North of the line, meanwhile, Vancouver's Island and the mainland colony were merged into "British Columbia" in 1866, with the capital being assigned to Victoria. Next, in 1871 British Columbia joined the new Canadian federation (founded 1867). In 1872, the emperor of Germany, acting as arbitrator of the San Juan Islands dispute, ruled in favor of the American position, establishing the present boundary in Haro Strait.

The Fraser River gold rush was a prime factor in these developments. The discovery of precious metal had led to the creation of British Columbia and ultimately provided Britain's West Coast possessions with the basis for sustained economic vitality. The original gold rush excitement, however, had predominantly involved American miners and merchants passing north of the 49th parallel where English sovereignty was, at least momentarily, potentially threatened. Colonel Richard Moody, in fact, had warned that British Columbia would become "an American country before long."[26] Perhaps, if the 1858 rush had lived up to its greater, outlandish expectations (and if level-headed, competent leaders had not prevailed), a mainland version of the San Juan crisis might have erupted, precipitating a border conflict between Britain and the United States.

In the long term, a significant number of the California and other foreign miners did not desire to return to San Francisco. They settled in the vast

Northwest region, providing both British Columbia and Washington Territory with a substantial additional population and labor force. Enduring stereotypes remained, however, as California residents continued to dismiss the North Pacific coast as being economically third rate, and generally an uncouth backwoods. In counterpoint, local residents on both sides of the 49th line often thought of the Golden State migrants as persons more interested in gaining undeserved quick wealth than in earning a decent sustained income; as more inclined to complaint than to doing hard work; and as more likely to give up than to persevere in the face of hardships.

Notes

Abbreviations

BCHQ   *British Columbia Historical Quarterly*

BCS   *BC Studies*

BL   Bancroft Library, University of California, Berkeley

EHFRM   Howay, Frederic W. *The Early History of the Fraser River Mines*, Archives of British Columbia Memoir No. VI. Victoria: Charles F. Banfield, 1926.

HBCA   Hudson's Bay Company Archives, Provincial Archives of Manitoba

NA   National Archives

OHQ   *Oregon Historical Quarterly*

PABC   Public Archives of British Columbia

PNQ   *Pacific Northwest Quarterly*

PRABC   *Papers Relative to the Affairs of British Columbia*, Parts I–IV. London: George Edward Eyre and William Spottiswoode, 1859–62.

PRO   Public Record Office

UBC   University of British Columbia Library

UW   University of Washington Library

WHQ   *Washington Historical Quarterly*

Introduction

1. San Francisco *Bulletin*, July 16, 1858; James Douglas to William G. Smith, July 23, 1858, B.226/b/15, HBCA.
2. T. A. Rickard, "Indian Participation in the Gold Discoveries," *BCHQ*, 2(1938), 3; Netta Sterne, *Fraser Gold 1858! The Founding of British Columbia* (Pullman: Washington State University Press, 1998).

3. *Wall Street Journal*, Aug. 9, 2000; *New York Times*, July 18, 2000.

4. For examples of cross border historiography, see Carlos A. Schwantes, *Radical Heritage: Labor, Socialism, and Reform in Washington and British Columbia, 1885–1917* (Seattle: University of Washington Press, 1979); Robin Fisher, "Indian Warfare and Two Frontiers: A Comparison of British Columbia and Washington Territory during the Early Years of Settlement," *Pacific Historical Review*, 50(1981), 31–51; Norbert MacDonald, *Distant Neighbors: A Comparative History of Seattle and Vancouver* (Lincoln: University of Nebraska Press, 1987).

Chapter One
An Unsettled Boundary

1. Jan. 8, 1853.

2. Mainland areas adjacent to the Fraser drainage, as well, soon came to be considered part of New Caledonia. H. H. Bancroft, *History of British Columbia, 1792–1887* (San Francisco: History Company, 1887), 35–36; F. W. Howay, *British Columbia: The Making of a Province* (Toronto: Ryerson Press, 1928), 54, 72; E. E. Rich, ed., *Part of Dispatch from George Simpson … to the Governor & Committee of the Hudson's Bay Company* (Toronto: Champlain Society, 1947), 16–25; E. Graham Alston, *A Handbook to British Columbia and Vancouver Island* (London: F. Algar, 1870), 2; Douglas to E. B. Lytton, Oct. 26, 1858, *PRABC*, 2:9–10. On British Columbia's several distinct regions, see Jean Barman, *The West beyond the West: A History of British Columbia* (Toronto: University of Toronto Press, rev. ed., 1996), 4–11. For full details on the Fraser River, historical and otherwise, see Richard C. Bocking, *Mighty River: A Portrait of the Fraser* (Vancouver: Douglas and McIntyre, 1997).

3. Despite the legendary hazards in crossing the Columbia's bar, steamers served the lower river by the early 1850s, toiling upstream to Portland on the Willamette River and to the Columbia River gorge and the Cascade Rapids. Service above The Dalles, conveying military supplies and prospectors to the mouth of the Walla Walla River, commenced in 1859. George Henry Richards to Douglas, Oct. 23, 1858; Douglas to Lytton, Nov. 3, 1858, both *PRABC*, 2:15–16, 19; W. Kaye Lamb, ed., *The Letters and Journals of Simon Fraser, 1806–1808* (Toronto: Macmillan of Canada, 1960), 109; Rich, ed., *Part of Dispatch*, 45; London *Times*, Aug. 14, 1858; "The Navigation of the Frazer River, and Its Approaches," *Nautical Magazine*, 28(1859), 325; Alfred Waddington, "On the Geography and Mountain Passes of British Columbia in Connection with an Overland Route," *Journal of the Royal Geographical Society*, 38(1868), 122; Sir George Simpson, *Narrative of a Journey Round the World, during the Years 1841 and 1842* (London: Henry Colburn, 2 vols., 1847), 1:182; San Francisco *Bulletin*, May 18, 1858.

4. The Fraser River entrance, though relatively free of hazard, was not entirely without danger. In 1850, for instance, the H.B.C. vessel *Cowlitz* was condemned after grounding on the bottom. The Fraser and Columbia rivers are the only regional streams that cut, east to west, entirely through the rugged Cascade Range. Douglas to James Murray Yale, B.113/c/1, HBCA; to Lord Stanley, July 26, 1858; to Lytton, Nov. 3, 1858; Richards to Douglas, Oct. 23, 1858, all *PRABC*, 1:23; 2:15, 19; "Navigation of the Frazer River," 325; Rich, ed., *Part of Dispatch*, 45; San Francisco *Alta Califor-*

nia, April 19, 1858; Alfred Waddington, *The Fraser Mines Vindicated, or, The History of Four Months* (Victoria: P. DeGarro, 1858), 7.

5. Waddington, *Fraser Mines Vindicated*, 7; Richard C. Mayne to Richards, July 7, 1859, ADM 1/5744, PRO; William Geo. Cox to Chartres Brew, April 6, 1859, *EHFRM*, 100–2; Douglas and John Work to H.B.C., London, Nov. 6, 1847, in "Fort Langley Correspondence: 1831–1858," *BCHQ*, 1(1937), 191.

6. W. Kaye Lamb, ed., *The Journals and Letters of Sir Alexander Mackenzie* (Cambridge: Cambridge University Press, 1970), 314, 319, 321–22; and *Fraser Letters and Journals*, 61–128. Also see Barry M. Gough, *First Across the Continent: Sir Alexander Mackenzie* (Norman: University of Oklahoma Press, 1997), 133–40.

7. "I cannot help thinking," Simpson observed in the early stages of his tour, "that no economy has been observed, that little exertion has been used, and that sound judgment has not been exercised but that mismanagement and extravagance has been the order of the day." Howay, *Making of a Province*, 101; Frederick Merk, ed., *Fur Trade and Empire: George Simpson's Journal* (Cambridge: Harvard University Press, rev. ed., 1968), 65, 123–24; Gov. and Com. to John McLoughlin, July 27, 1825; to George Simpson, Jan. 16, 1828, in Ibid., 252–53, 294–95. Also see James R. Gibson, *Farming the Frontier: The Agricultural Opening of the Oregon Country, 1786–1846* (Seattle: University of Washington Press, 1985), chaps. 4–6; John S. Galbraith, "The Early History of the Puget's Sound Agricultural Company, 1838–43," *OHQ*, 55(1954), 234–59.

8. Destroyed by fire, the original Langley post was replaced in 1841 by a "much more spacious structure." Morag Machlachlan, ed., *The Fort Langley Journals, 1827–30* (Vancouver: University of British Columbia Press, 1998), 36–37; Rich, ed., *Part of Dispatch*, 28, 41, 79; Simpson to McLoughlin, March 15, 1829, in Merk, ed., *Fur Trade and Empire*, 308; Yale to Simpson, Feb. 10, 1841, in "Fort Langley Correspondence," 190–91.

9. Rich, ed., *Part of Dispatch*, 28, 35–37, 39; Simpson, *Narrative of a Journey*, 1:182–83.

10. Ideally located for the refurbishment of horseflesh and the conciliation of important Indian tribes, Kamloops grew in importance. Rich, ed., *Part of Dispatch*, 25, 30–31; Instructions from the London office of H.B. Co. to officer in charge of N.W. Coast, n.d., James Douglas Papers, PABC; Robie L. Reid, ed., "To the Fraser River Mines in 1858: A Letter from C. C. Gardiner," *BCHQ*, 1(1937), 247; E. Colvile to Board of Management, Columbia District, July 10, 1851, B.226/c/1, HBCA; San Francisco *Alta California*, July 16, 1858. For complete details on the New Caledonia-Vancouver connection, see James R. Gibson, *The Lifeline of the Oregon Country: The Fraser-Columbia Brigade System, 1811–1847* (Vancouver: University of British Columbia Press, 1997). Also see Richard Somerset Mackie, *Trading beyond the Mountains: The British Fur Trade on the Pacific, 1793–1843* (Vancouver: University of British Columbia Press, 1997), 21–22, 60.

11. Simpson to Gov. and Com., Dec. 25, 1841, in Glyndwr Williams, ed., *London Correspondence Inward from Sir George Simpson, 1841–42* (London: Hudson's Bay Company Record Society, 1973), 75–76; to McLoughlin, June 25, 1836, in "Fort Langley Correspondence," 188–89; Douglas to McLoughlin, July 12, 1842, *Copies of Correspondence between the Chairman of the Hudson's Bay Company and the Secretary of State for the Colonies, Relative to the Colonization of Vancouver's Island*, House of Commons, 10 August 1848, 5–7; W. Kaye Lamb, "The Founding of Fort Victoria," *BCHQ*, 7(1943), 71–92.

12. Simpson to Charles Ross, June 20, 1844, in "Five Letters of Charles Ross," *BCHQ*, 7(1943), 117; London *Times*, Aug. 27, 1858; San Francisco *Alta California*, Feb. 2, 1858; Extract of a Report from Lieutenant Vavasour to Colonel Holloway, March 1, 1846, *Copies of Dispatches and other Papers Relative to Vancouver's Island*, House of Commons, 7 March 1849, 10–11; Original Indian Population, Vancouver's Island, in Papers of James Douglas, BL; W. Colquhon Grant, "Description of Vancouver Island," *Journal of the Royal Geographical Society*, 27(1857), 293–95; Roderick Finlayson Reminiscences, 48, BL; Colvile to Board of Management, July 10, 1851, B.226/c/1, HBCA.

13. For key documents, see Earl of Aberdeen to H. S. Fox, Oct. 18, 1842; Daniel Webster to Fox, Nov. 25, 1842; Statements of American and British Plenipotentiaries, Sept. 3, 12, 1844; James Buchanan to Pakenham, July 12, 1845; Feb. 4, 1846; Pakenham to Buchanan, July 29, 1845, all in *Correspondence Relative to the Negotiation of the Question of Disputed Right to the Oregon Territory* (London: T. R. Harrison, 1846), 1–2, 13–23, 34–35, 70. The annexationist quotations are from *Congressional Globe*, 28th Cong., 1st sess., 160, 678.

14. Fayette McMullin to Lewis Cass, Nov. 3, 1857; Charles H. Mason to Cass, Dec. 23, 1858, both U.S. State Department, Washington Territorial Papers, NA; A. Colvile to Earl of Clarendon, Dec. 6, 1855; Wodehouse to Colvile, Dec. 11, 1855, both B.226/c/1, HBCA; George Gibbs to A. Van Dusen, Sept. 4, 1852, Oregon and Washington Territorial Papers, House File, Records of the House of Representatives, RG 233, NA.

15. Douglas to Simpson, Feb. 2, 1858, B.226/b/15; Simpson to Dugald Mactavish, May 1, 1857, B.223/c/2; A. Barclay to P. S. Ogden, et al., Aug. 4, 1849, B.226/c/1, all HBCA; William F. Tolmie to Thomas M. Chambers, Dec. 20, 1849, Thomas M. Chambers Papers, Washington State Historical Society; to Isaac I. Stevens, Dec. 27, 1853; Stevens to Tolmie, Jan. ? 1854, both Isaac I. Stevens Papers, UW.

16. Simpson to Ogden, April 17, 1849; to Board of Management, Columbia District, March 31, 1851; May 27; Dec. 30, 1852, B.226/c/1; to Mactavish, Aug. 17, 1857; March 16, 1858, B.223/c/2, all HBCA. For an informed summary of the talks, see San Francisco *Alta California*, Jan. 28, 1856. Also see Frank E. Ross, ed., "Sir George Simpson at the State Department," *BCHQ*, 2(1938), 131–35.

17. The original ambiguous language called upon the H.B.C. to "dispose of the land...as may be necessary for the purpose of promoting settlements." The company nominated James Douglas as its choice for the governorship. J. H. Pelly to Earl Grey, Sept. 7, 1846; March 5, 1847; March 4; July 20, enclosing draft charter; Sept. 9, 1848; to B. Hawes, Oct. 24, 1846; Hawes to Pelly, Oct. 3, 1846; Feb. 2, 1847; Feb. 25; July 31; Sept. 4, 1848; Report from the Committee of Her Majesty's Privy Council, Oct. 31, 1848, all in *Copies of Correspondence ... Relative to the Colonization of Vancouver's Island*, 3–5, 9–17, 19–20; Douglas to Lytton, Sept. 30, 1858, *PRABC*, 1:36; Charter of Grant of Vancouver's Island to the Hudson's Bay Company, Jan. 13, 1849," *Copies of Despatches ... Relative to Vancouver's Island*, 13–16; Willard E. Ireland, "The Appointment of Governor Blanshard," *BCHQ*, 8(1944), 213–26; Barclay to Douglas, Dec. 6, 1850, B.226/c/1, HBCA; Margaret A. Ormsby, *British Columbia: A History* (Vancouver: Macmillan of Canada, 1958), 99–106; W. Kaye Lamb, "The Governorship of Richard Blanshard," *BCHQ*, 14(1950), 1–40. For the H.B.C. nomination of Douglas, see Pelly to Grey, Sept. 13, 1848, *Copies of Despatches ... Relative to Vancouver's Island*, 18.

18. Although some British Columbia historians once claimed that James Douglas was born in Scotland, his actual birthplace was in Guiana, to a white father and a black mother. San Francisco *Alta California*, Feb. 2; May 8; June 21; July 20, 1858; John B. Good Reminiscences, 10, BL; Douglas to Blackwood, Dec. 27, 1858, *EHFRM*, 3. Simpson quoted in B. A. McKelvie, "Sir James Douglas: A New Portrait," *BCHQ*, 7(1943), 93–94. Also see Barry M. Gough, "Sir James Douglas as Seen by His Contemporaries: A Preliminary List," *BCS*, 44(1979–80), 32–40.

19. The wealthy Blanshard was unsalaried—though he did receive a 1,000-acre land grant—but Douglas was paid £800 a year as governor of Vancouver's Island. London *Times*, Aug. 28, 1858; Douglas to Lytton, Sept. 29, 1858, *PRABC*, 1:35–36; A. G. Dallas to Thomas Fraser, Nov. 10, 1859, B.226/b/20; Barclay to Douglas, Aug. 3, 1849, B.226/c/1, both HBCA; Howay, *Making of a Province*, 111. For an argument that Douglas successfully balanced his private and public responsibilities, see Richard Mackie, "The Colonization of Vancouver Island, 1849–1858," *BCS*, 96(1992–93), 11–12.

20. London *Times*, July 9, 1858; Matthew Macfie, *Vancouver Island and British Columbia: Their History, Resources, and Prospects* (London: Longman, Green, 1865), 91; James Bell to John Thomson, Feb. 27, 1859, in Willard E. Ireland, ed., "Gold-rush Days in Victoria, 1858–1859," *BCHQ*, 12(1948), 242; Douglas to Duke of Newcastle, May 13, 1854, BT 1/515/1468, PRO.

21. Until the end of 1855, American citizens and foreigners willing to claim U.S. citizenship secured farms in Washington and Oregon territories virtually free of charge under the Donation Land Act passed by the U.S. Congress. Barclay to Ogden, et al., June 28, 1849, B.226/c/1, HBCA; San Francisco *Alta California*, Nov. 15, 1853; Oct. 22, 1858; W. Colquhon Grant to William Brodie, Aug. 8, 1851, in James E. Hendrickson, "Two Letters from Walter Colquhon Grant," *BCS*, 26(1975), 10; Grant, "Description of Vancouver Island," 269; London *Times*, May 31, 1858; Douglas to Lytton, May 23, 1859, *PRABC*, 3:12; Edward Ellice to W. A. G. Dallas, Sept. 14, 1859, Newcastle Papers, copies in G. P. V. Akrigg and Helen Akrigg Fonds papers, UBC. On the relative impact of poor quality land and high prices, see Mackie, "Colonization of Vancouver Island," 36–37.

22. Douglas and Work to H.B.C., London, Nov. 6, 1847, in "Fort Langley Correspondence," 191–92; Ormsby, *British Columbia*, 91; W. Kaye Lamb, "Early Lumbering on Vancouver Island," *BCHQ*, 2(1938), 31–53, 95–97; Grant, "Description of Vancouver Island," 312–13. Douglas is quoted in Howay, *Making of a Province*, 100. The early day merchant cited was James Strange of the East India Company in a 1786 letter quoted in W. A. Carrothers, "Forest Industries of British Columbia," in A. R. M. Lower, *The North American Assault on the Canadian Forest* (Toronto: Ryerson Press, 1938), 254. On the abandonment of Fort Yale, see Douglas to William G. Smith, June 7, 1858, B.226/b/15, HBCA.

23. With "the exclusive licence not extending beyond the trade of the natives," H.B.C. directors worried about competing interests "taking possession of the coal field." Grant, "Description of Vancouver Island," 275–79, 313; Barclay to Douglas, Nov. 1; Dec. 6, 1850; Simpson to Board of Management, Columbia District, Dec. 31, 1852, B.226/c/1; Douglas to Barclay, Sept. 21, 1853; May 18, 1855; to Smith, Feb. 25, 1856, B.226/b/14, all HBCA; San Francisco *Alta California*, Jan. 12, 1858; J. M. S. Careless, "The Lowe Brothers, 1852–70: A Study in Business Relations on the North Pacific Coast," *BCS*, 2(1969), 6–7.

24. Although the H.B.C. cultivated 150 acres at Victoria, company employees were "miserable farmers" according to Grant. "They ruin the land by paying no attention to the succession of crops, & never applying manure, & they ruin their stock by paying no attention to breeding and allowing the majority to run wild in the woods." "The Census of Vancouver Island, 1855," *BCHQ*, 4(1940), 51–58; Grant, "Description of Vancouver Island," 269–70, 274; Douglas to Lytton, Nov. 5, 1858, *PRABC*, 2:22; Olympia *Columbian*, Dec. 18, 1852; April 30, 1853; San Francisco *Alta California*, Nov. 21, 1853; Earl Fitzwilliam to Newcastle, June 29, 1853, Newcastle Papers; Simpson to Mactavish, March 16, 1858, B.223/c/1, HBCA; Grant to Brodie, Aug. 8, 1851, in Hendrickson, "Two Letters from Grant," 11.

25. Salem *Oregon Statesman*, Sept. 14, 1858; Olympia *Columbian*, Nov. 3, 1852.

26. J. Ross Browne to James Guthrie, Sept. 4, 1854, in Donald Michael Goodman, *A Western Panorama, 1849–1875: The Travels, Writings and Influence of J. Ross Browne* (Glendale: Arthur H. Clarke, 1966), 58; Olympia *Pioneer and Democrat*, Feb. 4, 1854; San Francisco *Alta California*, July 3, 1857; Olympia *Washington Pioneer*, Dec. 17, 1853.

27. The Puget Sound mills produced a combined 170,000 feet of lumber per day, nearly a quarter of this total coming from Port Gamble, the Kitsap Peninsula headquarters of the Pope and Talbot Company. San Francisco *Alta California*, Dec. 10, 1853; June 2, 1854; Douglas to Barclay, Oct. 15; Dec. 27, 1853; March 15, 1854; March 22, 1855; to Smith, Feb. 25; May 16; Dec. 19, 1856, B.226/b/14, HBCA; Olympia *Pioneer and Democrat*, May 13; Dec. 16, 1854.

28. "A direct conflict ... is seriously threatened," asserted the *Alta California* in the spring of 1858, after rioting against British sailors in New Orleans and retaliatory Royal Navy interference with U.S. shipping in the Gulf of Mexico. McLoughlin to John Gordon, Sept. 15, 1845, in Leslie M. Scott, ed., "Report of Lieutenant Peel on Oregon, 1845–46," *OHQ*, 29(1928), 58; San Francisco *Alta California*, June 29, 1858. On the Irish presence in gold rush California, see Roger W. Lotchin, *San Francisco, 1846–1856: From Hamlet to City* (New York: Oxford University Press, 1974), 104–5; Malcolm J. Rohrbough, *Days of Gold: The California Gold Rush and the American Nation* (Berkeley: University of California Press, 1997), 227.

29. "Slacum's Report on Oregon, 1836–37," *OHQ*, 13(1912), 186, 189–92; Jason Lee to Corr. Sec., Sept. 23, 1841, Methodist Missionary Society Records, microfilm, UW; Henry Spalding to David Greene, Feb. 12, 1846; to Mr. and Mrs. Stephen Prentiss, April 6, 1848; to Dudley Allen, Sept. 6, 1848, Henry Spalding Papers, Oregon Historical Society; Charles Henry Carey, ed., "Diary of Reverend George Gary," *OHQ*, 24(1923), 317–18; E. Ruth Rockwood, ed., "Diary of Rev. George H. Atkinson, D.D., 1847–1858," *OHQ*, 40(1939), 278; Notes Copied from the Hudson's Bay Company Account Books at Fort Nisqually, 1830–1850, UW; Victor J. Farrar, ed., "The Nisqually Journal," *WHQ*, 10(1919), 226; 11(1920), 60, 148; Oregon City *Oregon Spectator*, Jan. 11, 1849; Tolmie to Douglas, Nov. ? 1848, enclosing Newmarket petition, B.226/c/1, HBCA; Memorial of the Legislative Assembly, July 26, 1849, Oregon and Washington Territorial Papers; Olympia *Pioneer and Democrat*, Jan. 6; Oct. 19, 1855; J. B. Chapman to Webster, Sept. 24, 1852, Letters Received from the Surveyors General of Washington, 1854–1883, RG 49, NA. On settler ingratitude, see also Frank E. Ross, "The Retreat of the Hudson's Bay Company in the Pacific Northwest," *Canadian Historical Review*, 18(1937), 262–66.

30. Democratic supporters preparing to run their candidate, Isaac I. Stevens, for congressional delegate in 1858 accused incumbent Columbia Lancaster of the grossest misdeed imaginable—friendliness toward the Hudson's Bay Company. Olympia *Washington Pioneer*, Dec. 24, 1853; Olympia *Pioneer and Democrat*, July 8, 1854; Jan. 13, 20, 1855; Address to Citizens of Thurston County, Dec. 19, 1853, Stevens Papers; Stevens to Ogden, Dec. 20, 1853, Washington Territorial Papers.

31. The fact that Indians did not attack H.B.C. posts or personnel provided all the evidence needed, in the view of many settlers, proving the firm's guilt. Olympia *Pioneer and Democrat*, July 8, 1855; James Tilton to Douglas, Nov. 1, 1855; Douglas to Tilton, Nov. 6, 19, 1855; Tolmie to Silas Casey, March 26, 1856, all in Clarence B. Bagley, "Attitude of the Hudson's Bay Company during the Indian War of 1855–1856," *WHQ*, 8(1917), 297–99, 303–4; Simpson to Mactavish, Dec. 1, 15, 1856; to Geo. W. Manypenny, Nov. 20, 1856, B.223/c/2, HBCA; San Francisco *Alta California*, Nov. 27, 1855.

32. James Douglas claimed to have provided the identities and locations of Ebey's killers to Washington Territory, which failed to make effective use of the intelligence. McMullin to Buchanan, Oct. 20, 1857, in *WHQ*, 1(1907), 52; San Francisco *Alta California*, June 10, 1854; Portland *Oregonian*, Aug. 27, 1859; Douglas to Tolmie, June 13, 1854, in Bagley, "Attitude of the Hudson's Bay Company," 294; to Barclay, June 5, 1854; to Smith, Aug. 13, 1857; Jan. 14, 1858; to William H. McNeill, Feb. 19, 1858, B.226/b/14–16, HBCA; Mason to Douglas, Aug. 26, 1857, in "Defending Puget Sound Against the Northern Indians," *PNQ*, 36(1945), 71.

33. Another British ship, the *Albion*, was confiscated while loading spars on the southern shore of the Strait of Juan de Fuca. A Treasury Department ruling returning the vessel came only after it had been sold at auction. Insisting that the treaty applied just to the mainstream Columbia, the U.S. refused to allow H.B.C. access to any of the tributaries. The relevant legal issue was whether or not American officials could tax goods bound eventually to company forts in British territory. H.B.C. ships clearing customs at Astoria were also subject to a $220 fee assessed by bar pilots. Douglas to Yale, June 12, 1850; Nov. 7, 1854, B.113/c/1; Simpson to Board of Management, Columbia District, May 27, 1852; to Ogden, et al., June 25, 1850, B.226/c/1, all HBCA; Wm. Strong to Thomas Corwin, Oct. 17, 1850, Oregon and Washington Territorial Papers. On the *Albion* affair, see Lamb, "Early Lumbering on Vancouver Island," 33–35. Also see William L. Lang, *Confederacy of Ambition: William Winlock Miller and the Making of Washington Territory* (Seattle: University of Washington Press, 1996), 30.

34. An influential American witness to the seizures, Hugh Goldsborough, considered the "entire transaction as pitiful[,] trifling and utterly unworthy of official action." E. Colvile to Board of Management, Columbia District, July 10, 1851; Simpson to Board of Management, March 31; May 27, 1852, B.226/c/1; Douglas to Barclay, April 3, 1854, B.226/b/14, all HBCA; Portland *Oregonian*, March 6, 27, 1852. For full details on H.B.C. customs issues, as well as the Goldsborough quotation, see Lang, *Confederacy of Ambition*, 30–43.

35. Steilacoom *Puget Sound Herald*, July 23, 1858.

Chapter Two
Our Peculiar Field of Operations

1. To Dugald Mactavish, Sept. 30, 1856, B.223/c/2, HBCA.
2. In 1853, the H.B.C. transported gold dust worth $80,000 to Victoria for shipment to England. George Simpson to Board of Management, Columbia District, March 31, 1851; to P. S. Ogden, et al., June 25, 1850; A. Barclay to James Douglas, Dec. 6, 1850, all B.226/c/1, HBCA; E. Colvile to J. H. Pelly, Oct. 26; Dec. 8, 1849; to Simpson, Oct. 15, 1849, in E. E. Rich, ed., *London Correspondence Inward from Eden Colvile, 1849–1852* (London: Hudson's Bay Company Record Society, 1956), 7–8, 15, 181; E. Huggins, "How eighty thousand dollars ... worth of Gold Dust, was, in 1853, conveyed from Fort Vancouver ... to Fort Victoria," manuscript in Huntington Library.
3. Simpson to Board of Management, May 27; Aug. 30, 1852; Barclay to Ogden, et al., Sept. 13, 1850, all B.226/c/1, HBCA; Colvile to Gov. and Com., July 21, 1852, in Rich, ed., *London Correspondence Inward*, 138–39; Oregon City *Oregon Spectator*, June 27; July 11, 1850.
4. English merchant George Dixon acquired 1,800 skins in the Queen Charlotte Islands in 1789. The American John Ingraham purchased 1,400 in 1791. Governmental matters were formalized to a certain extent in July 1852 with the appointment of James Douglas as governor—the title is sometimes given as lieutenant governor—of the Queen Charlotte Islands. "There was in fact," the H.B.C. directors explained to James Douglas, who now held three positions, "no other way of creating the authority necessary to direct measures of protection in regard to that island." Portland *Oregonian*, Jan. 31; April 3, 1852; Richard Blanshard to Earl Grey, Aug. 18, 1850, *Copies or Extracts of Correspondence Relative to the Discovery of Gold at Queen Charlotte's Island*, House of Commons Command Paper 788, 1; F. W. Howay, *British Columbia: The Making of a Province* (Toronto: Ryerson Press, 1928), 117–18; Barclay to Douglas, July 2, 1852, B.226/c/1, HBCA; Robin Fisher, *Contact and Conflict: Indian-European Relations in British Columbia, 1774–1890* (Vancouver: University of British Columbia Press, 1977), 3, 9. The Spaniard is quoted in Iris H. W. Engstrand, *Spanish Scientists in the New World: The Eighteenth Century Expeditions* (Seattle: University of Washington Press, 1981), 64.
5. Presumably in an effort to shore up the H.B.C. position under the 1838 Indian trade monopoly grant, James Douglas informed the colonial office that the gold had been acquired from the natives, rather than excavated directly by company employees. Colvile to Board of Management, Columbia District, July 10, 1851; W. H. McNeill to Douglas, Nov. 20, 1851, both B.226/c/1, HBCA; London *Times*, April 2, 1852; Douglas to Grey, Oct. 31, 1851; Jan. 29, 1852, *Correspondence Relative to the Discovery of Gold*, 1–3. For details on Indian involvement in the Queen Charlotte rush, see Fisher, *Contact and Conflict*, 69–70; T. A. Rickard, "Indian Participation in the Gold Discoveries," *BCHQ*, 2(1938), 5–9.
6. Portland *Oregonian*, Jan. 31; Feb. 28, 1852; London *Times*, May 7, 1852; Sept. 23, 1853; Douglas to Grey, Oct. 31; Dec. 16, 1851; May 28, 1852; to Rear-Admiral Moresby, Jan. 29, 1852; John Ballenden to Barclay, Feb. 3, 1852, all *Correspondence Relative to the Discovery of Gold*, 1–2, 5–6, 8–9.
7. James Douglas also considered the navigation ban just retaliation for American interference with English shipping on Puget Sound. Simpson to Board of Management,

Columbia District, March 31, 1851, B.226/c/1, HBCA; Douglas to Grey, Dec. 16, 1851; Jan. 29; May 28, 1852; to Moresby, Jan. 29, 1852; John S. Pakington to Douglas, Sept. 27, 1852, all *Correspondence Relative to the Discovery of Gold*, 1–3, 6, 9, 13–14; London *Times*, Sept. 23, 1853.

8. Douglas to Grey, Jan. 29; April 15; May 28, 1852; to Pakington, Aug. 2, 1852, *Correspondence Relative to the Discovery of Gold*, 3, 8–10; Portland *Oregonian*, April 3, 17; July 3, 1852; Olympia *Columbian*, Jan. 1, 1853; London *Times*, Sept. 23, 1853; Simpson to Board of Management, May 27, 1852, B.226/c/1, HBCA.

9. London *Times*, Sept. 23, 1853; Simpson to Board of Management, Columbia District, Dec. 31, 1852, B.226/c/1, HBCA. Also see Barry M. Gough, *The Royal Navy and the Northwest Coast of North America, 1810–1914: A Study of British Maritime Ascendancy* (Vancouver: University of British Columbia Press, 1971), 133–34.

10. "The danger is not ... completely removed," James Douglas advised with respect to the Americans, as "any prospect of success" on the part of the H.B.C. would "set them all in motion" again. The Indians "have been spoiled by the H.B.Co.," a failed Queen Charlotte miner reported upon returning to American territory, "and want in barter more than twice the value of their gold." Barclay to Board of Management, Columbia District, Jan. 7, 1853; Simpson to Board of Management, Oct. 15; Dec. 31, 1852, all B.226/c/1, HBCA; London *Times*, Sept. 23, 1853; Douglas to Pakington, Aug. 2, 1852, *Correspondence Relative to the Discovery of Gold*, 10; Portland *Oregonian*, April 3, 1852.

11. California's population increased from 14,000 in 1848 to 100,000 in 1849, and to 223,000 in 1852. At just over 50 per cent, San Francisco had the third highest ratio of foreign born residents of any American city, behind only Milwaukee and St. Louis. San Francisco *Alta California*, Dec. 22, 1853; March 20; Oct. 21, 1854; Rodman W. Paul, *California Gold: The Beginning of Mining in the Far West* (Cambridge: Harvard University Press, 1947), 16, 23–25; Malcolm J. Rohrbough, *Days of Gold: The California Gold Rush and the American Nation* (Berkeley: University of California Press, 1997), 94; Roger W. Lotchin, *San Francisco, 1846–1856: From Hamlet to City* (New York: Oxford University Press, 1974), 103; J. S. Holliday, *Rush for Riches: Gold Fever and the Making of California* (Berkeley: University of California Press, 1999), 116.

12. Paul, *California Gold*, 345; Rohrbough, *Days of Gold*, 185–90, 192–96; Lotchin, *San Francisco*, 48–52, 83–84, 190–201, 220; Peter R. Decker, *Fortunes and Failures: White-Collar Mobility in Nineteenth-Century San Francisco* (Cambridge: Harvard University Press, 1978), 63–66; San Francisco *Alta California*, July 12, 1857; London *Times*, July 14, 1858; Kevin Starr, *Americans and the California Dream, 1850–1915* (New York: Oxford University Press, 1973), 94–95; Rohrbough, *Days of Gold*, 187; Decker, *Fortunes and Failures*, 64–65; Paul, *California Gold*, 84.

13. Rohrbough, *Days of Gold*, 262–66; Holliday, *Rush for Riches*, 153–54; San Francisco *Alta California*, July 1, 1854. Sacramento newspaper quoted in Paul, *California Gold*, 84–85.

14. San Francisco *Alta California*, July 9, 12, 29, 1853; June 5; July 15, 1854; Jan. 5, 1855; Lindsey Applegate to Joseph Lane, May 12, 1852, Joseph Lane Papers, Oregon Historical Society.

15. The Walla Walla treaties extinguished Indian title to much of the area east of the Cascades, allowing white settlement to proceed, once Congress ratified the documents. The Hudson's Bay Company diverted a substantial portion of the trade from U.S. to British outlets via a new trail connecting the gold country with Langley and Victoria.

Steilacoom *Puget Sound Courier*, June 21; July 5, 20, 27; Aug. 10, 17, 1855; San Francisco *Alta California*, July 14, 27; Aug. 25; Sept. 17, 1855; Olympia *Pioneer and Democrat*, Sept. 21, 28, 1855; Douglas to James Murray Yale, March 29, 1856, B.113/c/1; Simpson to Mactavish, Sept. 30, 1856, B.223/c/2, both HBCA.

16. Terence O'Donnell, *An Arrow in the Earth: General Joel Palmer and the Indians of Oregon* (Portland: Oregon Historical Society Press, 1991), 251–55; San Francisco *Alta California*, Feb. 6, 1854; Oct. 1, 1855; C. H. Mason to Isaac I. Stevens, Oct. 3, 1855, Records of the Washington Superintendency of Indian Affairs, 1853–1874, M5, NA; John D. B. Ogilvey to Ed. Huggins, March 13, 1856, Ms. FN724, Huntington Library.

17. Although some accounts date the Indian gold discovery to 1852, James Douglas told visiting journalists that the trade commenced at mid-decade. Douglas to William G. Smith, July 20, 1857, B.226/b/15; Simpson to Mactavish, May 1, 1857, B.223/c/2, both HBCA; San Francisco *Alta California*, May 28; July 16, 17, 20, 1858; Rickard, "Indian Participation in the Gold Discoveries," 9–10; Roderick Finlayson Reminiscences, 50, BL; *Victoria Gazette*, July 10, 1858.

18. Douglas to Smith, Sept. 1, 1857, B.226/b/15; Donald Mclean to Yale, Aug. 20, 1857, B.113/c/1, both HBCA. Also see Alfred Waddington, *The Fraser Mines Vindicated, or, The History of Four Months* (Victoria: P. DeGarro, 1858), 4–5.

19. In July 1857, Thomas Lowe, a California merchant with family commercial connections in Victoria, reported that rumors of Thompson River gold were circulating in San Francisco. Miners on the scene advised that, from the lack of "means of conveyance" on the Fraser, persons heading for the Thompson "will be compelled to travel *via* Colville Valley." San Francisco *Alta California*, Oct. 12; Dec. 5, 1857; Douglas to Yale, Dec. 26, 1857, B.113/c/1; to Smith, Sept. 1; Oct. 22; Nov. 27, 1857, B.226/b/15, HBCA; J. M. S. Careless, "The Lowe Brothers, 1852–70: A Study in Business Relations on the North Pacific Coast," *BCS*, 2(1969), 9–10.

20. Simpson to Mactavish, Oct. 14, 1857; Jan. 2, 1858; Douglas to Smith, July 20; Nov. 27, 1857, B.226/b/15, all HBCA.

21. Douglas to Smith, Nov. 27, 1857, B.226/b/15, HBCA; Rickard, "Indian Participation in the Gold Discoveries," 10–11.

22. Douglas to Smith, Oct. 22; Nov. 27; Dec. 28, 1857; Jan. 14, 1858, B.226/b/15; to Yale, Dec. 26, 1857, B.113/c/1, HBCA.

23. Americans charged that the H.B.C. had attempted to keep the gold finds secret in the interest of maintaining a monopoly over the new wealth. Douglas to Smith, Nov. 27; Dec. 28, 1857; Jan. 4, 14, 1858; to Simpson, June 17, 1858, B.226/b/15, HBCA; Arthur Wellesley Vowell and Thomas Spence, "Mining Districts of British Columbia," 17, BL.

Chapter Three
A Mad Crowd Thronging with Eager Steps

1. To Lewis Cass, Jan. 8, 1859, U.S. State Department, Washington Territorial Papers, NA.

2. George Simpson also wanted a fort built midway between Kamloops and the Pend Oreille River, controlling access to the Thompson from the direction of Fort Colvile. James Douglas to William G. Smith, Jan. 14; Feb. 3, 1858; to Dugald Mactavish,

April 16, 1858; to Donald Mclean, Feb. 9; April 19, 1858; to George Simpson, March 30, 1858, B.226/b/15, 16, HBCA.

3. Douglas to Smith, Feb. 18, 1858, B.226/b/15, HBCA.
4. Charles Adams was killed by his prospecting partner at Point Roberts in May 1858. In a more colorful account, he supposedly perished at the hands of Indians after marrying and abusing the daughter of a tribal leader. Douglas to Smith, Jan. 4, 1858; to Mclean, Feb. 9, 1858; to P. S. Ogden, Feb. 9, 1858, B.226/b/15, 16, HBCA; San Francisco *Bulletin*, May 31; June 5, 1858; San Francisco *Alta California* July 16, 1858.
5. Resigning at the end of 1858, McMullin claimed that "the climate of the Territory of Washington is unfavorable to my health." San Francisco *Alta California*, March 8, 1854; Jan. 20; Feb. 3, 12, 23; March 5, 1858; Oregon City *Oregon Argus*, June 12, 19, 1858; Steilacoom *Puget Sound Herald*, March 12; May 7; Oct. 22, 29, 1858; Fayette McMullin to President of the United States, Feb. 18, 1859, Washington Territorial Papers.
6. San Francisco *Alta California*, Jan. 12, 25; Feb. 3, 1858; Olympia *Pioneer and Democrat*, April 30, 1858.
7. "Gold," a Puget Sound settler wrote, "is all the talk here." Douglas to Simpson, March 1, 1858, B.226/b/15, HBCA; Olympia *Pioneer and Democrat*, March 5, 1858; Steilacoom *Puget Sound Herald*, April 2, 23, 1858; A. J. Chambers to T. M. Chambers, April 22, 1858, Thomas M. Chambers Papers, Washington State Historical Society.
8. Douglas to Simpson, March 1, 1858; to Smith, March 25; April 19, 1858; to James Murray Yale, March 30, 1857, B.226/b/15, 16, HBCA.
9. Olympia *Pioneer and Democrat*, March 5, 12, 1858; Steilacoom *Puget Sound Herald*, March 26; April 9, 16, 23, 1858; Douglas to Smith, March 10, 22, 25, 1858, B.226/b/15, HBCA.
10. Salem *Oregon Statesman*, April 27, 1858; Portland *Oregonian*, April 10, 24; May 1, 1858; Oregon City *Oregon Argus*, June 26, 1858.
11. San Francisco *Alta California*, Nov. 12, 1857; April 19, 21, 23, 1858; London *Times*, Aug. 4, 5, 1858. Also see Rodman W. Paul, *California Gold: The Beginning of Mining in the Far West* (Cambridge: Harvard University Press, 1947), 177.
12. Maintaining the need for a cautious approach, the *Alta California* expressed another common theme, California's obvious and deserved predominance on the Pacific coast. The new mines, after all, were merely "a continuation of our own mineral chain of mountains far into the British Possessions." San Francisco *Alta California*, March 9; April 4, 12, 17, 19, 1858.
13. San Francisco *Herald*, June 5, 1858; *New York Times*, July 15, 1858; Portland *Oregonian*, June 16, 1858; London *Times*, Aug. 4, 1858; San Francisco *Alta California*, April 27, 1858.
14. London *Times*, June 26; Aug. 4, 5, 1858; *New York Times*, July 15, 1858; San Francisco *Alta California*, June 21, 1858.
15. San Francisco *Alta California*, May 6, 31; June 21, 28; July 5, 1858; James Bell to John Thomson, Feb. 27, 1859, in Willard E. Ireland, ed., "Gold-rush Days in Victoria, 1858–1859," *BCHQ*, 12(1948), 235; London *Times*, May 31; June 26; Aug. 4, 1858; F. W. Howay, "The Negro Immigration to Vancouver Island in 1858," *BCHQ*, 3(1939), 113.
16. A company was organized at Yreka to make the complete trip from northern California along the eastern slope of the Cascades. Residents of Vancouver, Washington Territory, attempted to open a variant of the Columbia River route, blazing a trail across

the mountains to the Yakima Valley. Douglas to Lord Stanley, May 19, 1858, *PRABC*, 1:11; Portland *Oregonian*, April 24; May 1, 15; June 12, 26; July 17, 1858; San Francisco *Alta California*, May 3, 9, 27; June 3, 22, 1858; Oregon City *Oregon Argus*, July 31, 1858.

17. James Douglas worried that the Steptoe affair would inspire an Indian war north of the 49th parallel. San Francisco *Alta California*, May 23; June 9, 1858; John Mullan to S. H. Long, Nov. 12, 1862, Records of the Topographical Engineers, Letters Received, RG 77, NA; Edward Steptoe to W. W. Mackall, May 23, 29, 1858, Letters Received by the Office of the Adjutant General, 1822–1860, M567, NA; Oregon City *Oregon Argus*, June 26, 1858; Portland *Oregonian*, July 3; Sept. 18, 1858; R. H. Lansdale to James Nesmith, June 30, 1858, Records of the Washington Superintendency of Indian Affairs, 1853–1874, M5, NA; Robert Frost, "Fraser River Gold Rush Adventures," *WHQ*, 22(1931), 203–4, 206; Robie L. Reid, ed., "To the Fraser River Mines in 1858: A Letter from C. C. Gardiner," *BCHQ*, 1(1937), 245; Olympia *Pioneer and Democrat*, July 23, 1858; Steilacoom *Puget Sound Herald*, July 16, 1858; Douglas to Stanley, June 15, 1858, *PRABC*, 1:17. On the Steptoe retreat and the 1858 conflict, see Robert Ignatius Burns, S.J., *The Jesuits and the Indian Wars of the Northwest* (New Haven: Yale University Press, 1966), chaps. 6–8.

18. London *Times*, July 14; Aug. 4, 5, 1858; San Francisco *Alta California*, May 21; June 20, 24; July 3, 1858; Salem *Oregon Statesman*, June 29, 1858; San Francisco *Herald*, June 5, 1858.

19. San Francisco *Alta California*, April 21; June 6, 23, 29; July 4, 1858; Salem *Oregon Statesman*, June 29, 1858; San Francisco *Herald*, June 5, 1858; London *Times*, Aug. 4, 5, 1858.

20. San Francisco *Alta California*, April 20, 21; July 15, 1858; Salem *Oregon Statesman*, Aug. 3, 1858.

21. San Francisco *Alta California*, Aug. 12, 1858; *New York Times*, July 15, 1858; F. W. Howay, ed., "To the Fraser River! The Diary and Letters of Cyrus Olin Phillips, 1858–1859," *California Historical Society Quarterly*, 11(1932), 152; J. S. Holliday, *Rush for Riches: Gold Fever and the Making of California* (Berkeley: University of California Press, 1999), 215.

22. San Francisco *Alta California*, June 22, 1858; London *Times*, Aug. 4, 27, 1858; *New York Times*, July 15, 1858.

23. London *Times*, Aug. 4, 27, 1858; San Francisco *Alta California*, April 21; May 6; June 22, 1858.

24. Repaired and again named the *Brother Jonathan*, the *Commodore* returned to service in 1859, running between San Francisco and Puget Sound until sinking, with nearly 300 fatalities, off Humboldt Bay in 1865. Bell to Thomson, Feb. 27, 1859, in Ireland, ed., "Gold-rush Days in Victoria," 241; San Francisco *Alta California*, July 15, 26; Aug. 2, 3, 1858; Howay, ed., "Diary and Letters of Cyrus Olin Phillips," 152; Portland *Oregonian*, March 19, 1859; Victoria *British Colonist*, April 16, 1859; Olympia *Washington Standard*, Aug. 5, 19, 1865; Olympia *Pacific Tribune*, Aug. 12, 1865.

25. San Francisco *Alta California*, June 26, 1858; London *Times*, Aug. 27, 1858; George F. Stanley, ed., *Mapping the Frontier: Charles Wilson's Diary of the 49th Parallel, 1858–1862, while Secretary of the British Boundary Commission* (Toronto: Macmillan of Canada, 1970), 23; George Henry Richards to Douglas, Oct. 23, 1858, *PRABC*, 2:13; Dorothy Blakey Smith, ed., "The Journal of Arthur Thomas Bushby, 1858–1859," *BCHQ*, 21(1957–58), 128.

26. F. W. Howay, *British Columbia: The Making of a Province* (Toronto: Ryerson Press, 1928), 120; Jean Barman, *The West beyond the West: A History of British Columbia* (Toronto: University of Toronto Press, rev. ed., 1996), 65–66; Walter N. Sage, "The Gold Colony of British Columbia," *Canadian Historical Review*, 2(1921), 340; Douglas to Smith, June 20, 1858, B.226/b/15, HBCA; to Robert L. Baynes, May 12, 1858, ADM 1/5696, PRO; to Stanley, July 1, 1858, *PRABC*, 1:19.

27. Nineteenth century observers believed, from the evidence on the ground, that the Fraser had once flowed into Bellingham Bay. San Francisco *Alta California*, June 7, 9, 12, 23; July 10, 1858; London *Times*, Aug. 4, 1858; Steilacoom *Puget Sound Herald*, July 2, 1858; Eldridge Morse Notebooks, 20:7–8, BL.

28. Douglas to Stanley, July 1, 1858, *PRABC*, 1:19; to Allen Lowe and Co., April 29, 1858, B.226/b/16, HBCA; London *Times*, Aug. 4, 10, 1858; San Francisco *Alta California*, May 6; July 7, 17, 1858; Bell to Thomson, Feb. 27, 1859, in Ireland, ed., "Gold-rush Days in Victoria," 242, 246; Howay, ed., "Diary and Letters of Cyrus Olin Phillips," 153.

29. Despite the "intricate and shallow entrance," Captain George Henry Richards reported of conditions at Victoria, "vessels of considerable draught can enter by attending to the tides." Only a narrow bit of land separated the interior extremities of Victoria and Esquimalt harbors, leading naval officers to recommend constructing a connecting canal. San Francisco *Alta California*, June 26; July 2, 3, 7, 21, 23; Sept. 10, 1858; Richards to Douglas, Oct. 23, 1858; Douglas to E. B. Lytton, Jan. 15, 1859, both *PRABC*, 2:13–14, 56; London *Times*, Aug. 27, 1858; W. Colquhon Grant, "Description of Vancouver Island," *Journal of the Royal Geographical Society*, 27(1857), 281; Bell to Thomson, Feb. 27, 1859, in Ireland, ed., "Gold-rush Days in Victoria," 240–41. Already a favored resort of the Royal Navy, Esquimalt Harbour became Pacific station headquarters in 1862. See Barry M. Gough, *The Royal Navy and the Northwest Coast of North America, 1810–1914: A Study of British Maritime Ascendancy* (Vancouver: University of British Columbia Press, 1971), 186–91.

30. With the only bank safe in the British possessions, Fort Victoria served as the repository for all-important documents. London *Times*, Aug. 27, 1858; San Francisco *Alta California*, June 22, 26; July 20, 1858; Margaret A. Ormsby, *British Columbia: A History* (Vancouver: Macmillan of Canada, 1958), 141; San Francisco *Bulletin*, June 28, 1858; Roderick Finlayson Reminiscences, 51, BL; Douglas to Yale, July 3, 1858, B.226/b/16, HBCA.

31. Smith, ed., "Journal of Arthur Thomas Bushby," 120; Finlayson Reminiscences, 48; San Francisco *Alta California*, June 26, 1858; *Victoria Gazette*, July 10, 1858.

32. The first real estate was sold at Esquimalt in early July, with Chinese purchasers buying approximately a third of the lots sold. San Francisco *Alta California*, June 22, 23, 26; July 7, 8, 20, 1858; Douglas to Smith, June 14, 23, 1858, B.226/b/15, HBCA; London *Times*, Aug. 14, 27, 1858; San Francisco *Bulletin*, June 28, 1858.

33. London *Times*, Aug. 27, 1858; San Francisco *Alta California*, June 27, 28; July 12, 19, 1858.

34. Stanley, ed., *Mapping the Frontier*, 25; Alfred Waddington, *The Fraser Mines Vindicated, or, The History of Four Months* (Victoria: P. DeGarro, 1858), 17–18; San Francisco *Alta California*, July 7, 26, 1858; *Victoria Gazette*, July 10, 1858; San Francisco *Bulletin*, June 28, 1858; Douglas to Smith, Aug. 4, 1858, B.226/b/15, HBCA.

35. Composed, as a visitor unkindly wrote, of "Yesler's mill and the shacks of a half dozen employees," Seattle was not a scheduled mail steamer port of call. San Francisco *Alta*

California, June 6, 22, 28; July 3, 21; Aug. 14, 22, 1858; London *Times*, June 26, 1858; Steilacoom *Puget Sound Herald*, May 14, 21; June 11, 25; July 2, 16, 1858; Olympia *Pioneer and Democrat*, June 25; July 2, 1858; Oregon City *Oregon Argus*, Aug. 14, 1858; William S. Lewis, ed., "Reminiscences of Joseph H. Boyd: An Argonaut of 1857," *WHQ*, 15(1924), 249.

36. An American captain, who had no passengers or freight for Port Townsend, paid a heavy fine after being caught sailing direct from Victoria to Bellingham Bay. A pre-gold rush British visitor observed that Port Townsend "bids fair to become one of the most thriving little towns in the district." San Francisco *Alta California*, June 26; July 16, 1858; Lewis, ed., "An Argonaut of 1857," 248; F. W. Pettygrove Reminiscences, 10–11, BL; Grant, "Description of Vancouver Island," 317.

37. Howay, ed., "Diary and Letters of Cyrus Olin Phillips," 152; San Francisco *Bulletin*, May 3, 1858; Steilacoom *Puget Sound Herald*, March 12; April 30, 1858; San Francisco *Alta California*, May 4, 10, 18; June 26, 1858.

38. San Francisco *Alta California*, May 4, 10; June 6, 9, 23, 26; July 3, 1858; San Francisco *Bulletin*, May 3; June 19, 1858.

39. Edward T. Coleman, "Mountaineering on the Pacific," *Harper's New Monthly Magazine*, 39(1869), 795; Grant, "Description of Vancouver Island," 315; San Francisco *Alta California*, May 3, 4; June 9, 11, 22; Aug. 22, 1858; Steilacoom *Puget Sound Herald*, June 4, 1858; Olympia *Pioneer and Democrat*, April 23, 1858; Portland *Oregonian*, June 26, 1858.

40. Once the wharf was in place, all passengers for Bellingham Bay landed at Sehome. San Francisco *Alta California*, May 18; June 3, 9, 26; July 2, 3, 1858; Grant, "Description of Vancouver Island," 315; Steilacoom *Puget Sound Herald*, May 14, 21, 28, 1858; Portland *Oregonian*, June 26, 1858; *Victoria Gazette*, July 10, 1858; Whatcom *Northern Light*, July 3, 1858; San Francisco *Bulletin*, June 19, 1858.

41. The original settlers built their mill on Whatcom Creek, a stream that turned out to have an irregular flow, seriously hampering operations. San Francisco *Alta California*, June 6, 9, 12, 26; July 9, 10; Aug. 22, 1858; Olympia *Pioneer and Democrat*, May 7, 28, 1858; Howay, ed., "Diary and Letters of Cyrus Olin Phillips," 152; Salem *Oregon Statesman*, May 28, 1858; Whatcom *Northern Light*, July 3, 1858; Steilacoom *Puget Sound Herald*, May 28, 1858; Henry Roeder Reminiscences, 8–12, 28–45, BL; Edward Eldridge Reminiscences, 2–4, BL.

42. San Francisco *Alta California*, June 11, 12, 26; July 19, 15, 1858, the last date reprinting from the Whatcom *Northern Light*; Salem *Oregon Statesman*, May 28, 1858; Howay, ed., "Diary and Letters of Cyrus Olin Phillips," 152.

43. Olympia *Pioneer and Democrat*, July 30; Aug. 13, 1858; Reid, ed., "To the Fraser River Mines in 1858," 245; Steilacoom *Puget Sound Herald*, June 4, 1858; Howay, ed., "Diary and Letters of Cyrus Olin Phillips," 152; London *Times*, Aug. 27, 1858; Waddington, *Fraser Mines Vindicated*, 9–10.

44. San Francisco *Alta California*, April 19; May 3, 18; July 2, 1858; Whatcom *Northern Light*, July 3, 1858; Steilacoom *Puget Sound Herald*, April 16, 23, 1858; Olympia *Pioneer and Democrat*, April 16; May 14, 1858; James C. Prevost to Baynes, June 7, 1858, ADM 1/5696, PRO; Douglas to Smith, July 23, 1858, B.226/b/15, HBCA.

45. Gold prospects on Burrard Inlet and Howe Sound also had attracted H.B.C. interest. San Francisco *Alta California*, May 4, 8, 18; June 24; July 22, 1858; Richards to Douglas, Oct. 23, 1858; Douglas to Stanley, June 19, 1858, both *PRABC*, 1:17; 2:16; to

Smith, June 20, 1858, B.226/b/15, HBCA; Olympia *Pioneer and Democrat*, April 23, 1858.

46. Douglas to Yale, April 27, 1858, B.226/b/16, HBCA; San Francisco *Alta California*, May 4, 1858; San Francisco *Bulletin*, May 3, 1858; London *Times*, Aug. 27, 1858.

47. Although contemporary accounts claiming that "numbers" perished while "attempting to cross that stormy and dangerous Gulf" exaggerated matters, a combination of unstable watercraft, inexpert navigation, and variable weather certainly made the passage dangerous. San Francisco *Bulletin*, May 18, 1858; San Francisco *Alta California*, June 7; July 12, 1858; "The Navigation of the Fraser River, and Its Approaches," *Nautical Magazine*, 28(1859), 324–25; *Victoria Gazette*, July 10, 1858; Nugent to Cass, Jan. 8, 1859, Washington Territorial Papers.

48. When two gold hunters were found shot to death next to their tidewater campfire, suspicion immediately focused on the local Lummi Indians. A number of tribal members were locked up in Whatcom in a vain attempt to compel surrender of the supposed murderers. San Francisco *Alta California*, June 20, 23; July 7, 15, 20, 1858; Portland *Oregonian*, June 26, 1858; Whatcom *Northern Light*, Aug. 28, 1858.

49. The northern part of the Point Roberts peninsula was on the British side of the 49th parallel, but the main landing places were south of the line. San Francisco *Alta California*, June 22; July 6, 1858; London *Times*, Aug. 14; Nov. 30, 1858; Alfred Waddington, "On the Geography and Mountain Passes of British Columbia in Connection with an Overland Route," *Journal of the Royal Geographical Society*, 38(1868), 122; Steilacoom *Puget Sound Herald*, May 14, 1858.

50. Portland *Oregonian*, Aug. 14, 1858; Olympia *Pioneer and Democrat*, May 14, 1858; San Francisco *Alta California*, June 22, 23; Sept. 10, 1858; London *Times*, Nov. 30, 1858.

51. San Francisco *Alta California*, July 16; Aug. 21; Sept. 10, 1858; Reid, ed., "To the Fraser River Mines in 1858," 247; London *Times*, Nov. 30, 1858.

52. Douglas to Yale, April 27, 1858; to Allan Lowe and Co., April 29, 1858; to Wm. McNeill, Aug. 27, 1858; to Smith, June 9, 1858, B.226/b/15, 16, HBCA; to Stanley, May 19; July 26, 1858; James Yates, et al. to Douglas, June 9, 1858, all *PRABC*, 1:11, 15–16, 22; London *Times*, Aug. 14, 1858; San Francisco *Alta California*, May 31, 1858.

53. San Francisco *Alta California*, May 4, 6; June 6, 7, 1858; Portland *Oregonian*, June 19, 1858; London *Times*, Aug. 14, 1858.

54. Douglas to Lytton, Sept. 9; Oct. 11, 1858; to Stanley, May 19; July 26, 1858, *PRABC*, 1:11–12, 22, 34, 37–38; to McLean, April 19, 1858; to Smith, May 11, 1858, B.226/b/15, 16, HBCA.

55. Suspicious Americans thought the British firm intent upon "buying up" the steamship company. Proclamation, May 8, 1858; Douglas to Stanley, May 19; July 26, 1858, all *PRABC*, 1:11–12, 23; to Smith, May 11; June 20, 1858, B.226/b/15, HBCA; Norman R. Hacking, "'Steamboat 'Round the Bend': American Steamers on the Fraser River in 1858," *BCHQ*, 8(1944), 258–59; London *Times*, Aug. 14, 1858; Steilacoom *Puget Sound Herald*, July 9, 1858.

56. Douglas to Smith, June 9, 20, 1858; to Richard M. Jessop and R. I. Vanderwater, June 23, 1858, B.226/b/15, 16, HBCA; to Stanley, June 19, 1858, enclosing agreement of June 18, 1858; to Lytton, April 12, 1859, *PRABC*, 1:18–19; 3:7; Hacking, "'Steamboat 'Round the Bend,'" 257, 259–60, 262; Steilacoom *Puget Sound Herald*, April 2, 1858; San Francisco *Alta California*, May 27, 1858.

57. Returning to California, the *Surprise* eventually ended up in Chinese waters. Hacking, "'Steamboat 'Round the Bend,'" 260–64; Douglas to Stanley, June 19, 1858, *PRABC*, 1:18; to Smith, June 20, 1858, B.226/b/15, HBCA; San Francisco *Bulletin*, June 19, 1858; San Francisco *Alta California*, June 6, 28; July 16; Aug. 26, 1858; Portland *Oregonian*, July 24; Aug. 14, 1858.

58. Hacking, "'Steamboat 'Round the Bend,'" 262–63; San Francisco *Alta California*, June 20, 22; July 9, 16; Sept. 10, 17, 26, 1858; San Francisco *Bulletin*, July 16, 1858; Portland *Oregonian*, Aug. 14, 1858; Robie L. Reid, ed., "Extracts from Dr. Carl Freisbach, *An Excursion through British Columbia in the Year 1858*, pub. in Gratz, Austria, 1875," *BCHQ*, 5(1941), 223–24.

59. Ainsworth soon became one of the most powerful magnates in the Pacific Northwest as co-founder of the Oregon Steam Navigation Company. San Francisco *Alta California*, June 6; July 20; Aug. 2; Sept. 7, 14, 26, 1858; Hacking, "'Steamboat 'Round the Bend,'" 264–65, 272–73; London *Times*, Nov. 30, 1858; Oregon City *Oregon Argus*, July 17, 1858; Douglas to Smith, June 7, 20, 1858, B.226/b/15, HBCA; Randall V. Mills, *Stern-Wheelers Up Columbia: A Century of Steamboating in the Oregon Country* (Palo Alto: Pacific Books, 1947), 130–31, 202.

60. San Francisco *Alta California*, June 6, 20, 22; July 3, 9, 12, 16, 23, 1858; London *Times*, Nov. 30; Dec. 1, 1858; Olympia *Pioneer and Democrat*, May 14, 1858.

61. Douglas to Stanley, June 10, 1858, *PRABC*, 1:13; Olympia *Pioneer and Democrat*, Aug. 20, 1858; San Francisco *Alta California*, May 31; June 6, 1858; Portland *Oregonian*, May 29; June 19, 1858; San Francisco *Bulletin*, May 31, 1858.

62. Olympia *Pioneer and Democrat*, Aug. 20, 1858; San Francisco *Bulletin*, May 31, 1858; San Francisco *Alta California*, June 23, 1858; Steilacoom *Puget Sound Herald*, May 14, 1858.

63. "It is not absolutely necessary that a *Palace* should be built here," a company officer reported from Hope, "but if it is intended that a Gentleman should be stationed here he would require somewhat of a better kind of Dwelling House." Douglas to Smith, June 7, 1858, B.226/b/15; Mclean to Yale, June 22, 1858, B.113/c/1, both HBCA; San Francisco *Alta California*, July 9, 23, 1858; London *Times*, Dec. 25, 1858.

64. San Francisco *Alta California*, July 16, 23; Aug. 8, 1858; Douglas to Yale, April 27, 1858; to Smith, May 8; June 7, 1858, B.226/b/15, 16, HBCA; London *Times*, Aug. 14, 1858.

65. Olympia *Pioneer and Democrat*, July 2, 1858; Douglas to Smith, June 7, 1858, B.226/b/15, HBCA.

Chapter Four
Gold Is King

1. May 8, 1858.
2. Walter N. Sage, "The Gold Colony of British Columbia," *Canadian Historical Review*, 2(1921), 340; San Francisco *Alta California*, May 31; June 28, 1858; *New York Times*, July 15, 1858; Steilacoom *Puget Sound Herald*, May 21, 1858.
3. James Douglas to George Simpson, March 31, 1858; to William G. Smith, May 8, 1858; to George Henry Richards, April 5, 1858, B.226/b/15, 16, HBCA; London *Times*, Aug. 5, 1858; San Francisco *Alta California*, April 19, 23; May 12; June 6, 1858.

4. Douglas to Lord Stanley, May 19; June 10; Aug. 19, 1858, *PRABC*, 1:11, 13, 27; to Smith, Aug. 12, 1858, B.226/b/15, HBCA; Diary of Gold Discovery on Fraser River, May 24, 1858, James Douglas Papers, PABC; San Francisco *Alta California*, May 18, 1858; Olympia *Pioneer and Democrat*, Aug. 20, 1858.
5. San Francisco *Alta California*, July 9, 23; Aug. 2, 1858; London *Times*, Aug. 14, 1858.
6. London *Times*, Aug. 4; Dec. 1, 24, 1858; James C. Prevost to Robert L. Baynes, June 7, 1858, ADM 1/5696, PRO; San Francisco *Alta California*, June 7, 23; Aug. 2, 1858; Douglas to Stanley, June 10, 1858, *PRABC*, 1:14; Olympia *Pioneer and Democrat*, May 14, 1858.
7. San Francisco *Alta California*, June 7, 22, 23, 1858; Prevost to Baynes, June 7, 1858, ADM 1/5696; Douglas to E. B. Lytton, Oct. 12, 1858, ADM 1/5721, PRO.
8. Governor Douglas ordered the "ominous" Murderer's Bar renamed. Denouncing the "impudent assumption" of the prospectors at Fifty-four Forty Bar—the name referred to the extreme American position during the Oregon boundary crisis—Donald Fraser reported that a British officer tore the offensive "placard" to shreds and threw the pieces in the river. Douglas to Stanley, June 10, 1858, *PRABC*, 1:13; Prevost to Baynes, June 7, 1858, ADM 1/5696; San Francisco *Alta California*, June 3, 7; Aug. 19, 24; Sept. 26, 1858; London *Times*, Dec. 1, 24, 25, 1858; Olympia *Pioneer and Democrat*, Aug. 20, 1858; "The Discovery of Hill's Bar in 1858," *BCHQ*, 3(1939), 217–18. For the female population figure, see Robie L. Reid, ed., "Extracts from Dr. Carl Friesbach, *An Excursion through British Columbia in the Year 1858*, pub. in Gratz, Austria, 1875," *BCHQ*, 5(1941), 227.
9. San Francisco *Alta California*, May 18; June 7, 9, 23, 1858; Douglas to Stanley, June 10, 1858, *PRABC*, 1:13; Diary of Gold Discovery, May 28, 1858.
10. San Francisco *Alta California*, June 20, 21; Aug. 8, 19, 1858; London *Times*, Dec. 1, 1858; Douglas to Stanley, June 10, 1858, *PRABC*, 1:13; Robie L. Reid, ed., "To the Fraser River Mines in 1858: A Letter from C. C. Gardiner," *BCHQ*, 1(1937), 251; Mary Hill, *Gold: The California Story* (Berkeley: University of California Press, 1999), 72.
11. San Francisco *Alta California*, June 7, 20, 21; July 9; Aug. 8, 19, 1858; Diary of Gold Discovery, May 31, 1858; Prevost to Baynes, June 7, 1858, ADM 1/5696; Douglas to Stanley, June 10, 1858, *PRABC*, 1:14; John Nugent to Lewis Cass, Jan. 8, 1859, U.S. State Department, Washington Territorial Papers, NA; Olympia *Pioneer and Democrat*, May 14, 1858; Portland *Oregonian*, Sept. 4, 1858; Reid, ed., "To the Fraser River Mines," 251; London *Times*, Dec. 1, 1858.
12. The gold was "so plentiful and so generally diffused," Captain Prevost of the Royal Navy advised, that new arrivals had no problem locating profitable sites. San Francisco *Alta California*, June 6, 20, 22; July 8, 29, 1858; London *Times*, Dec. 1, 25, 1858; Diary of Gold Discovery, May 24, 27, 1858; Prevost to Baynes, June 7, 1858, ADM 1/5696. On the California experience, see Malcolm J. Rohrbough, *Days of Gold: The California Gold Rush and the American Nation* (Berkeley: University of California Press, 1997), 15–16, 125–27; Rodman W. Paul, *California Gold: The Beginning of Mining in the Far West* (Cambridge: Harvard University Press, 1947), 213–17.
13. The H.B.C. shipped over 1,000 ounces of Indian gold from Kamloops to Victoria in early fall 1858. *Victoria Gazette*, Oct. 2, 1858; San Francisco *Alta California*, June 20; July 3, 8, 9, 12, 23–25; Aug. 2, 1858; San Francisco *Bulletin*, June 19, 1858.

14. Douglas to Stanley, June 10; July 1, 1858, *PRABC*, 1:13–14, 19–20; to Smith, June 23, 1858, B.226/b/15, HBCA; Diary of Gold Discovery, June 1, 1858; San Francisco *Alta California*, June 23; July 3; Aug. 8, 1858.
15. San Francisco *Alta California*, May 8, 31; June 6, 7, 9, 12, 21, 22; July 7, 1858; Olympia *Pioneer and Democrat*, July 23, 1858; Steilacoom *Puget Sound Herald*, July 2, 1858; Douglas to Stanley, June 19, 1858, *PRABC*, 1:18; to Smith, July 23, 1858, B.226/b/15, HBCA; Diary of Gold Discovery, May 29, 1858; Portland *Oregonian*, June 19, 1858; Prevost to Baynes, June 7, 1858, ADM 1/5696.
16. San Francisco *Alta California*, May 31; June 7; July 7, 9, 12, 16, 1858; Steilacoom *Puget Sound Herald*, July 2, 1858.
17. San Francisco *Bulletin*, May 3, 18, 1858; Douglas to Duncan Finlayson, July 9, 1858, B.226/b/15, HBCA; to Stanley, July 1, 26, 1858, *PRABC*, 1:19, 22–23; San Francisco *Alta California*, July 19, 1858; Portland *Oregonian*, June 26, 1858.
18. San Francisco *Alta California*, May 4, 18; June 6, 22, 1858; Douglas to Stanley, July 1, 1858, *PRABC*, 1:19–20; Diary of Gold Discovery, May 27, 28, 1858.
19. San Francisco observers were mystified by the small amounts of gold dust carried on returning steamers. The H.B.C. shipped 2,688 ounces of gold direct to London during July alone. Douglas to Stanley, July 26, 1858, *PRABC*, 1:23; to Smith, July 7, 23, 26, 1858, B.226/b/15, HBCA; San Francisco *Alta California*, June 20, 29; July 7, 1858.
20. On the basis of personal observation and scores of reports from the interior, James Douglas was convinced that "the whole country situated to the eastward of the Gulf of Georgia ... is one continued land of gold." London *Times*, Aug. 10, 1858; San Francisco *Alta California*, May 31; June 6, 20, 22, 1858; Douglas to Stanley, June 10; July 26, 1858, *PRABC*, 1:14, 23; to Smith, July 23, 1858, B.226/b/15, HBCA; Diary of Gold Discovery, May 27, 1858; Prevost to Baynes, June 7, 1858, ADM 1/5696.
21. San Francisco *Alta California*, July 3, 4, 7, 12, 16; Aug. 10, 1858; *Victoria Gazette*, Aug. 14, 1858; Douglas to Lytton, Oct. 12, 1858, ADM 1/5721; Olympia *Pioneer and Democrat*, July 23; Aug. 20, 1858.
22. San Francisco *Alta California*, July 3, 7, 16, 21, 1858; Olympia *Pioneer and Democrat*, Aug. 20, 1858; Douglas to James Murray Yale, April 27, 1858, B.226//b/16, HBCA.
23. London *Times*, Aug. 4, 1858; San Francisco *Alta California*, July 3, 23; Aug. 2, 9, 1858.
24. A Hill's Bar prospector wrote of "few miners making more than expenses," the "great mass ... lolling listlessly" while "their slim means were rapidly diminishing." Douglas to Stanley, Aug. 19, 1858, *PRABC*, 1:27; to Smith, Aug. 12, 1858, B.226/b/15; Ovid Allard to Yale, Aug. 20, 1858, B.113/c/1, both HBCA; Olympia *Pioneer and Democrat*, Aug. 20, 1858; San Francisco *Alta California*, July 8, 12, 16; Aug. 9, 1858; Portland *Oregonian*, Aug. 14, 1858; *Victoria Gazette*, July 7, 1858.
25. San Francisco *Alta California*, July 7, 16, 17, 23; Aug. 6, 1858. For a compilation of the reporter's accounts, see Henry DeGroot, *British Columbia: Its Condition and Prospects, Soil, Climate, and Mineral Resources* (San Francisco: Alta California Job Office, 1859).
26. London *Times*, Dec. 24, 1858; San Francisco *Alta California*, July 3, 24; Aug. 2, 8; Sept. 10, 26, 1858; Douglas to Lytton, Oct. 12, 1858, ADM 1/5721; Reid, ed., "Extracts," 226; Steilacoom *Puget Sound Herald*, Aug. 13, 1858.

27. San Francisco *Alta California*, Aug. 8; Sept. 26, 1858; Douglas to Lytton, Oct. 12, 1858, ADM 1/5721; Allard to Yale, Aug. 20, 1858, B.113/c/1, HBCA; London *Times*, Dec. 24, 25, 1858.

28. San Francisco *Alta California*, July 3, 9, 16, 23, 25, 1858; San Francisco *Bulletin*, July 16, 1858; Portland *Oregonian*, July 24, 1858; Douglas to Lytton, Oct. 12, 1858, ADM 1/5721.

29. London *Times*, Aug. 27, 1858; San Francisco *Alta California*, July 9, 12, 16, 19, 1858; *Victoria Gazette*, July 10, 1858.

30. San Francisco *Alta California*, July 12, 17, 19; Aug. 9, 22; Sept. 6, 7, 10, 15, 1858; San Francisco *Bulletin*, Sept. 25, 1858; London *Times*, Oct. 12, 1858.

31. F. W. Howay, ed., "To the Fraser River! The Diary and Letters of Cyrus Olin Phillips, 1858–1859," *California Historical Society Quarterly*, 11(1932), 152; Whatcom *Northern Light*, July 15, 1858; San Francisco *Alta California*, May 3; June 9, 20, 22, 26; July 2, 20, 1858; Douglas to Smith, July 3, 1858, B.226/b/15, HBCA; Olympia *Pioneer and Democrat*, Aug. 13, 1858.

32. San Francisco *Alta California*, May 6, 8, 31; June 9, 26, 28; July 2, 9, 16, 1858; Olympia *Pioneer and Democrat*, May 14, 1858; Portland *Oregonian*, May 29; Sept. 4, 1858; Prevost to Baynes, June 7, 1858, ADM 1/5696; Whatcom *Northern Light*, July 3, 1858. For complete details on the planning and execution of the trail project, see R. L. Reid, "The Whatcom Trails to the Fraser River Mines in 1858," *WHQ*, 18(1927), 199–206, 271–76.

33. Olympia *Pioneer and Democrat*, June 25; July 23, 1858; San Francisco *Alta California*, June 22, 23, 26; July 15; Aug. 2, 1858; Whatcom *Northern Light*, July 31; Aug. 19, 1858. On DeLacy's army work, see W. Turrentine Jackson, *Wagon Roads West: A Study of Federal Road Surveys and Construction in the Trans-Mississippi West, 1846–1869* (New Haven: Yale University Press, 1964), 103–4.

34. Whatcom *Northern Light*, Aug. 19, 1858; Reid, "Whatcom Trails," 276; Portland *Oregonian*, July 24, 1858; San Francisco *Alta California*, June 26; July 3, 9, 20, 23, 1858; San Francisco *Bulletin*, June 28, 1858; Steilacoom *Puget Sound Herald*, Aug. 6, 1858.

35. San Francisco *Alta California*, July 25; Aug. 22; Sept. 26, 1858; Portland *Oregonian*, Aug. 7; Oct. 2, 1858; Salem *Oregon Statesman*, Oct. 5, 1858; Whatcom *Northern Light*, Aug. 19, 1858; Victoria *British Colonist*, Dec. 18, 1858; Roderick Finlayson Reminiscences, 52, BL.

36. San Francisco *Alta California*, June 6, 26; July 3, 9, 16, 19; Aug. 2, 1858; Olympia *Pioneer and Democrat*, Aug. 13, 1858; Steilacoom *Puget Sound Herald*, July 23, 30, 1858; George F. Stanley, ed., *Mapping the Frontier: Charles Wilson's Diary of the 49th Parallel, 1858–1862, while Secretary of the British Boundary Commission* (Toronto: Macmillan of Canada, 1970), 27, 30; Victoria *British Colonist*, April 30, 1859; London *Times*, Nov. 30, 1858.

37. A regular reader of the California papers, James Douglas was well aware of the complaints against this administration. "I cannot see," Donald Fraser wrote after affirming that the grant language said nothing about restricting non-Indian activities, "that any such power can be construed from the recital therein." Even so, Fraser thought that "the intention of the parties to the charter, at the time it was granted, was to exclude all persons from trading in the Company's territory in opposition to its interests." San Francisco *Alta California*, June 6, 9, 11, 26; July 21, 1858; R. W. Walker to Cass, June 18, 1858, Washington Territorial Papers; Steilacoom *Puget Sound Herald*,

June 18, 1858; London *Times*, Aug. 4, 1858; Douglas to Smith, July 23, 1858, B.226/b/15, HBCA.

38. Isaac I. Stevens to Cass, July 21, 1858, Isaac I. Stevens Papers, UW; San Francisco *Alta California*, May 6; June 6, 26; Aug. 20, 1858; San Francisco *Bulletin*, May 18, 1858.

39. San Francisco *Alta California*, June 26; July 3, 20; Aug. 22; Sept. 7, 1858; Steilacoom *Puget Sound Herald*, June 18, 1858; San Francisco *Bulletin*, June 5, 1858.

40. James Douglas blamed "the pressure of public business ... and irregular mail facilities" for his habit of making independent decisions prior to consultation with the colonial office. One problem caused by the lack of funds was the failure to provide for official recording of land titles, an administrative lapse potentially harmful to the integrity of real estate transactions. Douglas to Lytton, Oct. 11; Nov. 27, 1858, *PRABC*, 1:37; 2:37; to Simpson, June 17, 1858, B.226/b/15, HBCA; London *Times*, Aug. 10, 1858; Jan. 19, 1859; Prevost to Baynes, June 7, 1858, ADM 1/5696; Victoria *British Colonist*, Dec. 18, 1858; Jan. 15; Feb. 5, 12; March 19, 1859; James Bell to John Thomson, Feb. 27, 1859, in Willard E. Ireland, ed., "Gold-rush Days in Victoria, 1858–1859," *BCHQ*, 12(1948), 241; San Francisco *Alta California*, Aug. 6, 1858.

41. Parliament eventually supplied over £3,000 to cover extra pay for the officers and crews of the naval vessels, removing what Douglas called "an intolerable burden on our limited income." Lytton to Douglas, Sept. 16, 1858; Douglas to Lytton, Sept. 30; Dec. 9, 1858; to Duke of Newcastle, Aug. 4, 1860; to Stanley, May 19; June 15; July 26, 1858, all *PRABC*, 1:11, 16, 22–23, 27, 34, 36–37, 66; 2:43–44; 4:14; to Smith, May 11, 1858, B.226/b/15, HBCA; to Baynes, May 12, 1858, ADM 1/5696. On the *Satellite* and the *Plumper*, see Barry M. Gough, *The Royal Navy and the Northwest Coast of North America, 1810–1914: A Study of British Maritime Ascendancy* (Vancouver: University of British Columbia Press, 1971), 135.

42. London *Times*, Nov. 30; Dec. 24, 1858; Address of the Governor, Fort Yale, Sept. 12, 1858, *EHFRM*, 1; San Francisco *Alta California*, May 8; June 21; July 26, 1858.

43. In California, the mining tax was primarily used to harass Chinese and other non-white miners. London *Times*, Aug. 10, 14, 1858; June 3; Sept. 8, 1859; Douglas to Lytton, Sept. 9; Oct. 11, 1858, *PRABC*, 1:34, 38; San Francisco *Alta California*, Jan 23, 1855; May 20; Oct. 14, 1858; San Francisco *Bulletin*, April 28, 1858; Portland *Oregonian*, Jan. 30, 1858; Margaret A. Ormsby, *British Columbia: A History* (Vancouver: Macmillan of Canada, 1958), 147. On taxation of miners in California, see Rohrbough, *Days of Gold*, 228.

44. The governor's request for reinforcements from Admiral Robert Baynes, commander-in-chief of Her Majesty's Pacific squadron, was rejected. Douglas and Prevost worried that sailors would desert the *Satellite* for the mines. Douglas to Stanley, May 19; June 10; Aug. 19, 1858; to Prevost, June 14, 1858, *PRABC*, 1:11, 13, 25, 27; May 15, 21, 1858; to Baynes, May 12, 1858; Prevost to Douglas, May 18, 1858; to Baynes, June 7, 1858, all ADM 1/5696; San Francisco *Alta California*, June 6, 1858. Also see Gough, *Royal Navy and the Northwest Coast*, 134–36.

45. Douglas to Stanley, June 10, 19; July 1, 26, 1858, *PRABC*, I:13, 18–19, 22; to Smith, July 23, 1858; to Thomas Fraser, Nov. 16, 1858, B.226/b/15, HBCA; Gough, *Royal Navy and the Northwest Coast*, 135–36; San Francisco *Alta California*, June 6, 23; July 3, 1858; San Francisco *Bulletin*, June 19, 1858; London *Times*, Nov. 30, 1858.

46. Stevens to Cass, July 21, 1858, Stevens Papers; Portland *Oregonian*, June 19, 1858; Victoria *British Colonist*, Dec. 11, 1858; Jan. 15, 1859; San Francisco *Alta California*, June 6, 9, 26, 28, 1858; Steilacoom *Puget Sound Herald*, June 11, 1858; Walker to

Cass, June 18, 1858, Washington Territorial Papers; Douglas to Smith, July 23, 1858, B.226/b/15, HBCA; London *Times*, Nov. 30, 1858.

47. Douglas to Stanley, June 19; July 1, 1858; to Lytton, Sept. 9, 1858, *PRABC*, 1:18–19, 34–35; San Francisco *Alta California*, June 20, 23, 28; July 3, 1858; Richard Hicks to Douglas, Oct. 17, 1858, *EHFRM*, 4–5.

48. San Francisco *Alta California*, July 2, 9, 1858; Douglas to Stanley, July 26, 1858, *PRABC*, 1:22; Olympia *Pioneer and Democrat*, Aug. 20, 1858; C. O. Phillips to A. D. Merritt, Nov. 12, 1858, in Howay, ed., "Diary and Letters of Cyrus Olin Phillips," 154.

49. San Francisco *Alta California*, July 16, 1858; Douglas to Stanley, June 15; July 26, 1858; to Lytton, Sept. 9, 1858, *PRABC*, 1:15, 23, 25; Oct. 12, 1858, ADM 1/5721; to Fraser, Nov. 16, 1858; to Smith, June 9; July 23; Aug. 12, 1858; to Yale, July 3, 1858, B.226/b/15, 16, HBCA.

50. San Francisco *Alta California*, June 23; July 7, 10, 20, 23, 1858; London *Times*, Jan. 19, 1859; Victoria *British Colonist*, Dec. 11, 1858.

51. The H.B.C. also refused to take advantage of opportunities for land speculation, holding initial lot prices at $100. Douglas to Stanley, June 15, 1858; James Yates, et al. to Douglas, June 9, 1858, both *PRABC*, 1:15–16; *Victoria Gazette*, July 7, 1858; San Francisco *Alta California*, July 9, 12, 26, 1858; Bell to Thomson, Feb. 27, 1859, in Ireland, ed., "Gold-rush Days in Victoria," 241.

52. San Francisco *Alta California*, June 22; July 2, 1858; London *Times*, Aug. 27, 1858; Douglas to Stanley, June 15, 19; July 1, 26, 1858; to Lytton, Oct. 26; Nov. 30, 1858, *PRABC*, 1:16–18, 20, 22–23; 2:10, 40.

53. Douglas to Stanley, June 10, 1858; to Lytton, Oct. 11, 1858, *PRABC*, 1:14–15, 38; Oct. 12, 1858, ADM 1/5721; to Yale, Aug. 5, 10, 1858, HBCA; Address of the Governor, Fort Yale, Sept. 12, 1858, *EHFRM*, 1–2; San Francisco *Alta California*, May 23, 1858.

54. In exaggerated support of his claims regarding H.B.C. avarice, Isaac Stevens estimated the various fees to be worth, on the basis of full compliance, $2,400,000 a year. Douglas to Lytton, Oct. 12, 1858, ADM 1/5721; Sept. 9; Oct. 11, 26, 1858; to Newcastle, Nov. 14, 1861, *PRABC*, 1:34–35, 38; 2:9; 4:62; San Francisco *Alta California*, Sept. 3, 1858; Stevens to Cass, July 21, 1858, Stevens Papers.

55. Douglas to Smith, Dec. 28, 1857, B.226/b/15; to Yale, Dec. 26, 1857, B.113/c/1, HBCA; to Stanley, July 26, 1858; to Lytton, Oct. 26, 1858, *PRABC*, 1:23; 2:9–10; Oct. 12, 1858, ADM 1/5721; Hicks to Douglas, Nov. 12, 1858, *EHFRM*, 15; Richard C. Mayne to Richards, July 7, 1859, ADM 1/5744, PRO; San Francisco *Alta California*, Aug. 2; Sept. 14, 1858; Diary of Gold Discovery, June 1, 1858.

56. Some H.B.C. critics contended that Ainsworth actually discovered the route. San Francisco *Alta California*, Aug. 2, 9, 20; Oct. 23, 1858; Douglas to Stanley, July 26; Aug. 19, 1858; to Lytton, Oct. 26, 1858, *PRABC*, 1:23, 28; 2:9–10; to Smith, Aug. 4, 1858; to Donald McLean, July 24; Aug. 4, 1858; to Yale, July 30, 1858, B.226/b/15, 16; Aug. 5, 1858, B.113/c/1, HBCA.

57. Douglas to Lytton, Nov. 9, 30; Dec. 24, 1858; April 8, 1859, *PRABC*, 2:29, 39, 46; 3:1; San Francisco *Alta California*, Sept. 26; Oct. 5, 23; Dec. 2, 1858; London *Times*, June 3, 1859; Victoria *British Colonist*, Jan. 29; Feb. 19, 1859. Also see Reid, ed., "To the Fraser River Mines," 247–51.

58. Simpson to Dugald Mactavish, March 16, 1858, B.223/c/2, HBCA; Douglas to Stanley, June 10, 1858; Lytton to Douglas, July 16; Aug. 14; Sept. 2, 16, 1858, all *PRABC*, 1:14, 42, 47, 49, 61, 66.

59. Anticipating "remedial measures" on the part of Great Britain, the *Alta California* had for weeks urged American miners and merchants to acquiesce in H.B.C. exactions. Lytton to Douglas, July 1, 16, 31; Aug. 14, 1858, *PRABC*, 1:41–42, 46, 50; San Francisco *Alta California*, May 6; June 6, 11, 23; July 7, 1858.

60. Unification of Vancouver's Island and British Columbia made sense to many observers. The fact that the former had free trade and the latter did not, however, was a serious obstacle to union. Lytton to Douglas, July 16; Aug. 14; Sept. 2, 16, 1858; An Act to provide for the Government of British Columbia, Aug. 2, 1858; Instrument under the Royal Sign Manual, Sept. 2, 1858; Douglas to Lytton, Nov. 3, 1858, all *PRABC*, 1:1–2, 9–10, 43, 47, 56, 65: 2:19; Fraser to Joseph D. Pemberton, Nov. 25, 1858, B.226/c/1, HBCA; Jean Barman, *The West beyond the West: A History of British Columbia* (Toronto: University of Toronto Press, rev. ed., 1996), 69–70; Matthew Macfie, *Vancouver Island and British Columbia: Their History, Resources and Prospects* (London: Longman, Green, 1865), 95–97.

61. James Douglas waited until May 1859 to finally terminate his H.B.C. connection. Lytton to Douglas, July 16, 1858; Letters Patent, Sept. 2, 1858; Douglas to Lytton, Sept. 29; Oct. 4, 26, 27, 1858, all *PRABC*, 1:3–5, 35–36, 43; 2:1, 9, 17; to Simpson, Dec. 11, 1858; to Governor and Committee, Oct. 12, 1858; to McLean, April 23, 1859, B.226/b/15, 16; H. H. Berens to Douglas, Oct. 22, 1858, B.226/c/1; A. G. Dallas to Fraser, June 20; Aug. 8, 1859; to Yale, Feb. 16, 1859, B.226/b/19, all HBCA.

62. Instructions to James Douglas, Sept. 2, 1858; Orders of the Queen in Council, Sept. 2, 1858; Lytton to Douglas, Aug. 14; Sept. 2; Oct. 16; Dec. 16, 1858; Douglas to Lytton, Nov. 8, 1858, all *PRABC*, 1:5–9, 47–48, 61, 71; 2:25, 73.

63. Douglas to Fraser, Nov. 16, 1858, B.226/b/15, HBCA; to Lytton, Oct. 12, 1858, ADM 1/5721; Nov. 4, 8, 9, 27, 1858; Lytton to Douglas, July 31; Aug. 14; Sept. 2, 16; Oct. 16, 1858, all *PRABC*, 1:45, 47, 62, 66, 70; 2:21, 24–26, 37; Victoria *British Colonist*, Jan. 15, 29, 185; Frances M. Woodward, "The Influence of the Royal Engineers on the Development of British Columbia," *BCS*, 24(1974–75), 13–16, 36. On Begbie, see Sydney G. Pettit, "Judge Begbie in Action: The Establishment of Law and Preservation of Order in British Columbia," *BCHQ*, 11(1947), 113–48; Barman, *West beyond the West*, 77–78.

64. Langley purchasers made a required 10 percent down payment. Douglas to Lytton, Oct. 11, 12; Nov. 3, 8, 27, 29; Dec. 4, 14, 1858; May 12, 1859, *PRABC*, 1:38; 2:2, 20, 26, 34, 37, 41, 45; 3:11; C. H. Mason to Cass, Nov. 29, 1858, Washington Territorial Papers; Hicks to Douglas, Nov. 9, 12, 1858, *EHFRM*, 13; Victoria *British Colonist*, Dec. 27, 1858; Jan. 1, 1859; London *Times*, June 3, 1859; "The Navigation of the Fraser River, and Its Approaches," *Nautical Magazine*, 28(1859), 326.

65. Donald Walker, the H.B.C. trader at Fort Hope, estimated a population of 10,000 Indians on the Fraser River between the Gulf of Georgia and the mouth of the Thompson River. At the time of first white contact, 75,000 Indians, in the best scholarly estimate, lived in modern-day British Columbia. Declining primarily through disease to 26,000 by 1870, the number still represented approximately two-thirds of the total population. British Columbia was the only province to have a majority Indian population when it joined the Canadian federation. San Francisco *Alta California*,

June 21; Aug. 2, 11, 1858; Andrea Laforet and Annie York, *Spuzzum: Fraser Canyon Histories, 1808–1939* (Vancouver: University of British Columbia Press, 1998), 3–5; Olympia *Pioneer and Democrat*, Aug. 20, 1858; Matthew B. Begbie, "Journey to the Interior of British Columbia," *Journal of the Royal Geographical Society*, 31(1861), 243; R. L. Carlson, "The First British Columbians," in Hugh J. M. Johnston, *The Pacific Province: A History of British Columbia* (Vancouver: Douglas and McIntyre, 1996), 31; Sharon Meen, "Colonial Society and Economy," in Ibid., 112; Hugh Johnston, "Native People, Settlers and Sojourners, 1871–1916," in Ibid., 165. On the inherent problems of native demographics, see Robin Fisher, "Contact and Trade, 1774–1889," in Ibid., 61. Also see, for further details on Indian population and village locations, Cole Harris, "The Fraser Canyon Encountered," *BCS*, 94(1992), 8–15.

66. Richard Hicks reported that some of the Hill's Bar Indians possessed "thousands of dollars in gold." The Fort Langley salmon house, which normally packed 5,000 barrels of fish a year, closed when the Indians ceased supplying the facility. Douglas to Stanley, June 10, 1858, *PRABC*, 1:13; to Yale, July 24, 1858; John Work to McLean, April 19, 1859; to Fraser, April 25; May 10, 1859, B.226/b/16, 17, HBCA; San Francisco *Alta California*, June 20, 22; July 16, 23; Aug. 21, 1858; Olympia *Pioneer and Democrat*, May 14, 1858; San Francisco *Bulletin*, May 31, 1858. Also see Robin Fisher, *Contact and Conflict: Indian-European Relations in British Columbia, 1774–1890* (Vancouver: University of British Columbia Press, 1977), 100–1.

67. Douglas to Lytton, Sept. 9; Oct. 11; Nov. 5, 1858, *PRABC*, 1:34, 38–39; 2:23; John McLoughlin to Gov. and Com., Nov. 15, 1843, in E. E. Rich, ed., *The Letters of John McLoughlin from Fort Vancouver to the Governor and Committee, Second Series, 1839–44* (London: Champlain Society, 1943), 118; John Dunn, *History of the Oregon Territory and British North-American Fur Trade* (London: Edwards and Hughes, 1844), 81; San Francisco *Alta California*, July 9; Sept. 26, 1858; Olympia *Pioneer and Democrat*, Aug. 20, 1858.

68. A California merchant thought Amelia Douglas "an estimable person ... willing to give advice to those who ask it." For the contention that Douglas, concerned for social status, kept his wife in the background and tried to make his daughters into proper young Englishwomen, see Barman, *West beyond the West*, 46–47. San Francisco *Alta California*, June 20; July 19, 29; Aug. 2, 1858; Olympia *Pioneer and Democrat*, Aug. 20, 1858; Portland *Oregonian*, Aug. 14, 1858; Steilacoom *Puget Sound Herald*, May 14, 1858; San Francisco *Bulletin*, May 31, 1858; London *Times*, Nov. 30, 1858; Hicks to Douglas, Oct. 26, 1858, *EHFRM*, 9.

69. David Blaine to Parents, Dec. 6, 1853, Blaine Family Letters, UW; W. C. Talbot to Charles Foster, Sept. 4, 1853, Josiah Keller Papers, Western Americana Collection, Yale University Library; Olympia *Columbian*, Jan. 15, 1853; London *Times*, Dec. 1, 1858; San Francisco *Alta California*, July 23; Aug. 9, 21, 1858; Howay, ed., "Diary and Letters of Cyrus Olin Phillips," 155; Olympia *Pioneer and Democrat*, Aug. 20, 1858; S. Baxter to P. B. Cornwall, Dec. 13, 1875, Sehome Coal Company Records, Center for Pacific Northwest Studies, Western Washington University.

70. Portland *Oregonian*, Sept. 18, 1852; *Port Townsend Register*, March 28, 1860; Olympia *Columbian*, Jan. 15, 1853; Victor J. Farrar, ed., "Diary and Letters of Colonel and Mrs. I. N. Ebey," *WHQ*, 7(1916), 321; 8(1917), 132–33, 135; Catherine Blaine to Seraphina, Aug. 4, 1854; to ?, Nov. 23, 1854, Blaine Family Letters; San Francisco *Alta California*, Nov. 25, 1855; Feb. 23; April 4, 5, 1856; Sept. 8, 1857.

71.   "It has grown into a proverb," a Seattle newspaper remarked in an 1890 retrospective, "that no white man has ever been hung for the murder of an Indian." Edward Starling to Stevens, Dec. 4, 1853, Records of the Washington Superintendency of Indian Affairs, 1853–1874, M5, NA; Steilacoom *Puget Sound Herald*, Oct. 15, 1858; C. Blaine to ?, Oct. 30, 1854, Blaine Family Letters; Edmond S. Meany, ed., "Van Ogle's Memory of Pioneer Days," *WHQ*, 8(1922), 280–81; G. I. Rains to E. Townsend, Jan. 19, 1854, Pacific Division Records, U.S. Army Continental Commands, RG 393, NA; *Seattle Post-Intelligencer*, Feb. 6, 1890.

72.   Olympia *Pioneer and Democrat*, May 14, 1858; Steilacoom *Puget Sound Herald*, May 14, 1858; San Francisco *Bulletin*, May 31, 1858; San Francisco *Alta California*, June 6, 7, 9; July 9, 29, 1858.

73.   Olympia *Pioneer and Democrat*, May 14; Aug. 20, 1858; San Francisco *Alta California*, June 6, 20, 23; July 12, 1858; Portland *Oregonian*, Sept. 4, 1858.

74.   Fisher, *Contact and Conflict*, 100–1; Dorothy Blakey Smith, ed., "The Journal of Arthur Thomas Bushby, 1858–1859," *BCHQ*, 21(1957–58), 150; London *Times*, Dec. 1, 24, 25, 1858; Olympia *Pioneer and Democrat*, Aug. 20, 1858.

75.   Douglas to Stanley, June 15, 1858; to Lytton, Nov. 5, 1858, *PRABC*, 1:16; 2:23; Oct. 12, 1858, ADM 1/5721; to Smith, Aug. 27, 1858; to Yale, July 24, 1858, B.226/b/15, 16, HBCA; San Francisco *Alta California*, June 20; Aug. 19, 1858; London *Times*, Dec. 1, 24, 1858.

76.   San Francisco *Alta California*, Aug. 8; Sept. 2, 3, 7, 8, 26, 1858.

77.   Ibid., July 7; Aug. 2, 6, 9; Sept. 2, 1858; Hicks to Yale, Aug. 22, 1858, B.113/c/1; Douglas to Yale, July 27, 30, 1858, B.226/b/16, both HBCA; to Stanley, Aug. 27, 1858, *PRABC*, 1:29.

78.   Donald Fraser later reported that the two floating corpses were Frenchmen, killed for molesting Indian women. San Francisco *Alta California*, Sept. 3, 7, 8, 1858; *Victoria Gazette*, Aug. 27, 1858; Hicks to Yale, Aug. 22, 1858, B.113/c/1, HBCA; London *Times*, Dec. 25, 1858. Also see Fisher, *Contact and Conflict*, 99.

79.   Douglas to Stanley, Aug. 27, 1858, *PRABC*, 1:29; to McNeill, Aug. 27, 1858, B.226/b/16, HBCA; San Francisco *Alta California*, Sept. 8, 14, 17, 1858; *Victoria Gazette*, Aug. 27, 1858; London *Times*, Dec. 24, 25, 1858.

80.   Douglas to Smith, Aug. 12, 1858, B.226/b/15, HBCA; San Francisco *Alta California*, Aug. 12, 1858; Victoria *British Colonist*, May 17, 1860.

81.   Douglas to Smith, Aug. 12, 1858, B.226/b/15, HBCA; Oregon City *Oregon Argus*, July 31, 1858; San Francisco *Alta California*, Aug. 9, 19; Sept. 8, 27, 1858; Olympia *Pioneer and Democrat*, Aug. 20, 1858; Portland *Oregonian*, Aug. 14, 1858. Also see Sage, "Gold Colony of British Columbia," 353–55.

82.   Olympia *Pioneer and Democrat*, July 23, 30, 1858; Steilacoom *Puget Sound Herald*, Aug. 20, 27, 1858; San Francisco *Alta California*, Aug. 12, 21, 1858.

83.   Douglas to Stanley, July 26; Aug. 19, 1858, *PRABC*, 1:23, 27; to Smith, July 23; Aug. 12, 27, 1858, B.226/b/15, HBCA; to Lytton, Oct. 12, 1858, ADM 1/5721; Olympia *Pioneer and Democrat*, Aug. 20, 1858; San Francisco *Alta California*, Aug. 8, 9, 19; Sept. 9, 11, 1858; London *Times*, Dec. 24, 1858.

84.   San Francisco *Alta California*, Aug. 2, 10, 19, 21, 1858; Olympia *Pioneer and Democrat*, July 23, 1858.

85.   Douglas to Lytton, Sept. 9, 1858, *PRABC*, 1:34; Oct. 12, 1858, ADM 1/5721; San Francisco *Alta California*, Sept. 7–9, 11, 1858; London *Times*, Nov. 30, 1858.

86. San Francisco *Alta California*, Sept. 11, 26, 27; Oct. 2; Nov. 13, 1858; Hicks to Douglas, Oct. 16, 1858, *EHFRM*, 6; Douglas to Lytton, Nov. 9, 1858, *PRABC*, 2:27.
87. Hicks to Douglas, Oct. 26, 28; Nov. 9, 1858, *EHFRM*, 7–8, 10, 12; Douglas to Lytton, Nov. 9, 1858, *PRABC*, 2:27.
88. Hicks to Douglas, Oct. 26, 1858, *EHFRM*, 5–7; Douglas to Lytton, Nov. 9, 1858, *PRABC*, 2:27.
89. Hicks to Douglas, Oct. 26, 1858, *EHFRM*, 6–7; San Francisco *Alta California*, Aug. 19, 1858; London *Times*, Dec. 24, 1858.
90. Douglas to Lytton, Oct. 12, 1858, ADM 1/5721; Nov. 9, 1858, *PRABC*, 2:28; to Fraser, Nov. 16, 1858, B.226/b/15, HBCA; Hicks to Douglas, Oct. 26, 1858, *EHFRM*, 7–8.
91. Douglas to Lytton, Oct. 12, 1858, ADM 1/5721; Oct. 26; Nov. 9, 1858, *PRABC*, 2:9, 28; London *Times*, Dec. 24, 1858; San Francisco *Alta California*, Sept. 27, 1858.
92. Douglas to McLean, Jan. 18, 1859; to Fraser, Dec. 14, 1858, B.226/b/15, 16, HBCA; to Lytton, Nov. 30, 1858, *PRABC*, 2:39; Hicks to Douglas, Nov. 12, 1858, *EHFRM*, 15; San Francisco *Alta California*, Aug. 2; Nov. 13; Dec. 31, 1858.
93. Douglas to Lytton, Dec. 24, 1858, *PRABC*, 2:46–47; San Francisco *Alta California*, Dec. 12, 31, 1858.
94. Robert Frost, "Fraser River Gold Rush Adventures," *WHQ*, 22(1931), 209; Douglas to Lytton, Oct. 12, 1858, ADM 1/5721; to Fraser, Dec. 27, 1858, B.226/b/15; Donald Walker to Yale, Oct. 10, 1858, B.113/c/1, both HBCA; Reid, ed., "To the Fraser River Mines," 251.
95. Bell to Thomson, Feb. 27, 1859, in Ireland, ed., "Gold-rush Days in Victoria," 235; Douglas to Lytton, Dec. 24, 1858, *PRABC*, 2:46; San Francisco *Alta California*, Oct. 1, 2, 23, 1858; Oregon City *Oregon Argus*, Dec. 25, 1858; London *Times*, Feb. 17, 1859.
96. Douglas to Lytton, Nov. 9, 1858, *PRABC*, 2:29–30; Steilacoom *Puget Sound Herald*, Oct. 1, 1858; Portland *Oregonian*, Oct. 9, 23, 1858.
97. Many of the returnees demanded that Governor Douglas refund their mining license fees, since they had found no gold. San Francisco *Alta California*, Oct. 1, 2, 14, 16, 1858.
98. Ibid., Sept. 26; Oct. 16, 23, 26; Nov. 3, 23, 29, 1858; Douglas to Lytton, Dec. 14, 1858, *PRABC*, 2:45.
99. San Francisco *Alta California*, Nov. 23, 1858; Roger W. Lotchin, *San Francisco, 1846–1856: From Hamlet to City* (New York: Oxford University Press, 1974), 253, 260; Arthur Quinn, *The Rivals: William Gwin, David Broderick, and the Birth of California* (New York: Crown Publishers, 1994), 194; Robie L. Reid, "John Nugent: The Impertinent Envoy," *BCHQ*, 8(1944), 59–60; Oregon City *Oregon Argus*, Sept. 11, 1858; Salem *Oregon Statesman*, Sept. 18, 1858; Napier to Douglas, July 29, 1858, PABC.
100. Nugent also was offended by the governor's refusal to fire a cannon salute in his honor. Nugent to Douglas, Oct. 6; Nov. 12, 1858, PABC; to Cass, Jan. 8, 1859, Washington Territorial Papers; San Francisco *Alta California*, Sept. 27; Oct. 13, 1858; Victoria *British Colonist*, Jan. 22; Feb. 12, 1859; Steilacoom *Puget Sound Herald*, Nov. 26, 1858; Douglas to Lytton, Jan. 6, 1859, *PRABC*, 2:52. The agent's Victoria speech is reprinted in Reid, "Nugent," 74–76.
101. The Douglas figure, which he regarded as an understatement, does not include late shipments, such as the 10,000 ounces exported to San Francisco aboard the *Pacific* in

December. The governor passed along a clipping from one of the San Francisco papers, reporting the receipt of $511,000 at the U.S. mint in that city. San Francisco *Alta California*, Aug. 19; Sept. 9, 1858; Donald Sage, "Gold Rush Days on the Fraser River," *PNQ*, 44(1953), 165; Douglas to Lytton, Nov. 30; Dec. 14, 1858, *PRABC*, 2:40, 45; to Simpson, Dec. 11, 1858, B.226/b/15, HBCA; Paul, *California Gold*, 345. For another contemporary estimate, $705,000 through October, see Alfred Wadddington, *The Fraser River Mines Vindicated, or, The History of Four Months* (Victoria: P. DeGarro, 1858), 44.

102. San Francisco *Alta California*, Sept. 7, 14, 27; Oct. 5, 23, 1858.

103. Rodman Paul, the dean of western mining historians, dismissed Fraser as "10 per cent truth and 90 per cent humbug." A more recent survey of gold mine history concludes that "the rush had fallen flat as a flapjack" by the fall of 1858. London *Times*, Aug. 3; Dec. 1, 1858; San Francisco *Alta California*, Oct. 26, 28; Nov. 24, 30, 1858; Douglas to Simpson, Oct. 26, 1858, .226/b/15; Fraser to Douglas, Aug. 20, 1858, B.226/c/1, both HBCA; Steilacoom *Puget Sound Herald*, Nov. 12, 26; Dec. 31, 1858; Paul, *California Gold*, 178; Paula Mitchell Marks, *Precious Dust: The American Gold Rush Era: 1848–1900* (New York: William Morrow, 1994), 32.

Chapter Five
A Gradually Augmenting Yield

1. April 16, 1859.

2. James Douglas to E. B. Lytton, Dec. 14, 1858; Jan. 21, 1859, *PRABC*, 2:45, 67; London *Times*, Feb. 17, 1859; Portland *Oregonian*, Jan. 8; Feb. 19, 1859; San Francisco *Alta California*, Jan. 11, 1859; Matthew B. Begbie to Douglas, Feb. 3, 1859, *EHFRM*, 40–41.

3. John Work to Ovid Allard, March 31, 1859, B.226/b/17, HBCA; London *Times*, Feb. 3, 1859; Begbie to Douglas, Jan. 14; Feb. 3, 1859; Chartres Brew to R. C. Moody, Feb. 12, 20, 26; March 5, 1859, all *EHFRM*, 25–26, 33–34, 69–70, 80, 85, 87; Victoria *British Colonist*, Jan. 8, 1859; Dorothy Blakey Smith, ed., "The Journal of Arthur Thomas Bushby, 1858–1859," *BCHQ*, 21(1957–58), 127; Portland *Oregonian*, Jan. 8, 1859.

4. London *Times*, Feb. 17, 1859; Douglas to Lytton, Dec. 24, 1858, *PRABC*, 2:46; Brew to Moody, Jan. 30, 1859, *EHFRM*, 67; San Francisco *Alta California*, Jan. 11; Feb. 24, 1859; Work to James Murray Yale, Feb. 13, 1859, B.113/c/1, HBCA; Olympia *Pioneer and Democrat*, Feb. 24, 1859.

5. Brew to Moody, Jan. 30, 1859, *EHFRM*, 67; Douglas to Lytton, Nov. 30, 1858; Jan. 21; March 10, 1859, *PRABC*, 2:39, 57–58, 67; to Thomas Fraser, Dec. 14, 1858; Jan. 22, 1859, B.226/b/15, HBCA; Victoria *British Colonist*, Jan. 8; March 26, 1859; San Francisco *Alta California*, Dec. 31, 1858; May 18, 19, 1859; London *Times*, Feb. 17; June 3, 28, 1859.

6. Victoria *British Colonist*, Dec. 27, 1858; London *Times*, Jan. 19; Feb. 17, 1859; Smith, ed., "Journal of Arthur Thomas Bushby," 120; San Francisco *Alta California*, May 1, 1859.

7. Smith, ed., "Journal of Arthur Thomas Bushby," 127, 148–49; Victoria *British Colonist*, March 12; April 30, 1859; London *Times*, Dec. 24, 25, 1858.

8. Smith, ed., "Journal of Arthur Thomas Bushby," 127; Richard Hicks to Douglas, Oct. 17; Nov. 9, 12, 1858; Wm. H. Bevis to Douglas, Jan. 1, 1859; Brew to Douglas, Jan. 12, 1859; to Moody, Feb. 20, 1859, all *EHFRM*, 3–4, 13–14, 23–24, 64–65, 78; Victoria *British Colonist*, Dec. 27, 1858; Jan. 29; Feb. 26, 1859; San Francisco *Alta California*, May 30, 1859.

9. London *Times*, Dec. 24, 25, 1858; Victoria *British Colonist*, Jan. 8, 1859; Begbie to Douglas, Feb. 3, 1859; Hicks to Douglas, Oct. 28, 1858, both *EHFRM*, 10–11, 38–38; San Francisco *Alta California*, July 15; Sept. 26, 1858. On Ned McGowan's California activities, which included office-holding, ownership of a house of prostitution, and allegations of bank robbery, see Roger W. Lotchin, *San Francisco, 1846–1856: From Hamlet to City* (New York: Oxford University Press, 1974), 186, 220; Arthur Quinn, *The Rivals: William Gwin, David Broderick, and the Birth of California* (New York: Crown Publishers, 1994), 148, 150–51, 167–68, 182.

10. Lytton to Douglas, July 31; Aug. 14, 1858; Douglas to Duke of Newcastle, Oct. 18, 1859; to Lytton, Oct. 27, 1858; May 23, 1859, all *PRABC*, 1:45, 49; 2:17; 3:12, 67; Richard C. Mayne to George Henry Richards, July 7, 1859, ADM 1/5744, PRO; "Letter from Charles Major, dated Fort Hope, Sept. 20, 1859," *BCHQ*, 5(1941), 229.

11. Victoria *British Colonist*, Jan. 29; March 19; May 20; June 1, 22; July 22, 1859; Matthew B. Begbie, "Journey into the Interior of British Columbia," *Journal of the Royal Geographical Society*, 31(1861), 243; Smith, ed., "Journal of Arthur Thomas Bushby," 127; Hicks to Douglas, Nov. 9, 1858; April 30, 1859; Jas. H. Ross to C. Standish, May 9, 1859, all *EHFRM*, 12, 18–19, 58–59; Douglas to Lytton, Jan. 8, 1859, *PRABC*, 2:55–56.

12. Victoria *British Colonist*, Feb. 5; March 26, 1859; Begbie to Douglas, Jan. 14; Feb. 3; March 19, 1859; Brew to W. A. G. Young, April 16, 23, 1859; to Moody, Feb. 19, 1859; Hicks to Douglas, Oct. 26, 28; Nov. 12, 17, 24, 1859, all *EHFRM*, 6, 10–11, 14–16, 26–27, 37–38, 51, 70–71, 108, 110–11; Douglas to Lytton, Jan. 8, 1859, *PRABC*, 2:55.

13. Brew to Douglas, Nov. 11, 1858; Begbie to Douglas, Jan. 14; Feb. 3, 1859, all *EHFRM*, 25, 34–36, 60–61; Lytton to Douglas, Oct. 16, 1858; Douglas to Lytton, Jan. 8, 1859, both *PRABC*, 1:71; 2:55; Victoria *British Colonist*, Jan. 8, 1859. Also see, for details on the Whannell-Perrier "war," Sydney G. Pettit, "Judge Begbie in Action: The Establishment of Law and Preservation of Order in British Columbia," *BCHQ*, 11(1947), 138–42.

14. Moody to Douglas, Jan. 17, 1859, ADM 1/5721, PRO; Begbie to Douglas, Jan. 14, 18; Feb. 3, 1859; Resolution of a Meeting of Miners, Jan. ? 1859, all *EHFRM*, 25, 28–33; Victoria *British Colonist*, Feb. 5, 1859.

15. Begbie to Douglas, Feb. 3, 1859; Brew to Moody, Feb. 20, 26; March 5, 1859, all *EHFRM*, 36–37, 78, 84–86; Victoria *British Colonist*, Jan. 29, 1859; Douglas to Lytton, Jan. 8, 1859, *PRABC*, 2:55–56; Portland *Oregonian*, May 7, 1859.

16. Douglas to Lytton, July 26; Oct. 26; Nov. 9, 30; Dec. 24, 27, 1858; April 8, 11; May 8; June 8, 1859, *PRABC*, 1:23; 2:10, 28–29, 39, 46, 49; 3:2, 4–5, 10, 17; Victoria *British Colonist*, April 16, 1859.

17. Douglas to Lytton, Oct. 26, 1858; Jan. 15; July 2, 1859, *PRABC*, 2:9–10, 56–57; 3:26–28; Begbie to Douglas, Feb. 3, 1859, *EHFRM*, 41.

18. Douglas to Lytton, Nov. 4; Dec. 27, 1858; April 8, 1859; Lytton to Douglas, Dec. 16, 1858, all *PRABC*, 2:20–21, 49, 73; 3:1; London *Times*, June 3, 28; July 26, 1859; Victoria *British Colonist*, June 6, 1859.

19. Prepayment of the first $5 was abandoned at the instruction of the colonial office in October 1858. Lytton to Douglas, Dec. 16, 1858; Douglas to Lytton, Sept. 30; Nov. 9; Dec. 14, 30, 1858, all *PRABC*, 1:37; 2:28, 45, 51, 73; London *Times*, June 3; July 26, 1859; Hicks to Douglas, Oct. 17, 26; Nov. 9, 1858; Brew to Moody, March 5, 1859; to Young, April 2, 9, 23, 30, 1859, all *EHFRM*, 4–5, 8–9, 12, 87, 93–95, 97–100, 111, 114–17; San Francisco *Alta California*, May 13, 1859.

20. The name was sometimes spelled "Queensborough." London *Times*, June 3, 1859; Douglas to Lytton, Dec. 14, 1858; Feb. 4, 5; April 8, 1859; Moody to Douglas, Jan. 28, 1859; Lytton to Douglas, Feb. 11, 1859, all *PRABC*, 2:45, 59–61, 80; 3:1; San Francisco *Alta California*, May 25, 1859.

21. Douglas to Lytton, April 8; June 6; Aug. 17, 1859, *PRABC*, 3:2, 16, 39; Victoria *British Colonist*, Feb. 5, 19; April 23; May 20; June 1, 3, 1859; John B. Good Reminiscences, 38, BL; San Francisco *Alta California*, June 11, 1859; London *Times*, July 26, 1859. Also see Dorothy Blakey Smith, "The First Capital of British Columbia: Langley or New Westminster?" *BCHQ*, 21(1957–58), 15–50.

22. Brew to Young, April 2, 1859; William Geo. Cox to Brew, April 6, 1859, both *EHFRM*, 97, 101; Douglas to Lytton, April 25, 1859, *PRABC*, 3:9; Work to Donald McLean, April 19, 1859; to Fraser, April 25; May 10, 1859, B.226/b/17, HBCA.

23. Douglas to Lytton, June 8, 1859, *PRABC*, 3:17; Contract for cutting and clearing a line of road, June 17, 1859, PABC; London *Times*, Sept. 8, 1859; San Francisco *Alta California*, May 10, 1859; Brew to Young, March 26; April 2, 1859; Cox to Brew, April 6, 1859, all *EHFRM*, 95, 98, 100, 102; Mayne to Richards, July 7, 1859, ADM 1/5744; Frances M. Woodward, "The Influence of the Royal Engineers on the Development of British Columbia," *BCS*, 24(1974–75), 17–19.

24. Victoria *British Colonist*, March 26; May 16, 1859; Douglas to Lytton, May 8, 1859; Begbie to Douglas, April 25, 1859, both *PRABC*, 3:10, 18; Brew to Young, April 23, 1859, *EHFRM*, 109; Mayne to Richards, July 7, 1859, ADM 1/5744; San Francisco *Alta California*, May 27, 1859.

25. Work to Fraser, March 22, 1859; to Yale, April 13, 1859, B.226/b/17, HBCA; San Francisco *Alta California*, Jan. 11; Feb. 16; May 1, 3, 7, 1859; Victoria *British Colonist*, Feb. 12, 1859; Brew to Moody, March 5, 1859, *EHFRM*, 87.

26. The *Alta California*, which had largely ignored developments in the north since December, resumed detailed coverage in May 1859. London *Times*, June 3, 28, 1859; San Francisco *Alta California*, Oct. 26, 1858; Victoria *British Colonist*, April 9, 1859; Brew to Young, March 19, 1859, *EHFRM*, 94; Douglas to Lytton, July 4, 1859, *PRABC*, 3:28; Smith, ed., "Journal of Arthur Thomas Bushby," 152, 157, 159.

27. Donald Fraser complained of having to pay $40 a month in order to retain his servant, "a man who knows nothing in particular ... [and] who can do nothing well." Brew to Moody, March 5, 26, 1859, *EHFRM*, 87, 95; London *Times*, June 3, 1859; Victoria *British Colonist*, March 12, 1859; Douglas to Lytton, April 12, 1859, *PRABC*, 3:6; Work to Fraser, March 31, 1859, B.226/b/17, HBCA.

28. San Francisco *Alta California*, May 10, 16, 27, 1859; Victoria *British Colonist*, March 26, 1859; Begbie to Douglas, March 19, 1859; Brew to Young, April 9, 1859, both *EHFRM*, 52, 100.

29. Douglas to Lytton, March 10; April 12, 1859, *PRABC*, 2:67; 3:6; San Francisco *Alta California*, May 27; July 2, 1859; Portland *Oregonian*, July 23, 30; Aug. 27, 1859; Hicks to Douglas, April 5, 1859, *EHFRM*, 18. For details about mining-era trail

pioneering and Indian campaigns in central Washington Territory east of the Cascades, see H. Dean Guie, *Bugles in the Valley: Garnett's Fort Simcoe* (Portland: Oregon Historical Society, 1977), 111–23; Ron Anglin, *Forgotten Trails: Historical Sources of the Columbia's Big Bend Country*, ed. and with contributions by Glen W. Lindeman (Pullman: Washington State University Press, 1995), 125–70.

30. Begbie to Douglas, April 25, 1859, *PRABC*, 3:20–21; San Francisco *Alta California*, May 16; July 2, 1859; Smith, ed., "Journal of Arthur Thomas Bushby," 155. For the traditional version, holding that the Fountain was named after a natural feature, see G. P. V. and Helen B. Akrigg, *British Columbia Place Names* (Vancouver: University of British Columbia Press, 3rd ed., 1997), 86.

31. San Francisco *Alta California*, May 15, 1859; London *Times*, June 28, 1859; Victoria *British Colonist*, March 26, 1859; Hicks to Douglas, April 5, 1859, *EHFRM*, 17.

32. San Francisco *Alta California*, May 18, 27, 1859; Victoria *British Colonist*, April 9; May 16; June 6, 1859; Brew to Young, April 23, 1859, *EHFRM*, 115; Begbie to Douglas, April 25, 1859, *PRABC*, 3:19.

33. Brew to Young, April 23, 1859, *EHFRM*, 112; Douglas to Lytton, June 8, 1859, *PRABC*, 3:17; San Francisco *Alta California*, May 25, 27, 1859; Victoria *British Colonist*, May 7, 1859.

34. Douglas to Lytton, March 25, 1859, *PRABC*, 2:70; Work to Fraser, March 31; July 19, 1859, B.226/b/17, 20, HBCA; London *Times*, Sept. 8, 1859.

35. Douglas to Lytton, June 8; July 2, 1859, *PRABC*, 3:16–17, 28; London *Times*, June 28; July 26, 1859; Work to Fraser, May 25; June 8, 1859, B.226/b/17, HBCA.

36. Victoria *British Colonist*, May 16, 27, 1859; "Letter from Charles Major," 229–30; San Francisco *Alta California*, May 16, 27, 30, 1859.

37. San Francisco *Alta California*, June 11, 15; July 2, 1859; Victoria *British Colonist*, May 23, 27; June 20, 1859; London *Times*, July 26, 1859; Work to Fraser, May 25, 1859, B.226/b/17, HBCA.

38. London *Times*, July 26; Sept. 28, 1859; San Francisco *Alta California*, May 25; June 11, 1859; Douglas to Lytton, April 12; June 8, 1859, *PRABC*, 3:7, 17; Victoria *British Colonist*, May 20; June 6; July 11, 1859; Olympia *Pioneer and Democrat*, July 15, 1859.

39. San Francisco *Alta California*, May 30, 31; June 15; July 2, 1859.

40. Victoria *British Colonist*, July 13, 1859.

41. Ibid., July 27, 1859; W. S. Harney to S. Cooper, Aug. 29, 1859; to Assistant Adjutant General, July 19, 1859, Department of Oregon Records, U.S. Army Continental Commands, RG 393, NA; Work to Fraser, June 21, 1859; A. G. Dallas to Fraser, Aug. 24, 1859, B.226/b/19, 20, HBCA. For complete details on the San Juan affair, see Barry M. Gough, *The Royal Navy and the Northwest Coast of North America, 1810–1914: A Study of British Maritime Ascendancy* (Vancouver: University of British Columbia Press, 1971), chapt. 7.

42. Olympia *Pioneer and Democrat*, Aug. 19, 1859; Steilacoom *Puget Sound Herald*, July 29; Aug. 5, 19, 1859; Victoria *British Colonist*, Aug. 1, 3, 5, 1859; Work to Fraser, Aug. 8, 1859, B.226/b/20, HBCA; London *Times*, Jan. 30, 1860.

43. Douglas to Lytton, July 2, 1859, *PRABC*, 3:26.

Chapter Six
Becoming a Business

1. To Duke of Newcastle, June 6, 1860, *PRABC*, 4:12.
2. Although General Harney was personally disgraced, the new American army commander in the region, Colonel George Wright, endorsed his forward strategy against the northern Indians. San Francisco *Alta California*, Aug. 27, 1859; Steilacoom *Puget Sound Herald*, Oct. 28, 1859; George Wright to L. Thomas, July 28; Aug. 28; Sept. 20, 1860, Department of Oregon Records, U.S. Army Continental Commands, RG 393, NA; A. G. Dallas to James Douglas, Aug. 5, 1859, B.226/b/19, HBCA; Douglas to E. B. Lytton, Aug. 23, 1859, *PRABC*, 3:49; Victoria *British Colonist*, Feb. 5; Aug. 1860.
3. London *Times*, Sept. 8, 1859; John Work to Thomas Fraser, July 5, 1859 B.226/b/20, HBCA; Victoria *British Colonist*, Aug. 18, 1860; San Francisco *Alta California*, Sept. 20, 1859.
4. Portland *Oregonian*, Nov. 12, 1859; Victoria *British Colonist*, July 29; Oct. 17, 1859; Feb. 5, 1860.
5. Victoria *British Colonist*, Aug. 29, 1859; March 13, 1860; Douglas to Lytton, July 4, 1859; to Newcastle, Oct. 18, 1859, *PRABC*, 3:29, 66; Work to Fraser, Aug. 8, 1859, B.226/b/20, HBCA.
6. Douglas to Lytton, July 4, 1859; to Newcastle, Oct. 18, 1859, *PRABC*, 3:29, 66–67; San Francisco *Alta California*, Aug. 27, 1859; Victoria *British Colonist*, July 4, 15; Aug. 8, 1859; Work to Fraser, Aug. 8, 1859, B.226/b/20, HBCA.
7. London *Times*, Sept. 8, 1859; Victoria *British Colonist*, July 4, 1859; Work to Fraser, Nov. 11, 1859, B.226/b/20, HBCA; Douglas to Newcastle, Oct. 18, 1859, *PRABC*, 3:66.
8. The Quesnel River was named after one of Simon Fraser's traveling companions. London *Times*, Sept. 8, 1859; Jan. 30, 1860; Victoria *British Colonist*, Aug. 1, 8, 15, 24, 1859; San Francisco *Alta California*, Aug. 27, 1859; Douglas to Newcastle, Oct. 18, 1859; Jan. 24, 1860, *PRABC*, 3:66, 92–93; G. P. V. and Helen B. Akrigg, *British Columbia Place Names* (Vancouver: University of British Columbia Press, 3rd ed., 1997), 221.
9. San Francisco *Alta California*, Dec. 17, 1859; Douglas to Newcastle, Oct. 18, 1859, *PRABC*, 3:67; Work to Fraser, Oct. 26; Nov. 11, 26, 1859, B.226/b/20, HBCA; Victoria *British Colonist*, Oct. 21, 1859.
10. The H.B.C. supplemented Governor Douglas's official salary, which the home government declined to increase, with a private and presumably secret pension. Newcastle to Douglas, Sept. 5, 1859; Douglas to Lytton, July 2, 1859, both *PRABC*, 3:27, 100; Victoria *British Colonist*, Aug. 29, 31, 1859; Feb. 25; Dec. 12, 1860; Jan. 19, 1861; San Francisco *Alta California*, Jan. 23; Feb. 18, 1860; Dallas to Fraser, Sept. 13, 14, 1859, B.226/b/19, HBCA.
11. In a rare departure from its self-reliance dictum, the colonial office advanced money for lighthouse construction on the British side of the Strait of Juan de Fuca. Apparently miscomprehending previous correspondence on the subject, the Duke of Newcastle thought the 1858 pack trail expenditures more than sufficient and expressed muted displeasure over the new spending; the road was officially completed in the summer of 1860. Douglas to Lytton, July 2; Aug. 23, 1859; to Newcastle, Oct. 18, 1859; April 23, 1860; Newcastle to Douglas, Oct. 28, 1859, all *PRABC*, 3:27–28,

49, 68, 105; 4:4–5; Victoria *British Colonist*, Sept. 30, 1859; Feb. 14; April 21; July 24, 26, 1860; San Francisco *Alta California*, Dec. 17, 1859; London *Times*, Sept. 8, 1859.

12. The Goldfields Act was modified in January 1860 to take into account the requirements of miners working "bench diggings" located away from streams. Rules and Regulations for the Working of Gold Mines, n.d.; Douglas to Newcastle, Oct. 18, 1859; May 23, 31; Aug. 4; Oct. 9, 1860, all *PRABC*, 3:63–65, 67–68; 4:6–8, 14, 22; London *Times*, Nov. 1, 1859; March 15, 1860.

13. Douglas to Newcastle, Oct. 25, 1860, *PRABC*, 4:30–31; Victoria *British Colonist*, Aug. 17, 1860; London *Times*, Jan. 30, 1860; Steilacoom *Puget Sound Herald*, April 29, 1859; Feb. 24; June 6; Nov. 9, 1860; San Francisco *Alta California*, Feb. 23, 1860.

14. Victoria *British Colonist*, Jan. 24; Feb. 5, 1860; San Francisco *Alta California*, Jan. 14, 1860; Douglas to Newcastle, April 23, 1860, *PRABC*, 4:4.

15. San Francisco *Alta California*, Jan. 14, 1860; W. F. Tolmie to George Simpson, Jan. 8, 1860, B.226/b/20, HBCA; Victoria *British Colonist*, Jan. 28; Aug. 31; Dec. 21, 1860.

16. The first direct overland migrants from the eastern United States, a party of Minnesotans, reached British Columbia in the fall of 1859. Victoria *British Colonist*, Sept. 28, 1859; May 8; July 10, 1860; San Francisco *Alta California*, March 19, 1860; Douglas to Newcastle, Oct. 18, 1859; Jan. 24; April 23; July 6, 1860, *PRABC*, 3:66, 92–93; 4:5, 12; Henry M. Ball to Colonial Secretary of British Columbia, May 12, 1860, PABC; London *Times*, June 28, 1859.

17. Douglas to Newcastle, Feb. 28, 1861, *PRABC*, 4:45; Victoria *British Colonist*, Aug. 8, 1859; April 28; May 22; July 26; Aug. 3; Sept. 6, 12, 1860.

18. The usual uncertainties prevailed as to the actual end of winter; as indicated by a miner's report in late January 1860; "the weather has moderated during the past week from rain and snow to storm and blow." Douglas to Newcastle, April 23; July 6; Oct. 25, 1860, *PRABC*, 4:5, 12, 27; Victoria *British Colonist*, Feb. 25; March 13; April 7; May 1, 22; Aug. 31, 1860; London *Times*, March 15, 1860; San Francisco *Alta California*, Jan. 29, 1860.

19. "I have adopted the popular and more convenient orthography of the word," Governor Douglas reported regarding the name Cariboo, "though properly it should be written 'Cariboeuf' or Rein Deer, the country having been so named from its being a favourite haunt of that species of the deer." The Quesnel and Cariboo districts also were prime beaver regions, as dry diggings operators discovered to their dismay. The creatures, one claim holder wrote, "dam ditches and turn the water out in the night, and the miners damn the Beavers and turn it in again the next day." Douglas to Newcastle, Sept. 16; Oct. 24, 1861, *PRABC*, 4:57, 59; Victoria *British Colonist*, Sept. 11, 14; Dec. 15, 19, 1860.

20. Douglas to Newcastle, June 4; July 16; Sept. 16; Oct. 24, 1861, *PRABC*, 4:53, 56–57, 59, 61.

21. Douglas to Newcastle, Nov. 21, 1859; April 23; June 4; Aug. 16, 1860, *PRABC*, 3:71; 4:5, 10, 20; Work to Fraser, Jan. 27, 1860, B.226/b/20, HBCA; Portland *Oregonian*, Oct. 29; Dec. 3, 1859.

22. Victoria *British Colonist*, July 13; Aug. 7; Dec. 13, 28, 1860; Douglas to Newcastle, Aug. 16; Oct. 8, 25, 1860, *PRABC*, 4:20, 29.

23. With no public funds available for additional projects, Governor Douglas addressed the Fraser River disadvantages by urging Fort Hope merchants to open a road to the

Similkameen River, and asked Fort Yale interests to substantially improve links with the upper country. Acquiring a steamer designed specifically for local river conditions, the Yale people inaugurated the first regular service between tidewater and their community. Victoria *British Colonist*, Feb. 25; April 21; July 13; Aug. 23, 29, 31; Nov. 30, 1860; Douglas to Newcastle, June 5; July 6; Oct. 9, 25, 1860; J. F. Allison to P. O. O'Reilly, July 27, 1860, all *PRABC*, 4:9–14, 22, 28, 30; Tolmie to E. Huggins, March 15, 1860, B.226/b/21, HBCA.

24. Douglas to Newcastle, Oct. 8, 25, 1860, *PRABC*, 4:21, 30; Victoria *British Colonist*, Dec. 13, 28, 1860; Jan. 3, 1861.

25. F. W. Howay, *British Columbia: The Making of a Province* (Toronto: Ryerson Press, 1928), 136; Matthew Macfie, *Vancouver Island and British Columbia: Their History, Resources, and Prospects* (London: Longman, Green, 1865), 109.

26. Willard E. Ireland, "First Impressions: Letter of Colonel Richard Clement Moody, R.E., to Arthur Blackwood, February 1, 1859," *BCHQ*, 15(1951), 97–103, 106.

Sources

Archives and Repositories

Bancroft Library (University of California, Berkeley)
Center for Pacific Northwest Studies (Western Washington University, Bellingham)
Federal Records Center (Seattle)
Hudson's Bay Company Archives (Provincial Archives of Manitoba)
Huntington Library (California)
National Archives (U.S.)
Oregon Historical Society (Portland)
Public Archives of British Columbia
Public Record Office (U.S.)
University of British Columbia (Vancouver)
University of Washington (Seattle)
Washington State Historical Society (Tacoma)
Washington Territorial Papers (U.S. State Department)

Newspapers

London *Times*
New York Times
Olympia *Columbian*
Olympia *Pacific Tribune*
Olympia *Pioneer and Democrat*
Olympia *Washington Pioneer*
Olympia *Washington Standard*
Oregon City *Oregon Argus*
Oregon City *Oregon Spectator*
Portland *Oregonian*
Salem *Oregon Statesman*
San Francisco *Alta California*
San Francisco *Bulletin*
San Francisco *Herald*
Seattle Post-Intelligencer
Steilacoom *Puget Sound Herald*
Victoria *British Colonist*
Victoria *Victoria Gazette*
Whatcom *Northern Light*

Journals, Magazines, and Published Documents

Bagley, Clarence B. "Attitude of the Hudson's Bay Company during the Indian War of 1855–1856," *Washington Historical Quarterly*, 8(1917).
Begbie, Matthew B. "Journey to the Interior of British Columbia," *Journal of the Royal Geographical Society*, 31(1861).

Careless, J. M. S. "The Lowe Brothers, 1852–70: A Study in Business Relations on the North Pacific Coast," *BC Studies*, 2(1969).

Carey, Charles Henry, ed. "Diary of Reverend George Gary," *Oregon Historical Quarterly*, 24(1923).

"The Census of Vancouver Island, 1855," *British Columbia Historical Quarterly*, 4(1940).

Coleman, Edward T. "Mountaineering on the Pacific," *Harper's New Monthly Magazine*, 39(1869).

Copies of Correspondence between the Chairman of the Hudson's Bay Company and the Secretary of State for the Colonies, Relative to the Colonization of Vancouver's Island, House of Commons, 10 August 1848.

Copies of Dispatches and other Papers Relative to Vancouver's Island, House of Commons, 7 March 1849.

Copies or Extracts of Correspondence Relative to the Discovery of Gold at Queen Charlotte's Island, House of Commons Command Paper 788.

"Defending Puget Sound Against the Northern Indians," *Pacific Northwest Quarterly*, 36(1945).

"The Discovery of Hill's Bar in 1858," *British Columbia Historical Quarterly*, 3(1939).

Farrar, Victor J., ed. "Diary and Letters of Colonel and Mrs. I. N. Ebey," *Washington Historical Quarterly*, 7(1916), 8(1917).

_____, ed. "The Nisqually Journal," *Washington Historical Quarterly*, 10(1919), 11(1920).

Fisher, Robin. "Indian Warfare and Two Frontiers: A Comparison of British Columbia and Washington Territory during the Early Years of Settlement," *Pacific Historical Review*, 50(1981).

"Five Letters of Charles Ross," *British Columbia Historical Quarterly*, 7(1943).

Frost, Robert. "Fraser River Gold Rush Adventures," *Washington Historical Quarterly*, 22(1931).

Galbraith, John S. "The Early History of the Puget's Sound Agricultural Company, 1838–43," *Oregon Historical Quarterly*, 55(1954).

Gough, Barry M. "Sir James Douglas as Seen by His Contemporaries: A Preliminary List," *BC Studies*, 44(1979–80).

Grant, W. Colquhoun. "Description of Vancouver Island," *Journal of the Royal Geographical Society*, 27(1857).

Hacking, Norman R. "'Steamboat 'Round the Bend': American Steamers on the Fraser River in 1858," *British Columbia Historical Quarterly*, 8(1944).

Harris, Cole. "The Fraser Canyon Encountered," *BC Studies*, 94(1992).

Hendrickson, James E. "Two Letters from Walter Colquhoun Grant," *BC Studies*, 26(1975).

Howay, F. W. "The Negro Immigration to Vancouver Island in 1858," *British Columbia Historical Quarterly*, 3(1939).

_____, ed. "To the Fraser River! The Diary and Letters of Cyrus Olin Phillips, 1858–1859," *California Historical Society Quarterly*, 11(1932).

Ireland, Willard E. "First Impressions: Letter of Colonel Richard Clement Moody, R.E., to Arthur Blackwood, February 1, 1859," *British Columbia Historical Quarterly*, 15(1951).

_____, ed. "Gold-rush Days in Victoria, 1858–1859," *British Columbia Historical Quarterly*, 12(1948).

Lamb, W. Kaye. "Early Lumbering on Vancouver Island," *British Columbia Historical Quarterly*, 2(1938).

_____. "The Founding of Fort Victoria," *British Columbia Historical Quarterly*, 7(1943).

_____. "The Governorship of Richard Blanshard," *British Columbia Historical Quarterly*, 14(1950).

"Letter from Charles Major, dated Fort Hope, Sept. 20, 1859," *British Columbia Historical Quarterly*, 5(1941).

Lewis, William S., ed. "Reminiscences of Joseph H. Boyd: An Argonaut of 1857," *Washington Historical Quarterly*, 15(1924).

Mackie, Richard. "The Colonization of Vancouver Island, 1849–1858," *BC Studies*, 96(1992–93).

McKelvie, B. A. "Sir James Douglas: A New Portrait," *British Columbia Historical Quarterly*, 7(1943).

Meany, Edmond S., ed. "Van Ogle's Memory of Pioneer Days," *Washington Historical Quarterly*, 8(1922).

"The Navigation of the Frazer River, and Its Approaches," *Nautical Magazine*, 28(1859).

Pettit, Sydney G. "Judge Begbie in Action: The Establishment of Law and Preservation of Order in British Columbia," *British Columbia Historical Quarterly*, 11(1947).

Reid, Robie L., ed. "Extracts from Dr. Carl Freisach, *An Excursion through British Columbia in the Year 1858*, pub. in Gratz, Austria, 1875," *British Columbia Historical Quarterly*, 5(1941).

_____. "John Nugent: The Impertinent Envoy," *British Columbia Historical Quarterly*, 8(1944).

_____, ed. "To the Fraser River Mines in 1858: A Letter from C. C. Gardiner," *British Columbia Historical Quarterly*, 1(1937).

_____. "The Whatcom Trails to the Fraser River Mines in 1858," *Washington Historical Quarterly*, 18(1927).

Rickard, T. A. "Indian Participation in the Gold Discoveries," *British Columbia Historical Quarterly*, 2(1938).

Rockwood, E. Ruth, ed. "Diary of Rev. George H. Atkinson, D.D., 1847–1858," *Oregon Historical Quarterly*, 40(1939).

Ross, Frank E. "The Retreat of the Hudson's Bay Company in the Pacific Northwest," *Canadian Historical Review*, 18(1937).

_____, ed. "Sir George Simpson at the State Department," *British Columbia Historical Quarterly*, 2(1938).

Sage, Donald. "Gold Rush Days on the Fraser River," *Pacific Northwest Quarterly*, 44(1953).

Sage, Walter N. "The Gold Colony of British Columbia," *Canadian Historical Review*, 2(1921).

Scott, Leslie M., ed. "Report of Lieutenant Peel on Oregon, 1845–46," *Oregon Historical Quarterly*, 29(1928).

"Slacum's Report on Oregon, 1836–37," *Oregon Historical Quarterly*, 13(1912).

Smith, Dorothy Blakey. "The First Capital of British Columbia: Langley or New Westminster?" *British Columbia Historical Quarterly*, 21(1957–58).

_____, ed. "The Journal of Arthur Thomas Bushby, 1858–1859," *British Columbia Historical Quarterly*, 21(1957–58).

Waddington, Alfred. "On the Geography and Mountain Passes of British Columbia in Connection with an Overland Route," *Journal of the Royal Geographical Society*, 38(1868).

Woodward, Frances M. "The Influence of the Royal Engineers on the Development of British Columbia," *BC Studies*, 24(1974–75).

Books and Monographs

Akrigg, G. P. V. and Helen B. *British Columbia Place Names*. Vancouver: University of British Columbia Press, 3rd ed., 1997.

Alston, E. Graham. *A Handbook to British Columbia and Vancouver Island*. London: F. Algar, 1870.

Anglin, Ron; ed. and with contributions by Glen W. Lindeman. *Forgotten Trails: Historical Sources of the Columbia's Big Bend Country*. Pullman: Washington State University Press, 1995.

Bancroft, Hubert H. *History of British Columbia, 1792–1887*. San Francisco: History Company, 1887.

Barman, Jean. *The West beyond the West: A History of British Columbia*. Toronto: University of Toronto Press, rev. ed., 1996.

Bocking, Richard C. *Mighty River: A Portrait of the Fraser*. Vancouver: Douglas and McIntyre, 1997.

Browne, J. Ross: *A Peep at Washoe; or, Sketch of Adventure in Virginia City*. New York: Harper and Brothers, 1875 [reprinted Palo Alto, California: Lewis Osborne, 1968].

Burns, Robert Ignatius, S.J. *The Jesuits and the Indian Wars of the Northwest*. New Haven: Yale University Press, 1966.

Correspondence Relative to the Negotiation of the Question of Disputed Right to the Oregon Territory. London: T. R. Harrison, 1846.

Decker, Peter R. *Fortunes and Failures: White-Collar Mobility in Nineteenth-Century San Francisco*. Cambridge: Harvard University Press, 1978.

DeGroot, Henry. *British Columbia: Its Condition and Prospects, Soil, Climate, and Mineral Resources*. San Francisco: Alta California Job Office, 1859.

Dunn, John. *History of the Oregon Territory and British North-American Fur Trade*. London: Edwards and Hughes, 1844.

Engstrand, Iris H. W. *Spanish Scientists in the New World: The Eighteenth Century Expeditions*. Seattle: University of Washington Press, 1981.

Ficken, Robert E. *Washington Territory*. Pullman: Washington State University Press, 2001 .

Fisher, Robin. *Contact and Conflict: Indian-European Relations in British Columbia, 1774–1890*. Vancouver: University of British Columbia Press, 1977.

Gibson, James R. *Farming the Frontier: The Agricultural Opening of the Oregon Country, 1786–1846*. Seattle: University of Washington Press, 1985.

_____. *The Lifeline of the Oregon Country: The Fraser-Columbia Brigade System, 1811–1847*. Vancouver: University of British Columbia Press, 1997.

Goodman, Donald Michael. *A Western Panorama, 1849–1875: The Travels, Writings and Influence of J. Ross Browne*. Glendale: Arthur H. Clarke, 1966.

Gough, Barry M. *First Across the Continent: Sir Alexander Mackenzie*. Norman: University of Oklahoma Press, 1997.

_____. *The Royal Navy and the Northwest Coast of North America, 1810–1914: A Study of British Maritime Ascendancy*. Vancouver: University of British Columbia Press, 1971.

Guie, H. Dean. *Bugle's in the Valley: Garnett's Fort Simcoe*. Portland: Oregon Historical Society, 1977.

Hill, Mary. *Gold: The California Story*. Berkeley: University of California Press, 1999.

Holliday, J. S. *Rush for Riches: Gold Fever and the Making of California*. Berkeley: University of California Press, 1999.

Howay, F. W. *British Columbia: The Making of a Province*. Toronto: Ryerson Press, 1928.

_____. *The Early History of the Fraser River Mines*, Archives of British Columbia Memoir No. VI. Victoria: Charles F. Banfield, 1926.

Jackson, W. Turrentine. *Wagon Roads West: A Study of Federal Road Surveys and Construction in the Trans-Mississippi West, 1846–1869*. New Haven: Yale University Press, 1964.

Johnston, Hugh J. M. *The Pacific Province: A History of British Columbia*. Vancouver: Douglas and McIntyre, 1996.

Laforet, Andrea, and Annie York. *Spuzzum: Fraser Canyon Histories, 1808–1939*. Vancouver: University of British Columbia Press, 1998.

Lamb, W. Kaye, ed. *The Journals and Letters of Sir Alexander Mackenzie*. Cambridge: Cambridge University Press, 1970.

_____, ed. *The Letters and Journals of Simon Fraser, 1806–1808*. Toronto: Macmillan of Canada, 1960.

Lang, William L. *Confederacy of Ambition: William Winlock Miller and the Making of Washington Territory*. Seattle: University of Washington Press, 1996.

Lotchin, Roger W. *San Francisco, 1846–1856: From Hamlet to City*. New York: Oxford University Press, 1974.

Lower, A. R. M. *The North American Assault on the Canadian Forest.* Toronto: Ryerson Press, 1938.

MacDonald, Norbert. *Distant Neighbors: A Comparative History of Seattle and Vancouver.* Lincoln: University of Nebraska Press, 1987.

Macfie, Matthew. *Vancouver Island and British Columbia: Their History, Resources, and Prospects.* London: Longman, Green, 1865.

Machlachlan, Morag, ed. *The Fort Langley Journals, 1827–30.* Vancouver: University of British Columbia Press, 1998.

Mackie, Richard Somerset. *Trading beyond the Mountains: The British Fur Trade on the Pacific, 1793–1843.* Vancouver: University of British Columbia Press, 1997.

Marks, Paula Mitchell. *Precious Dust: The American Gold Rush Era, 1848–1900.* New York: William Morrow, 1994.

Mayne, Richard C. *Four Years in British Columbia and Vancouver Island.* London: John Murray, 1862.

Merk, Frederick, ed. *Fur Trade and Empire: George Simpson's Journal.* Cambridge: Harvard University Press, rev. ed., 1968.

Mills, Randall V. *Stern-Wheelers Up Columbia: A Century of Steamboating in the Oregon Country.* Palo Alto: Pacific Books, 1947.

O'Donnell, Terence. *An Arrow in the Earth: General Joel Palmer and the Indians of Oregon.* Portland: Oregon Historical Society Press, 1991.

Ormsby, Margaret A. *British Columbia: A History.* Vancouver: Macmillan of Canada, 1958.

Papers Relative to the Affairs of British Columbia, Parts I–IV. London: George Edward Eyre and William Spottiswoode, 1859–62.

Paul, Rodman W. *California Gold: The Beginning of Mining in the Far West.* Cambridge: Harvard University Press, 1947.

Quinn, Arthur. *The Rivals: William Gwin, David Broderick, and the Birth of California.* New York: Crown Publishers, 1994.

Rich, E. E., ed. *The Letters of John McLoughlin from Fort Vancouver to the Governor and Committee, Second Series, 1839–44.* London: Champlain Society, 1943.

_____, ed. *London Correspondence Inward from Eden Colvile, 1849–1852.* London: Hudson's Bay Company Record Society, 1956.

_____, ed. *Part of Dispatch from George Simpson . . . to the Governor & Committee of the Hudson's Bay Company.* Toronto: Champlain Society, 1947.

Rohrbough, Malcolm J. *Days of Gold: The California Gold Rush and the American Nation.* Berkeley: University of California Press, 1997.

Schwantes, Carlos A. *Radical Heritage: Labor, Socialism, and Reform in Washington and British Columbia, 1885–1917.* Seattle: University of Washington Press, 1979.

Simpson, Sir George. *Narrative of a Journey Round the World, during the Years 1841 and 1842.* London: Henry Colburn, 2 vols., 1847.

Stanley, George F., ed. *Mapping the Frontier: Charles Wilson's Diary of the 49th Parallel, 1858–1862, while Secretary of the British Boundary Commission.* Toronto: Macmillan of Canada, 1970.

Starr, Kevin. *Americans and the California Dream, 1850–1915.* New York: Oxford University Press, 1973.

Sterne, Netta. *Fraser Gold 1858! The Founding of British Columbia.* Pullman: Washington State University Press, 1998.

Waddington, Alfred. *The Fraser Mines Vindicated, or, The History of Four Months.* Victoria: P. DeGarro, 1858.

Williams, Glyndwr, ed. *London Correspondence Inward from Sir George Simpson, 1841–42.* London: Hudson's Bay Company Record Society, 1973.

Index